15/10/1992

MY EXIT VISA

MY EXIT VISA

Margaret Stansgate

HUTCHINSON

London

This edition first published in 1992 by
Hutchinson

Random House UK Limited
20 Vauxhall Bridge Road, London SW1V 2SA

Random House Australia (Pty) Ltd
20 Alfred Street, Milsons Point, Sydney, NSW 2061, Australia

Random House New Zealand Ltd
18 Poland Road, Glenfield, Auckland, New Zealand

Random House South Africa (Pty) Ltd
PO Box 337, Bergvlei, 2012, South Africa

A CIP catalogue record for this book is available from the British Library
ISBN 0 09 174754 6

Typeset in 10.5/12 Bembo
by Pure Tech Corporation, Pondicherry, India
Printed and bound in Great Britain by
Mackays of Chatham PLC, Chatham, Kent

CONTENTS

ILLUSTRATIONS

Daniel Turner Holmes
Margaret Eadie Holmes
Margaret Stansgate and her mother
Margaret Stansgate at the time of her engagement
Margaret Stansgate and her husband at their wedding reception
Margaret Stansgate with her sons
Margaret Stansgate's parents with her sister
Oswald Mosley and Lady Cynthia Mosley (Hulton–Deutsch)
Waldorf and Nancy Astor (Hulton–Deutsch)
Margaret Stansgate with Sir Ernest Benn (Hulton–Deutsch)
Earl and Countess of Oxford and Asquith (Hulton–Deutsch)
Sidney and Beatrice Webb (Hulton–Deutsch)
1929 Labour Cabinet (Hulton–Deutsch)
Michael and William Wedgwood Benn
With President Nasser of Egypt
With members of the Knesset
At the Taj Mahal
Mahatma Gandhi's memorial
Tony Benn refused entry to House of Commons
Charter of the Congregational Federation
Margaret Stansgate and her family
David and June Benn

(Unless otherwise attributed, all photographs come from the Benn family collection, copyright David, Tony and Stephen Benn.)

FOREWORD

'Now, my dear, sit down, make yourself comfortable and tell me about yourself. What are the things in your life that are most important to you?' With these words Lady Stansgate greeted me when I met her for the first time to assist with the writing of her memoirs. As the weeks went by I realised that this desire of hers to dig beneath the surface – to 'get understanding' – was what made her memories of all the people she had met and the places she had visited so fascinating.

She had begun her memoirs a few years before, filling many note-books, but arthritis and failing eyesight had now made it impossible for her to write or to check facts in libraries and Record Offices. So, armed with a tape-recorder, I was sent by Richard Cohen of Random Century to capture the rest of Lady Stansgate's memories and weave them into the notebooks.

I could not have been engaged in a more rewarding task. Here was a woman who could remember the death of Queen Victoria in 1901 and who had been caught up in the events of the whole century from then onwards. I was enthralled as she recounted her meetings with people as various as the Liberal Prime Minister, Asquith, and the last Emperor of China, Pu-yi. Her powers of description and ability to tell hilarious anecdotes with perfect timing often had me in fits of laughter.

I found myself involved in a certain amount of detection work and made an important discovery while looking for some documents in a box of Lord Stansgate's papers in the House of Lords Record Office. I came across about fifty charred typewritten pages: casualties of a fire at the Stansgates' home during the London Blitz. As I read them, I realised that they were a diary that Lady Stansgate had written on a portable typewriter during the travels she and her husband had made across the Middle East and the newly formed Soviet Union in 1926. She was delighted by my find, believing the diary to have been lost, and asked me to make it the basis of some chapters in the book.

Sadly, Lady Stansgate did not live to see the publication of her memoirs, but her voice and spirit live on in the following pages.

I was given every help and encouragement in my task by Lady Stansgate's sons, Tony Benn and David Benn; Richard Cohen, Kate Mosse, and Tony Whittome of Random Century; and the archivists at the House of Lords Record Office. I was also fortunate in being able to read transcripts of an interview Lady Stansgate gave to Rebecca Abrams for the National Life Story Collection, and of interviews she gave to the BBC.

Gill Shepherd

CHAPTER 1

1897–1911

I never really understood my parents or myself until quite mature middle life when I took up an offer in *The Times* for an in-depth calligraphy test. After copying out a column of the newspaper as instructed and sending it in with the £10 fee, I got back a fascinating analysis, containing a key paragraph: 'This writer is the child of parents of contrasting and even conflicting temperaments and points of view, and in consequence she is unable to accept anything on authority but has to try and think out everything for herself.' That is absolutely true.

My father, Daniel Turner Holmes, was born in 1863 in Irvine in Ayrshire, not very far from Robert Burns's birthplace. His father, James Holmes, was a tailor when I knew him but had been, at one time, a steeplejack. I always think that his deeply held religious beliefs were connected with the beautiful wide vistas which rewarded him after the arduous effort of climbing the spires.

My father always spoke of his mother, Elizabeth Turner, with great affection and gratitude, remembering how hard she worked and the many trials she had to bear. The greatest of these was the loss of five of her eight children. 'Every one of them could have been saved today,' my father would say. He never heard his mother complain, as it was believed at that time that all trials and sorrows were 'sent' and must be endured. But on all of the five anniversaries of her children's deaths she went to the cemetery. She had no means to buy flowers to put on the tiny graves, but her tears expressed everything. Her grief reached its peak with the death of her only surviving daughter, 'wee Jeanie', at the age of seven.

My grandparents' home was a tiny house called Friars' Croft. The kitchen was not only the living room and work room but also had two curtained recesses, each containing a large double bed. One was occupied by my grandparents, the other by my father and his elder brother, James. A second room, furnished with a dining table and a set of upright chairs, contained family photographs and copies of the Bible. The third room was really only half a room and was situated at the junction of two streets with windows looking on to each.

This was where my grandmother delighted to sit, with the family mending, on many afternoons a week when the shopping was done. She relaxed in the only piece of furniture in the house that could be called an armchair. I now have this in my flat and it is a much-cherished possession. Grandmother was interested in her neighbours, and watching them go to and fro relieved the tedium of the mending. Grandfather, well aware of this, shook his head at her 'worldly-mindedness'.

The greatest loss she experienced, short of death, was the emigration of her eldest son to America. James was a skilful carpenter, highly trained, interested in his trade, and ambitious to make his way. Irvine, in the last century, offered few opportunities to realise the future success for which he hoped, while tales abounded from those who had already taken the big step and found it paid. When James announced his decision, his mother could hardly believe it. Her response was: 'Oh, James, what for are you going to America? – you've got nothing to hide.' He was her beloved eldest, the one on whom she relied for every sort of help. Alec, the youngest, was a near invalid, tormented by chronic asthma, and was obliged to leave Scotland in later life for the warmer climate of South Africa; the middle son, my father, was a scholar.

James wrote regularly, and his letters were a great comfort for the rest of his parents' lives. I asked Grandmother when he was likely to come back for a holiday and she replied: 'Never, I hope.' He had come home once before, without warning, and the shock had nearly killed her; when he left, the grief was almost more than she could bear.

Unfortunately, I was unable to have any direct communication with my grandmother, because since the age of forty she had been profoundly deaf as a result of an illness that had not been adequately treated. My mother, who was clever at using her lips to form words, was the only member of the family, except Grandfather, who ever got in real touch with her.

Grandmother showed her affection by administering vigorous 'pats' on the back that almost sent us spinning. Kissing, even among close relatives, was unheard of in this older circle of my childhood. I never kissed my paternal grandparents, and when I asked my father if he had ever kissed his parents, he expressed the greatest distaste for the idea: 'Certainly not!' He was, however, never in doubt of their deep and sincere affection.

My father was totally unlike any other member of the family. Intensely impractical, he was unable to shut a window without jamming it or put a shovelful of coal on the fire without extinguishing it. I vividly recall my mother saying: 'Dan, do you not realise that fires are like human beings: they cannot live without air. If you pour on coal from the top without poking the fire from below, it will just go out.' As his brother James, whom I later encountered in America, said to me: 'Oh, Daniel! What a brain, and he can hardly tie his own shoelaces!' My mother was very capable, and I am sure her patience was sorely tried when she married.

My father went to school at a very early age – in fact they could not keep him away. I am told that he followed his elder brothers to school in Irvine and the teachers were so intrigued by this little boy, with his already wonderful powers of assimilating knowledge and his great thirst for acquiring information, that he was allowed to attend classes from the age of three or four.

Education always had a high priority in Scotland and people could be poor but not unlettered. This was for two reasons: the system of schooling with its well-qualified teachers; and the religious commitment common to the majority of the population, who were steeped in the ideas and the language of the King James Bible. Thanks to his little town school, my father became a pupil teacher and then made his way through the whole external degree course of London University, doing so well that he not only obtained first-class honours but was placed first of all those from all over the country who sat the examination. This was among the happiest times of his life and he treasured the BA certificate. In his last illness, when he was ninety-two, I used to cheer him up by talking of his achievement and asking him questions as, together, we looked at the document. 'It was a triumph!' he would say, smiling happily on his pillow. He had a wonderful aptitude for learning and, although he became an English teacher, his heart was in the Classics.

For a few years he travelled throughout the Highlands and Islands, lecturing to hundreds of literary societies in association with the establishment of libraries given by James Coats. My father recorded his experiences in his book, *Literary Tours in the Highlands and Islands of Scotland*, which is a fascinating account of life in the remoter parts of the country in the early years of the century, and shows the passion for education of the Scottish people.

My mother, Margaret Eadie, was the daughter of the much-respected Peter Eadie who was twice Provost of Paisley. Born in Perthshire of a family of crofters and stonemasons, he came to Paisley as a young engineer to seek more training. In 1864, at the time of my mother's birth, he was sent to Italy to supervise the erection of gasworks, and never forgot the perilous journey over the Alps in a horse-drawn vehicle. In Sicily he was in constant danger of attacks by brigands.

While living for a time in Galashiels, he developed, in 1871, an improved method for making ring travellers, devices which spin and twist yarn in order to give it greater strength. These were manufactured in his small two-roomed house with all the family lending a hand while nearly expiring from the heat of the improvised furnace. The demand increased so much that my grandfather set up Eadie Brothers in Paisley, where the company flourished.

I never knew my maternal grandmother, as she died before my mother's marriage, but she had a very definite first-hand influence on me. When I learnt to read and write and asked for a notebook, my mother gave me a commonplace book that had been kept by my grandmother. I remember this object vividly. It was a very beautiful book in which each of the pages, many of them unused, was of a different pastel shade, and should not really have been given to a child to scribble on. In this book my grandmother wrote down from time to time her most intimate thoughts about life and its problems. This showed her outlook to be a deeply religious one but revealed the existence of many painful doubts to which she could find no answer.

There was a mystery surrounding her birth, for she had never known a father and bore her mother's maiden name, Margaret Riddle. Unable to find her parents' marriage certificate, she was afraid that she had been born illegitimate. This made her feel unfit to enter the company of the 'saved', as there are passages in the Bible which say that the illegitimate will not come into the presence of the Lord to the third or fourth generation. Her only hope was that her parents' coming together had been after a Gretna Green type of marriage, favoured in Scotland in the last century, whereby the two people concerned declared before witnesses that they were man and wife and so entered into an irregular, but legal, married state. My mother's common-sense view of my grandmother's birth was: 'Am I not glad that my mother saw the light?'

My great-grandmother, with whom my grandmother lived until her marriage, had been housekeeper to a Scottish peer, Lord Torphichen, who lived on the outskirts of Edinburgh. She had complete responsibility for running a large household and twice a week rode on horseback into Edinburgh, accompanied by two grooms, to do all the extensive shopping.

My grandmother and her mother were both skilled seamstresses and together they set up a little business at home, making fine undergarments. At first this went well, but eventually it failed and they had to close down. This was done satisfactorily and there were no debts, but they were left penniless, without a morsel of food in the house. Together they knelt down in prayer, throwing themselves in complete trust on God. My grandmother never forgot what happened when, a few minutes later, there was a knock on the door and a neighbour appeared. 'Oh,' she said, 'I have just this minute remembered that a long time ago you lent me a loaf and so at last I'm bringing you one back.' After this things took a turn for the better when my grandmother was given a post as a teacher in a small private school. Later they went to Paisley so that her mother could escape from the man she had eventually married, an inebriate coachman who threatened her life.

In Paisley, my grandmother, at the age of twenty-seven, met Peter Eadie, a lad of nineteen. It was love at first sight and they plighted their troth by inscribing on a penny, melted in the fire, their initials and the date. They were engaged for five years and married in 1861. It was a singularly happy marriage and lasted until Margaret's death at the age of sixty-six. They had three surviving children: Peter, John and my mother.

My mother was a woman of great beauty, charm and vitality, but she had an unstable character and was quite unpredictable. Although she had great ability, she felt very underprivileged in comparison to her two brothers and, when they were out, would sometimes dress in their clothes. Girls were discouraged from doing anything adventurous and she was not allowed to have a bicycle, even at the age of thirty, because it was considered unladylike.

She had experienced the frustration of being removed from school at sixteen to look after her mother and take a main share in running the home, although adequate domestic help could have been well afforded. Both her brothers turned down the offer of a university education, whereas her one desire was to go on learning. Later, my mother was severely reproached for joining a course in English Literature at the newly opened women's college in Glasgow, Queen Margaret's. Returning home after the first lecture, she found a new, well-equipped work-basket in a prominent place in her bedroom. This was to remind her that the most important thing in life for a woman was the home.

In the year 1884, at the age of twenty, my mother, to her own surprise, succeeded in breaking away for a few months. It happened that a contemporary had just then met and married a young Austrian business-man and gone to live in Vienna. Here was a wonderful opportunity. My mother wrote to her friend asking her to find an Austrian family of impeccable reputation to whom she could give English lessons in exchange for learning German. The young Scottish friend warmly welcomed the idea and wrote to say she had found just the family: a Baron and Baroness Schlesinger who had young children and would be pleased to receive her.

With this letter in her hands, my mother began to put heavy pressure on her parents. The plan had everything to commend it: she had never been abroad, she wished to learn fluent German, and here was her chance. Her friend and the Austrian husband in Vienna would not be far away; they would keep a watchful eye on her, and rescue her if anything went wrong. My mother surprised her parents by the pressure she brought to bear on them, amounting to insistence that she should have her way for once. Finally it was agreed and she sailed for Austria.

After a few days in Vienna, she arrived at the Schlesingers' estate. It did not take long to discover that the Baron was a full-blown tyrant of whom everyone, especially his wife and children, went in fear and trembling. My mother found his table manners disgusting: she had never before seen anyone settle down, elbows on the table, to devour chicken legs with an end in each hand. After a month she realised that on the Baron's orders she had been obliged to speak nothing but English and not a single German word had been addressed to her. She then wrote to her friend in Vienna asking if a place as a paying guest could be found for her there. An immediate invitation followed and soon my mother had settled down for a memorable winter of opera, museum visits, lectures and German lessons. Her progress proved to be immediate and striking, and for the first time in her life she felt that she was 'getting somewhere'.

It was not to last. Letters from home became more and more demanding, and finally she was told: 'Your mother needs you back,' and was
asked: 'When is this selfishness to stop?' It always seemed to me that this
question might have been asked quite legitimately of the possessive
mother herself. My mother went home and stayed there for twelve more
years. She had many offers of marriage, but her mother told her: 'I hope
you will never marry. You are the only daughter and your place is at
home looking after your parents and running the house.' Finally, at the
age of thirty-two, she met my father and decided after much heart-
searching to marry him. A few weeks after she announced her engagement, her mother had a stroke and died – whereupon everybody said:
'You've killed your mother,' and, poor dear, she felt guilty about that
to the end of her life. My father used to say, in Greek: 'Your mother is
a self-tormentor.'

In my parents' house there was a much-enlarged photograph of my
maternal grandmother: a very severe-looking woman in a grey sequinned
dress with a brooch at the neck. If this portrait was looking down upon
us from the mantelpiece we knew that my mother felt that she had done
wrong to marry, but if my mother had it upside down on her knees
playing patience on it then we knew it was all right and she had not
regretted marrying after all.

My parents met when my father was head of the English Department
at Paisley Grammar School, and my mother, who had a great love of
literature, enjoyed talking to him. She used to say to me: 'I married your
father for his mind.' Even in my teens this remark made me very uneasy
and I used to tease her: 'It's no better than saying, "I married him for
his money!" ' I thought that a marriage should not take place for anything less than a love of the whole personality. Now I think this is really
what happened with them, for they adored each other. But they were
so different that it was almost impossible for them to run a house
together, and their married life of over fifty years was a long series of
lovers' quarrels and reconciliations.

I was born, the elder of two daughters, in Paisley in the festive month
of June 1897, a week or two before Queen Victoria's Diamond Jubilee.
Indeed, my mother had thoughts of calling me Victoria and then very
considerately did not, because she thought it would date me. I lived in
a very comfortable little home in Bridge of Weir. Our sandstone house,
with its two gables, overlooked the whole valley of the Clyde from the
spires of Glasgow University to the Kilpatrick Hills and a shoulder of
Ben Lomond, the Perthshire mountain that is covered in snow even in
June. The funnels of the ill-fated *Lusitania* could be seen as it was being
built in the shipyard in Glasgow. I used to stand by the wide open
bedroom window, entranced by the beautiful prospect: the hills in the
distance and, below, countless farmhouses and plots of land and lakes,
that looked so small.

Both my parents had desired a daughter, though for different reasons: my mother because she was an ardent feminist who had no time for boys and wanted to bring up a daughter in the cause of fighting for her rights as a woman; my father because he was just as ardent an anti-feminist. As a Greek scholar he was confirmed in his belief, by Aristotle and others, that women were by nature the inferior sex and that their calling was to make a comfortable home for the men of the family. He once remarked in my hearing that if he had had twelve children he would have liked them all to have been girls. How comfortable this would have made the home, had they been amenable, can well be imagined.

He had not the slightest interest in anything of a domestic nature. During all their long married life of fifty-seven years my mother ordered and bought most of his clothes. He took all this for granted and never showed the slightest interest in how they got into his possession. He was, however, a meticulously careful dresser, and during his long life of ninety-two years I never saw him without a collar or, indeed, in any sort of undress. I have an amusing photograph of my father, paddling with my son David at Bexhill, wearing carefully turned up, immaculate grey flannel trousers, and a black Homburg hat.

In those days women's inferior status could be observed in the Births columns of *The Times*. Whereas now an entry will read: 'To John and Jane Smith, a daughter,' then the announcement would say: 'The wife of John Smith of a daughter' – the 'of' being a shortened form of 'delivered of'. The most important person in the whole event was, of course, the husband.

At the time of my birth there had been some improvement in the position of women: the Married Women's Property Acts, the last of which had been passed in 1893, meant that my mother had control of her own money; and there was a slowly increasing number of women in the professions. My mother, taking advantage of the fact that women were now allowed to practise medicine, insisted on having a female doctor attend my birth. Unfortunately, my arrival was dangerously delayed and a male doctor had to be sent for in the middle of the night. My mother, when later teased about this by anti-feminists, always remarked: 'It wasn't because she was a woman but because she could neither see nor hear!'

Shortly after my birth, my mother found herself with a stepmother of her own age. In 1898, a few years after my grandmother died, my grandfather announced that he was going on a trip to the Holy Land. This was the second time he had done so; the first time had been some years before. It was no light undertaking in those days to visit Jerusalem and took a week by land and sea, unlike today when you can see the midday sun shining on the Thames and the sun setting the same day on the river Jordan.

When he returned, my grandfather had a long talk with my mother.

It was quite evident that he had something very important on his mind. After leaving Jerusalem he had gone on to Damascus and, among other visits, had spent twenty minutes in a mission run by the Church of Scotland. One class was presided over by a woman of early middle age, Emily, a Jewish convert to Christianity. She taught the little Druse children to sing 'Jesus loves me, this I know', and my grandfather was enchanted.

It was obvious to my mother that he had thought of nothing else since. His only fear was that if Emily agreed to marry him he would be taking her away from 'the Lord's work'. My mother suggested that he should write to the head of the mission and make some enquiries about her. He must have made his intentions crystal clear, because a personal letter soon arrived from Emily beginning 'Darling' and giving the measurements of her finger for engagement and wedding rings. He made arrangements to go out to Damascus and bring her home.

During his absence my mother undertook the not very congenial task of getting her old home ready for her stepmother. She organised the redecoration where it was necessary and replaced some articles of furniture that had been specially dear to her mother by others which she bought herself. A suitable staff was assembled and everything was in apple pie order when she greeted her father and his new wife on the doorstep. Sadly the two ladies, both of whom had been born in September 1864, took an instant dislike to each other that increased and deepened with the years.

Admittedly my mother was very critical, but the main trouble was that Emily would not share my grandfather's company. She wanted him all to herself, and when my mother called to see him Emily would plant herself firmly beside her husband and give my mother no chance of a personal conversation. The housekeeper, warmly sympathising with my mother, would ring her up: 'Come along quickly; Mrs Eadie has gone out shopping and you'll find Mr Eadie alone.' This my mother instantly did, but when her stepmother returned and found my mother there she suspected what had happened.

Emily showed her insecurity in other ways. My mother always dressed well and in good taste and possessed a few pieces of attractive jewellery. Her stepmother had to go one better in both cases, buying things that were identical in style but much more expensive.

Two children were born of this marriage, Eric and Noel. They absorbed a great deal of my grandfather's time and attention and deprived us of what would have been a grandfather's close relationship had they not been there. It always amused us to have as playmates an uncle and aunt younger than ourselves and we wondered why Grandfather did not like us to joke about it. We were fascinated when Emily's relatives came to stay from time to time, because they used to converse in Arabic, their native tongue, while my grandfather sat in complete silence.

Towards Grandfather, I fear that Eric and Noel were often insubordinate, and in his sixties and seventies he would have been glad of peace and quiet. One afternoon at our house they proved quite uncontrollable and when, finally, he gave up admonishing them, he merely remarked in broad Scots: 'I wonder who invented weans' (children). It was a cry from the heart.

Noel had a beautiful voice of great strength and, after my grandfather's death, she went with her mother to London for voice training. Eventually Madame Noel Eadie sang the part of the Queen of the Night in *The Magic Flute* at Covent Garden and went on to have a successful career.

I had a strict upbringing as my father was a real disciplinarian. Luckily, I was spared many a whipping by my mother because, although she used to snap a bit and was not entirely opposed to punishment, she was not as severe as my father.

For a long time my father was at home writing books. He would come out of his study and say: 'Now stop that noise.' Unfortunately he was tone deaf and even music was a noise; he only recognised the National Anthem because everyone stood up. 'Nobody's going to learn the piano on my nerves,' he insisted, and so I could only practise the piano when he was out of the house. I was not able to have parties of friends round for tea unless he was away. Brooms and brushes were not allowed to operate when he was studying, and we had to creep up and down stairs. Indeed, I was brought up on tiptoe and have had wobbly ankles ever since.

Fortunately, he took walks two or three times a day. My mother would call: 'Children, your father's out,' and with those words the house would fall into a state of happy bedlam, the maids would clatter away, and Hermione and I would sing and talk to our hearts' content, until my mother's warning shout: 'Your father's at the gate,' whereupon silence descended.

My mother had a very strange feature: she had one brown eye and one grey. One of them was always dominant and I used to wait and see which eye it would be. The grey eye was cold and critical, and if that was dominant then nothing I did was any use; I just could not please her. But if the warm and friendly brown eye was smiling at me, then I knew I was going to have a very happy and pleasant day. I might be taken into Glasgow for roller-skating, or for a little shopping at the Doll's House in the arcade, which I much loved, and then lunch at Cranston's.

I loved playing with my dolls, Lala and Karina, but my father disapproved of this. I think it may have been a strangely exaggerated puritanism, because he thought it 'unseemly', a favourite word of his, for little girls to pretend to be mothers. His attitude made me intensely vulnerable. If I did anything wrong he would lock up my dolls and, because they were so real to me, I thought that they could not breathe in the cupboard. I even developed symptoms of asthma out of empathy with them.

Life mellowed my father greatly, and by the time he had reached ninety he was a delightful companion to whom I could talk without inhibition. When I told him what an extremely repressive parent he had been he looked at me in amazement and said: 'My dear, it isn't possible.' I replied: 'It's more than possible, it happened!'

My father was a scholar, describing himself, in one of his many poems, as 'a worshipper at learning's shrine'. I loved the stories he told me about the Greeks, especially about Socrates drinking the hemlock. I was fascinated by the beauty of the Greek letters and I asked him to say a Greek word for me. Without an instant's hesitation he said: 'Lanthano' – 'I escape notice.' Later on, when I knew a little about Freud, I thought this incident was a key to my father's character, for he wished 'to escape notice'; he just wanted to be left alone with his books. My mother, however, was ambitious for him. She wanted to turn him into a sage, just as Jane Welsh Carlyle, a woman of independent means with whom my mother identified, had made her husband, Thomas Carlyle, 'the Sage of Chelsea'.

My mother was determined that my father should obtain further qualifications, as she had a tremendous belief in his ability to teach at a high level. The first step, she felt sure, was to get him away from Paisley Grammar School. If left there he would pass inevitably and – alas for my mother – quite contentedly on to retirement which he would spend with his beloved books. She wanted him to take an Oxford degree, but one of the requirements was that he would have to live in college and, although my mother said that she would move the family to Oxford, he would not do that.

Her next suggestion was that he should take a degree at the Sorbonne. He liked that idea very much and so, when I was about four, our home at Bridge of Weir was let furnished, and we went to France. The only voice raised in warning was that of my mother's father, Peter Eadie, who expressed grave doubts as to the wisdom of taking a man away from a settled career which brought a secure income and would lead to an equally certain pension. Why not use the adequately long school holidays for visits to France and elsewhere? My mother's response was final: 'I'll ask nobody's permission to go abroad.' She wanted to go for her own sake as well as for my father's. We lived in a guesthouse for students in the Latin Quarter and both my father and mother attended the Sorbonne. Unfortunately, my father's course of study was mismanaged and, sadly, he never got his doctorate.

I did not have a very happy time at first. My mother wanted to be free to attend lectures and go to her beloved opera, and so she engaged a *bonne* for me, called Mathilde. She had a young man who used to meet us on our walks, and he told me that, if I disclosed this to my parents, he would give me to the *charbonnier*, the man who delivered coal in the neighbourhood and was always covered in coal dust. For me, he was an object of terror. Once, when I was out walking with my mother,

Mathilde's boyfriend passed us and gave me a menacing glare. I clung to my mother and wept. She asked me what was the matter and I replied: 'Oh, c'est le jeune homme de Mathilde' – 'It's Mathilde's boyfriend!' Then I wept harder still and said: 'Now they'll give me to the *charbonnier!*' So my mother interviewed Mathilde and sent her back home, with a month's wages instead of notice.

My parents, realising that they should find a different kind of person to be my nurse, engaged Madame Le Clair, a woman of late middle age. Unfortunately she had just come from Martinique, where an earthquake had robbed her of all her possessions and many of her friends. She was very unhappy and I did not like her at all. We all spoke French and my mother kept asking me, 'Qu'est-ce qu'elle a?' – 'What's the matter with her?' Happily for me, I remembered an incomprehensible phrase Madame Le Clair often uttered. I quoted, triumphantly: 'Elle a des nuits blanches avec des idées noires,' which meant: 'sleepless nights with dark thoughts'. This startled my mother, and so Madame Le Clair was sent away, well compensated. After this my mother took care of me and I was very happy.

I found Paris delightful. One of my main pleasures was playing in the Luxembourg Gardens, particularly riding in one of the donkey carts. There were always visits to interesting museums and shops, but what I liked best of all was when my mother would say: 'Time for a rest and a cup of coffee.' This meant sitting for half an hour or so in a main street outside a café where chairs and tables invited us to pause and enjoy the pleasant, busy scene. I loved having orange juice and a brioche.

It was while we were in France, in 1901, that Queen Victoria died. My mother wept and wept when she heard the news, and I remember wondering why she was so upset when the old lady had not known us. None of us, I think, had actually seen Queen Victoria, but she somehow just stood for Britain. There were so few people alive then who could remember earlier sovereigns that it was just impossible to think of any other monarch ruling them. Years later I remember one of my little boys writing in an essay: 'Queen Victoria lived an unspeakably long time!'

After we came back to Scotland my sister, Hermione, was born in 1904. Having been a much-spoiled only child for seven years, I was quite shocked to learn, without any warning, that I had a sister. Although delighted, I had not been prepared for the change in my life that her arrival brought and could not understand what had happened to me. I was literally put down and Baby was always on Mother's knee. My reaction was to become troublesome and demanding, which was characterised by my parents as selfish and naughty. Then one day my mother announced: 'Oh, I know what we'll do. She needs discipline, we'll send her to school!' I was a little grown-up. I sat at table with my parents and listened to what they said and joined in the conversation. I knew the name of the Prime Minister and various members of the Cabinet and what was being discussed in Parliament. But at the age of seven I had received no formal education.

The education authorities in Scotland normally kept a very sharp look-out to see what people were doing about their children, but they had not interfered in our case. As my father had been Head of the English Department at Paisley Grammar School, they naturally assumed that he was looking after my education. As a matter of fact he took no interest in it whatsoever, and my mother used to say: 'Oh, a shoemaker's children are always ill-shod.' Had I been a boy he would have sent me to school early and kept me hard at it, but he had no interest in the education of daughters.

School was my first humiliation in life. It was a disaster. I was sent to St Columba's School, an excellent day school for girls in Kilmalcolm. I shall never forget that first day when all the new children were gathered together to be tested. When it came to my turn I could not read the test. All the other girls were soon sorted out according to their educational level, but I remained isolated. I heard a lot of whispering among the staff, who were, of course, discussing me. Here was Margaret, a well-grown, well cared for, obviously well-loved little girl, well into her eighth year, whom nobody had taught to read or write.

What to do with me was the problem. The girls of my own age were happily settled into Form I or just below in the Transition, but I suffered the indignity of being put with the babies of five years old. I was nearly eight and could hardly squeeze into the little seat. As a further humiliation my lovely sailor suit, bought from the Compagnie Anglaise in Brussels, had shining gold buttons which scratched the desk and I was told that I must either wear something else or have them cut off. I had to begin at the beginning and try to make sense of the picture of a cat beside which stood mysterious symbols reading CAT.

I dreaded going to school. Salt tears fell every morning into my already salted porridge as I wailed, being still bilingual: 'Vilain Kilmalcolm!' – 'Nasty Kilmalcolm!' Then I lingered and delayed so long that sometimes there would be a warning cry from my parents of: 'Hurry up! There's a puff of smoke at Houston.' I knew that once the train had arrived at Houston-Croslee, the station before ours, no matter how fast I ran it would reach Bridge of Weir before I could get there and then leave, unless it stayed for a long drink. Missing the train was a dreary experience. I had to get a note of excuse, go down alone by the next train, present myself to be reproved by the Head Mistress, and then go to my class and receive a mark of lateness.

I took refuge in illness. The school was very cold and my mother kept our house extremely warm, so it was quite easy to be ill and I got five attacks of bronchitis during the winter. My only happy times were in bed at home despite the heavy poulticing that my mother ceaselessly applied, with the assistance of a grim-faced nurse, and the nasty treatments our doctor prescribed such as blowing powder down my throat through a tube. If I protested too long I knew by the ominous sound of cracking knee joints on the bend in the stair that my father had been sent for and would appear round the door, saying: 'Now, I'll give you two minutes to swallow that.' In his outstretched hand he held a solid gold gentleman's watch. I could never bear the sight of that watch, which was also used in a similar fashion to make sure I was not late for meals.

My mother, deciding that I should be taught at home, engaged a governess. If my father had talked to her for ten minutes he would have seen that she was not the right person. She was a very tall, attractive, well-dressed woman and a good disciplinarian, but she was really only fitted to coach students who wanted to go to university. She knew nothing of what went on in an ordinary school. She taught me a bit of history, which I liked very much, but nothing at all about mathematics or science, and so I got into a permanent condition of being behind.

Soon Hermione, now three years old, joined us round the parlour table. She thus had more than a four-year start in education over me and never looked back until her Oxford degree at the age of twenty-two. Every tutor of hers whom I met spoke of her as a very bright litle girl and warned me to look to my laurels, as yet non-existent. This naturally added to my own self-despair.

When I returned to school I was put in a class of girls of my own age, and the first thing that I encountered was the forty-ninth theorem of Euclid about the square on the hypotenuse, which, of course, was Greek to me! At the end of the year the class was very angry with me because I spoilt their record: if I had not been in the class everyone would have received a prize.

Although my early education was, as my grandchildren tell me, 'a horror story', when, eventually, I learned to read I became a tremendous reader and took advantage of my parents' very well stocked library. I could tell who owned the books by their condition. Whereas my mother's books were well bound, my father neglected his. He used to read while taking long walks in the countryside, and if he did not want to take a whole book with him he would tear out a chapter. His books were always in fragments. The only book that I was forbidden to read was *Wuthering Heights*, which, I regret to say, was the first book I read! Under my mother's inspiration, my sister and I, early in life, eagerly devoured literary magazines, and so got some idea of what was going on in the wider world outside our hilltop home in lowland Scotland.

My mother was supremely efficient and frequently scolded me for the apparently incurable faults of absent-mindedness and procrastination. 'Behold, the dreamer cometh,' she would say to me, and constantly quoted a German proverb: 'Tomorrow, tomorrow, not today, say all the lazy folk.' At home my mother could produce more imaginative and delicious meals than any cook she ever employed; she could clean and turn out and spring-clean a room better than any housemaid; and she could clean the family silver tea service, used daily along with our Crown

Derby china, and serve afternoon tea, better than any parlourmaid. In consequence, she enjoyed the respect of those whom she employed. From time to time, after lunch, our cook would appear in the parlour and say: 'Mrs Holmes, the oven's just right and everything's ready. Will you come and make some cakes and scones for tea?' My mother would put down the silk and bead purse she was crocheting and repair to the kitchen. We enjoyed the results later. People whom she employed have told me that she was the most generous and considerate employer they had ever had. She hated class distinction, and the words 'sir' and 'madam' were banned in our house as 'servile'.

Alas! Her standards were so high and her tolerance of a child's ineptitude and clumsiness so limited that I could never satisfy her and gave up trying. 'You're just like your father,' she would say, which seemed to me unfair, as presumably I had no choice in the matter.

My mother was a woman of great courage. At my sister's birth, as at my own, she suffered much injury and, as well, some kind of shock. As a result of this latter event she woke up one morning, soon after Hermione's birth, feeling strangely ill with violent palpitations, and when she looked into the glass she could not recognise the face that looked back at her as her own. The neck was swollen and the eyes stared wildly. When the doctor saw her that day he diagnosed an illness of which he had read but had never seen until that moment. 'You have exophthalmic goitre,' he told her. It was not known how long she would survive. For years I hardly dared draw breath morning by morning until I had seen with my own eyes that she still lived. Throughout the whole of my life I have never suffered a period of greater insecurity and distress. Little children can suffer far more than they are given credit for, and in dealing with my own three I have never allowed myself to forget this.

My mother's characteristic reaction was quite different from my own. In her opinion little children should not be protected from the harsh threats that life presented. She therefore spoke of her own death as more than likely. Collapsing on the sofa during one attack of violent palpitations, she whispered: 'Don't be surprised if I slip away.' I was seven years old at the time and the agony of that moment is with me still. Turning to the window, I looked out on to a great storm playing over the wide valley of the Clyde and felt the whole weight of an inscrutable Providence. In fact my mother, then forty, lived to be nearly eighty-nine.

I shall never forget her great fortitude throughout the years of her struggle for health. I never once heard her complain or lament the great personal beauty she had lost. 'I got a humbling!' was all she ever said about it all. She wanted me to be prepared for all eventualities. 'If I go you must expect your father to marry again pretty soon,' she would say, adding as relish: 'And you know the kind of stepmother I got.' At this I would break down in anticipation of such horror.

She went a couple of times to Bad Neuheim in Germany for baths, and when her absence became intolerable I would sit in the wardrobe wearing her Jaeger dressing gown and weep. My father was too stern to be of any comfort, and Mother's absence made him even more morose than usual. Sometimes my mother would spend a month in a Glasgow nursing home, and on one Sunday afternoon my grandfather, Peter Eadie, took the tram from Paisley to see her. When he arrived he was taken into the Matron's office, to be met with the question: 'Provost Eadie, how did you get here?' On receiving my grandfather's reply she said: 'Am I to understand that, although you are a professing Christian, you travelled by tram on the sabbath?' She then turned him out without a sight of his sick daughter.

While my mother was away my sister and I and the household were left in the care of Nurse Watt, an elderly martinet who had no understanding of children whatsoever. I kept out of her way and found my greatest comfort and happiness in the company of my little cairn terrier, Cullie, named after the Cuillin hills of his birthplace on the Isle of Skye. Our friendship was a very warm and real factor in my daily life. Cullie, like me, detested Nurse Watt, who cared for dogs no more than for children. We each knew exactly how the other felt. Cullie to Nurse Watt was just a nuisance to be kept out of sight. In the daytime he was put out into the garden, and at night, after I had gone to bed, he was ordered into his basket and told to stay there. But Cullie and I had a different idea. As soon as Nurse Watt had gone into the sitting room he crept upstairs to my room, always lighted with a 'peep' of gas, and on to my bed. Should she be heard coming upstairs he got under the eiderdown with lightning speed and did not move an inch even when she patted it vigorously into place. As soon as she left he came out shaking and panting with laughter as real as mine, and we enjoyed half an hour or so of warm companionship. Then, when he thought I ought to go to sleep he gave me an affectionate lick and left.

He was a year old when he came to us, and we were warned that he had not yet had distemper. It was a risk we had to take if we were to accept an exceptionally fine little puppy. Sadly, he caught the disease very badly. We sent him to the vet and visited him daily, but one morning we heard that he had died in the night. I grieved at the sight of my beloved little playmate lying stiff and cold, and I have never been able to think of it since without remembering Kipling's lines: 'Brothers and Sisters, I bid you beware / Of giving your heart to a dog to tear.'

Many years later, after the First World War, when my parents, Hermione and I were living in Seaford in Sussex, we again possessed a puppy. Dugald was a West Highland terrier, also from Skye, and, despite travelling in a ventilated box that bore instructions to feed and water him on the journey, was a woebegone little creature on arrival. But he very soon recovered and made himself at home almost immediately. Like Cullie, he had great intelligence and could convey his own wishes very clearly. My father was the main walker in the family and Dugald always went with him. If my father delayed his morning or afternoon walk he would be reminded by loud barks from Dugald, who would then beg on his hind legs in front of my father's hat, stick and overcoat in the hall. This soon brought my father out and the walk began. Dugald always showed a good deal of independence, and Hermione and I secretly admired his courage in refusing to come when my father called him, or indeed to do anything he was ordered to do. It was a new experience for my father to be disobeyed, and find himself powerless to do anything about it.

At that time we also had a cat called Puss who had taken refuge with us as a stray and remained as a much-loved member of the family. Dugald, too, was on the friendliest of terms with her and every night they played the same game: Dugald would rise up suddenly and begin to chase Puss round the room; with a leisured air of great superiority she would halt just within reach and then swiftly leap on to the top of a desk or scamper up the arm of the sofa, neither of which things Dugald could do. This went on until both, tired out, would settle down together in front of the fire.

One day Puss gave birth to five lovely kittens of different colours whom we had not the heart to dispose of in any fashion. Dugald took a great interest from the first and soon made an arrangement with Puss whereby he would take a share in looking after them. This proved very amusing to watch. Every afternoon he approached Puss, who was resting in her basket, and, after some obvious communication had passed between them, he would take out all five kittens, carrying each very gently by the scruff of its neck, and deposit them in a wide circle round him on the lawn outside. There, for half an hour or so, he played with each one; turning it over, very gently, and tickling it with his paw, then turning it back. He went round them all as though they were toys to be played with. This over, he reversed the procedure and carried each tenderly back to be put beside Puss in her basket. His reward was a loud purr, of approval and thanks, for this kindly act of babysitting. Puss had evidently enjoyed a snooze on her own.

In recent years I had the delight of a visit from an Israeli friend, Ruth Horner, who in the course of some years in London had acquired a West Highland terrier, also called Dugald, whom she used to describe as 'the most important male in my life'. This Dugald was bilingual and would respond to commands given in both English and Hebrew. When they arrived at my flat, Ruth instructed him: 'Dugald, this is a nice lady; jump on her lap and talk to her.' This Dugald trustingly did and began to make friendly gurgling noises while looking me straight in the face. Then his mistress addressed him in Hebrew: 'Now show her how members of the Knesset talk to each other' – whereupon Dugald sat up straight and began to growl and bark fiercely for several moments. I hear that he has settled down well in Israel, and no doubt his knowledge of Hebrew has greatly increased. I fear, however, that owing to quarantine regulations I shall not see him again.

My parents gave me no Christian education of any sort because they felt that their own lives had been darkened and depressed by the very gloomy Calvinistic form of Christianity which was current in Scotland at that time. My mother said she used to come home from church and go to her room and just weep and weep. My father, who wanted me to know about Socrates rather than Christ on the Cross, had formed a distaste for his father's religion.

His father's Christian commitment came early in life, but he was not satisfied with the Presbyterian Church of Scotland, the 'Auld Kirk', into which he had been born, and so he changed churches several times. Finally, inspired by the American evangelists Moody and Sankey, who held revivalist meetings throughout the country in the 1870s, stirring up the keenest speculation and enthusiasm, my grandfather decided to found his own religious group: a branch of the Plymouth Brethren called the Irvine Brethren. For the time being they would meet in his own home and those of other members. My grandfather once described his conversion as seeing the 'whole plan of salvation', and being so thrilled that he ran all the way from Irvine to Killwinning. My grandmother was very 'pawky'. (I am not sure what the English translation would be, but I suppose it means independent and committed to her views. Her husband's brothers had lost their wives early and one had married three times. Grandfather said he 'didna ken how my brother could be bothered'. To which Grandmother replied that 'he hadna been tried'.)

At this point my grandmother, who had always been supportive of her husband's changes of religious allegiance, came into open revolt and expressed herself forcibly, in broadest Scots: 'You had me out of the Auld Kirk into the Free Kirk and then into the Relief Kirk, and now you want me into the Brethren, and I'm no going.' She fell very ill and when she recovered she said that she had changed her mind. His rejoinder was: 'And how would you have liked to have been parted from me for all eternity if you had died last week?'

My grandfather was the minister of the Brethren and he married and buried members of his flock. I possess the settee on which he sat to preside at meetings in his own kitchen, and although it is now covered with a 'worldly' material, very different from the sober horsehair of his own day, I feel that it still radiates a sense of peace and blessing and I would not part with it for anything.

Eventually, the Brethren were able to build their own meeting place where they held services on Sundays. It was their custom to baptise new members in the river Irvine in imitation of Christ's baptism in the Jordan. My father never directly admitted to this having taken place in his own case, but from the intense distaste with which he related his recollections of having seen such ceremonies I feel sure that he was not speaking at second hand. There were always mockers around making participants feel self-conscious. On one occasion an onlooker entered the river and made the pretence of baptising his dog.

On one of our visits to Irvine, my little sister, Hermione, went for a walk with Grandfather. They were approached by an unsteady individual who, placing his hand on Grandfather's shoulder, asked: 'What I want to know is, is there a hell?' Grandfather gently detached himself and walked on. Hermione wanted to know who the stranger was. 'It was your great-uncle Alistair.' 'Why did he say is there a hell?' asked Hermione, and Grandfather replied, enigmatically: 'Aye, the poor fella.'

Hermione and I discussed this at length. What was 'hell'? Evidently there was some mystery, into the knowledge of which we were not admitted. We made discreet enquiries and found that the maids had been warned not to mention the matter to us. In the course of time the subject came up in Bible classes at school, so it could now be openly discussed at home. From my father I learned that in his own home more had been heard about the Devil and hell than of the love of God. It would seem that every moment of daily life presented a trap for the unwary. Without any bad intention whatsoever one could do something that put one in danger of everlasting, unending retribution.

Sunday, known in the Scotland of those days as 'the sabbath', had to be lived through with the greatest circumspection, and no work of any kind was allowed. In my father's early days the blinds throughout the house remained drawn as though a death had just taken place. The family went to church three times during the day and no recreation of any kind was permitted in between.

Restrictions on liberty extended throughout the week. No literature, except the Bible and books about the Bible, was allowed in the house. Once, when my father was given three books as school prizes and brought them home to show to his mother, she gave them each one glance and remarked: 'I don't see anything about Jesus in these.' She turned away without handling them. No daily paper was taken, and no magazine permitted except *The Life of Faith*. All playing cards – 'the Devil's picture books' – were strictly forbidden. My father and his two brothers found a way round this prohibition. Small family photographs abounded in a box in the sitting room. These were duly marked on the back in pencil with the name of four classes of flowers so there were the King, Queen, Jack, and the numbered cards, of Roses, Daffodils, Tulips and Carnations. It was possible to play a fully intelligible game of whist without detection – I do not suppose they ever got as far as bridge! My mother's comment on this was brief and pithy: 'Imposing senseless restrictions that taught the young to deceive!' In general, religious practice has changed considerably since those days, but recently Lord Jakobovits, when he was Chief Rabbi, told me that on a visit to distant parts of Scotland he had found that a perfect model of an Orthodox Jewish sabbath was observed on Sunday.

Later on, when I knew my grandfather better, although I was astonished at the severity of his views on eternal, endless, torment after death I felt that in his religious commitment there was a deep and abiding joy. In his old age, when he would come with Grandmother to spend a day at our home, he was a delightful playmate for Hermione and me. He showed a side of himself never, apparently, suspected before. I can still see my father looking out of his study window in a kind of stupefied wonder at the sight of his austere father, whom he had never known to relax, now, in his eighties, laughing merrily as he played roly-poly down a steep grass slope with his two little granddaughters.

Only once did Grandfather try to convert me to his religion. On a walk when I was about twelve, he began to tell me how earnest a Christian my father had been in his teens. He then began to ask for information: 'Has your father, by any chance, become a backslider?' He pronounced the word, a new one to me, with such echoes of doom in his voice that I immediately determined not to give my father away in case he was, indeed, in some danger. I remained silent.

Then the conversation took an unexpected turn as my grandfather attempted to 'save' me. I remained woefully at sea while he tried to explain the difference between the once and the twice born. 'How', he quoted, 'can a man enter a second time into his mother's womb?' I was just learning the facts of life from friends of my own age – my mother, alas, being unwilling to discuss the matter – and this sudden plunge into the subject by a male grown-up was too much for me. 'Please don't, Grandfather,' I begged with scarlet face. Mercifully, he sensed an unjustified invasion of my privacy and he desisted, never returning to the attack.

My father softened greatly towards religion in old age, with the realisation that what had been presented to him as the Christian religion in his youth was full of flaws and grave errors. After a stay at my house he wrote to my mother about my theological books: 'There's medicine for the soul there,' and his last audible words were: 'Lord have mercy on me.' My mother, however, turned against Christianity more and more.

She was much concerned that I should be aware of science and the reliable non-spiritual information it gave us. One of the events she arranged that I greatly enjoyed was a visit to the Paisley observatory. There I was introduced to the wonders of space as the surface of the moon and the rings of Saturn were brought to me in close-up. I learned a great deal from my mother, who gave me a lasting interest in the great expanse of the universe and provided me with many fascinating books, such as the life of the astronomer William Herschel. She also told me about Eastern religions, for she had studied Sir Edwin Arnold's *The Light of Asia* and ever afterwards believed in reincarnation. For a time, unfortunately, she thought I was the returned spirit of her mother.

My mother also felt that children, rather than being sheltered, should be fully exposed to the distressing events of life so that they might realise the nature of this world and its challenges to them. I remember two occasions especially when this happened. Once, on a visit to Paris in my teens, my mother wished me to go to the morgue with her. Terrified, I cried: 'What good could such a spectacle do to anyone?' 'It shows you what life is like,' she replied and went by herself, calling me a coward.

The other occasion was when she decided to take me to see her own mother's grave in Hawkhead cemetery in Paisley. My father, whether unwillingly or not I do not know, came also. I must have been five or six at the time and was much impressed by the great structure before which we stood. At the top of it was a round copper plaque on which was engraved a profile of my grandmother with the Italian words *Dolce Madre*. Almost at once my mother broke down in a flood of agonised tears and was inconsolable. I got the impression that somehow her mother was imprisoned in this imposing building and could not be released.

I adored my own mother and knew how she must feel, and so I wept too. My father spoke urgently to my mother, obviously telling her not to frighten me, but she was beyond hearing. He took me on a little walk and tried to tell me a story but I would not listen. My father then took to action. He began to make little skips and jumps among those unfamiliar objects, the tombstones. Never having seen my dignified father behave in this fashion, I burst out laughing in the midst of my tears, took his hand, and was comforted. Looking back across the years I can understand my mother's distress. Mixed with her natural sorrow, and sharpening it cruelly, was the sense of guilt because her mother had not wanted her to marry.

Although my parents were agnostics, in early adulthood they had been bound by the social conventions of the day; especially the requirement that schoolmasters should be members of the established Church of Scotland. My father conformed to this and, at the time of her marriage, even though her family were devoted members of the Free Church, which had broken away from the Church of Scotland a few decades before, my mother joined him as a member of Paisley Abbey.

The Abbey stands in the centre of Paisley and is a gloriously beautiful building. My father always used to say that the Abbey gave its name to the town: *basilica* became in the course of time Pasilicum, and then Paisley. Some years ago when I was asked to broadcast in the 'Home on Sunday' series on the BBC, the Abbey authorities very kindly played the music I chose. It was an unforgettable experience.

My parents were married in my grandfather Eadie's house rather than the Abbey because of my mother's extreme dislike of public occasions. This characteristic, together with my mother's sadly poor health after my birth, meant that I was christened in my parents' drawing room.

My parents did not relate the details of my christening; indeed, I did not know its date, 17 July 1897, until I was middle-aged and, in order to enter for a course of study for the Archbishop's Diploma in Theology,

I had to present evidence that it had happened. But my mother did tell me that the distinguished Doctor of Divinity – a friend of William Gladstone – who officiated warned her severely when the ceremony was over that next time she must come to church 'like everybody else'. I still possess a much-engraved solid silver rose bowl, used for my baptism, and the beautifully embroidered christening robe given to me by my grandmother Holmes, which has been used by all my descendants.

By the time my sister, Hermione, was born, my parents had moved out to the village of Bridge of Weir, cutting all connections with the church. During the thirteen years that we lived there no minister entered our home. On the one occasion on which we entered a church, for a wedding, my little sister, remembering a visit to *Peter Pan*, remarked afterwards: 'We sat in the dress circle.' Hermione was not christened until she was sixteen. I was her godmother, and a contemporary of mine, St John Harmsworth, was her godfather. She was confirmed a few days after by the Bishop of Chichester who, seeing her alone afterwards, told her that while it would have been better had she been christened as an infant he hoped that she would now do her best to become a good Christian. I thought this most inept and wished that he might have told her how good it was that she had made her own choice.

Both my parents retained the moral standards taught by their parents, in particular their severe sexual ethics, and described themselves as 'puritan agnostic Humanists'. My mother impressed her strong ethical views upon Hermione and myself from our earliest years. 'Always remember,' she would say, 'others first.' And she would go on: 'Never grudge to do more for the people you are helping than you need to do.' As a little girl she had often been sent out with hot meals for sick or needy neighbours over whom her compassionate mother kept a watchful eye. These errands of mercy frequently took her into the risk of severe infection, but there was never any question of avoiding them for that reason. In consequence, she never had any fear of either illness or death, and if the patient had died she always went to the bedside to pay her last respects. I regret to say that she was never able to communicate these sentiments in their entirety to me when I was young. It was not until I married and experienced both illness and death in my own family that I was able to take them in my stride as part of life.

What made me turn towards religion goes back, I think, to our time in France. One year, when the Sorbonne was in vacation, we spent a holiday in the guesthouse of a Roman Catholic nunnery. The nuns were amused by this little girl who chattered in French and English so well, and my mother allowed them to look after me while they were tidying the chapel. When they passed the altar they dropped on to their knees and I dropped down too. I did not know what it was about, but it gave me the sense of otherness – the sense of the numinous – which has never left me.

When we arrived back in Scotland, although I was only about six or

seven years old, I started to look for a church to attend. On the hillside
below our house I found a little Scottish Episcopal church with a most
beautiful road down to it, covered with wild roses which we called dog
roses. I regularly attended services at this small church on a Sunday
morning. I loved the music, the silences and the unobtrusive ministry
of the priest in charge, so unlike the austere solemnity of the Presbyterian
parish church presided over by Mr Sandys, the minister, who never
seemed to smile. I used to meet him on weekdays walking the country
roads, resplendent in silk hat and frock coat. He had a formidable squint
and one never felt out of the range of his critical gaze. I fled at the sight
of him. I was not spoken to at the church, as far as I can remember,
and, with hindsight, it surprises me that nobody in the congregation took
any notice of a little girl coming on her own to worship.

At St Columba's School I received religious education from our headmistress, Miss Waugh. Religion was so important to her that she took
scripture classes throughout the school. She had been to Palestine several
times and I can still hear the commotion in her soul when she told us
about it. She said: 'Now, I hope every one of you visits the Holy Land
one day,' and I made up my mind that that was something I must do.

I found a great comfort from the little religion that I knew. My
mother, for some reason best known to herself, taught me the Lord's
Prayer; a fatal mistake from her own point of view. I liked the sound of
the words and I said them morning and night. In the course of time I
began to pray them as well as say them, and I have always found great
comfort and consolation and strength during all the difficulties of life in
this sense of otherness. I felt that life had another dimension altogether
so that what we saw and heard was not the whole story.

Although my parents had told me that they wanted me to decide for
myself about religion, they did not approve of my religious feelings. My
father told me he was 'disappointed' in me, and when catastrophes
occurred, such as the earthquakes at Messina and San Francisco, my
mother demanded of me in triumph: 'Where is now thy God?' I was
only a teenager and of course I could not give her an answer, but I felt
quite sure that there was one. The 'sense of presence' that went back to
the days in the convent chapel assured me.

As a child, however, the most important thing in my life was politics.
My parents were tremendous Liberals before the First World War and,
while I did not accept their religious views, I became an enthusiastic
supporter of their politics. I used to go to school with my pockets full
of pamphlets that I had obtained from the Liberal Publication Department, and have tremendous battles with the horrid little girls at St
Columba's, who were all Tories.

The amusing thing was that originally my father had been a member
of the Conservative Party, but as he could not marry an Eadie and
continue in that light he became a Liberal. Later on he reverted to his

original views and, to my surprise, began to express Tory opinions. As a classicist my father had always been an elitist, and I do not believe that he ever had much use for democracy as Liberals understood it. The prevalent fear of Russian Communism as being the logical conclusion of democracy led my mother into the Tory way of thinking too in later life.

The excitement of the general election of 1906 made a big impression on me. I was nine years old at the time and saw myself as a Gladstonian Liberal. My parents had a telephone installed so that we could get the results quickly. Our constituency was West Renfrew, but the candidate we were most interested in was Sir Thomas Glen Coates in Paisley, where my mother's family lived. I was allowed to sit up and hear the results and we were delighted when the election of Sir Thomas came through. In that era polling took place during several weeks, not all on one day as happens now. One result could, therefore, affect others. The Liberals won a tremendous victory at that election, and we were thrilled that the Prime Minister, Sir Henry Campbell-Bannerman, always known as C.B., who had come to power in December 1905, was now confirmed in office with a huge majority.

I first visited Parliament in the spring of 1910, before my father became a member. Sadly, Campbell-Bannerman had died in 1908 and so the Prime Minister was Herbert Henry Asquith. I was almost thirteen, and when my parents were going to spend a few days in London during the school term I begged them to take me. They did not want me to be away from school and so I rather craftily said: 'But Parliament is the place where history is made; surely it will put me in a very privileged position to have seen history being made?' Well, that was rather cute of me and they relented.

I was thrilled by the visit and fell in love with London and the House of Commons. We stayed at a little hotel in Bloomsbury that I think was called The Thackeray, and dined in the Harcourt Room at the House of Commons with an old family friend, Sir John McCallum, the MP for Paisley, and his wife. We travelled from the hotel in a four-wheeled horse-drawn vehicle known as a 'growler', as the other type of cab, the two-wheeled hansom, could carry only two passengers. There were some motor cars about but many of the buses were still horse-drawn. I remember the pride in my father's voice as he said: 'Cabbie, House of Commons!'

Our visit must have been on, or about, Primrose Day, 19 April, because, as we went through Parliament Square on our way to the St Stephen's Hall entrance, my attention was attracted by a statue decked with primroses. I asked my father whose it was and he said: 'Oh, that's Disraeli. Primroses were supposed to be his favourite flower, but Gladstone used to say, and I always agreed with him, that the gorgeous orchid would be much more Disraeli's flower than the humble primrose.'

It was an exciting time to visit Parliament, for it was a period of very live issues. Despite the landslide victory of 1906, much of the Liberal legislative programme had been thwarted by the large Conservative majority in the House of Lords. The Tories were not only resisting some social reforms, but in 1909 they went as far as voting against Lloyd George's budget. This crisis of 'peers versus the people' led Prime Minister Asquith to hold an election at the beginning of 1910 and to introduce a Parliament Bill to restrict the House of Lords' veto. Sadly for us the huge Liberal majority had been lost and the Government only held office with the votes of the Labour MPs and the Irish Nationalist MPs. The latter demanded Irish Home Rule as the price of their support, and the Conservatives were determined to fight against this as hard as they could.

When we entered the central hall my mother and I were separated from my father, whom we did not meet again until we left the House. He was told to wait until after prayers before he could enter the Strangers' Gallery, reserved in those days for men, while we were whisked off in a lift to the Ladies' Gallery. The suffragettes' campaign of 'Votes for Women!' was in full swing, and before we were allowed to enter, my mother and I had to sign, in a large book, a very solemn promise that we would not make a disturbance of any kind. The Ladies' Gallery was near the ceiling, behind the Speaker's chair, and contained three rows of seats placed behind a heavy gold-painted grille. If one happened to be lucky enough to get into the front row it was just possible by squinting through the grille to get a good bird's-eye view of the top of the Speaker's chair, the Treasury table, and the august all-male assembly of MPs. From either of the back rows there was very little to be seen clearly at all.

The Ladies' Gallery was for members' wives and ordinary women, while the Speaker's Gallery next to it was for Cabinet ministers' wives, ambassadors' wives and such like. These two galleries looked exactly the same, but in the more exclusive one the women could have a tray of tea and toasted teacakes on their knees, like matinée-goers at the theatre. As there was much heated discussion in the Ladies' Gallery between supporters of different parties, the usher frequently had to keep the situation under control with his 'Hush, ladies!' One Conservative MP appreciated how cramped the galleries were but expressed himself in a most patronising way: 'It is doubtful, Mr Speaker, whether ladies should be allowed to witness our proceedings, but if they are allowed they should at least be properly accommodated.' I shall never forget that horrible, heavy grille with its criss-crossed bars symbolising our inferior position.

My mother and I were furious at this state of affairs. We were fervent supporters of women's suffrage and were members of Millicent Fawcett's National Union of Women's Suffrage Societies, the suffragists. Being opposed to violence, we did not support the Women's Social and Political Union, the suffragettes, although we went to meetings addressed by the Pankhursts and were horrified by the forcible feeding inflicted on Mrs Pankhurst and others in prison.

The issue of votes for women split the country; nobody seemed indifferent to it. There were women, such as Mrs Humphry Ward, the novelist, who were as fervently opposed to it as some men. She and Lord Curzon founded the League for Opposing Women's Suffrage. Paradoxically, I was quite pleased about this because I have always thought that when people start organisations opposing things the battle is almost won. Margot Asquith, the wife of the Prime Minister, was a determined anti-feminist. Although a loyal friend to countless women, for women in general she was no use at all. Her stepdaughter, Violet Bonham-Carter, was almost as bad, remarking on one occasion: 'If I had the vote, and I don't think that I want one . . .'

My father was very much against women's suffrage and would not listen to the argument put forward by my mother that there should be no taxation without representation. When my mother said to him: 'Give me one good reason against it, Dan,' he replied: 'Well, you couldn't stand the long hours.' Given the number of hours women spend looking after a home and family, that really was nonsense. When I asked him why women should not have the vote he responded testily: 'Because man is the lord of creation!' On the outbreak of the First World War he announced, triumphantly: 'You'll never get the vote now!' whereas, of course, the war was one of the things that helped us get it. Without women's work the war could not have been won. As Mary Macarthur, the Secretary of the Women's Trade Union League, expressed it: 'What a pity that the vote was given to the hand that filled the shell rather than the hand that rocked the cradle.' When women over the age of thirty got the vote in 1918 my mother said to my father: 'Well, Dan?' Lifting his chin, he answered: 'We men may have to take it away from you.'

Looking back on it now, I wonder if the violence played some part in obtaining the vote. I do not like to think so, but even Margot Asquith, who was as opposed to the vote for women as was her husband, confided to me: 'I think the Pankhursts did help to get women the vote.' Recently, I was pleased that my son Anthony arranged for a plaque commemorating Emily Davison to be placed in a little room in the House of Commons. On the night of the census she hid herself in the room so that she was able to say that her address was the House of Commons. Later she was killed while trying to stop King George V's horse in the Derby. I hope this room will soon be on the regular visitors' circuit at the Commons, for I think it is right that women should know at what awful cost their emancipation was won.

Before women obtained the vote we did have one rather strange privilege. Parliament only recognises two types of people: Members and Strangers. In those days women were not even Strangers; we were 'non est'. Consequently, as we were not really there, we were allowed to be present at Members' Prayers, whereas men were excluded. At two-thirty precisely a hush fell on the House. The attendants on duty called out:

'Mr Speaker!' The main door opened and through it came the impressive figure of Mr Speaker Lowther. His train bearer and his secretary followed him to the chair, and then the prayers were read.

I loved the prayers. I can still hear the beautiful voice of the Chaplain of the House, old Archdeacon Basil Wilberforce, a relative of William Wilberforce who helped to emancipate the slaves, praying: 'Let all the people praise thee, oh Lord, yea let all the people praise thee. Oh, let the nations rejoice and be glad. God is our own God and shall give us his blessings and all the ends of the earth shall revere him.' That gave me not only a sense of otherness but also a sense of the world being one, which has never left me.

A few years ago when I dined with Mr Speaker Weatherill I mentioned this early experience and he gave me a copy of the service sheet with a charming inscription. I once told Cliff Michelmore in an interview that I got a great deal of spiritual inspiration from the House of Commons in my youth, and he obviously thought I was going off my rocker!

The Ladies' Tea Room also proved to be a source of inspiration. All the mantelpieces in the House of Commons carry inscriptions in Gothic lettering. The one in the Ladies' Tea Room bore the injunction 'Get Understanding', which at that time I did not realise came from the Old Testament Book of Proverbs. I thought to myself: 'That's what I want to do, understand what life is all about.' I have always made that my motto in life. If you meet people, get understanding of them. Do not just leave the contact to a casual thing but get understanding of what they are like and what they are interested in.

How I loved that visit to Parliament! The Government were reintroducing Lloyd George's budget and so I heard some very important speeches. It was fascinating to see the famous politicians of the day. In particular I was struck by Mr Balfour, the former Conservative Prime Minister, who was 'long, lean and languorous'. He always sat with his eyes shut and his feet on the Treasury table. He never appeared to be taking notice of anything, but when it came to his turn to speak he jumped up and was extremely lucid and to the point. It was said that at one time Margot Tennant, who later became Margot Asquith, wanted to marry him. When Balfour was asked why he had not married her he replied: 'I rather thought of having a career of my own.'

Shortly after our visit to London, two memorable events occurred: the appearance of Halley's comet, which was so much brighter than on its return visit in 1986; and, in May 1910, the death of King Edward VII. He had fallen ill in his beloved Biarritz, and his fondness for France had done a great deal to create good relations between our two countries such as had not existed for a very long time. He was a very honest man. Everyone knew that he had a number of mistresses, and he always said: 'I want people to take me as I am. I'm not going to pretend to be a puritan, because I am not.' There had been apprehension at his accession as he had not been greatly respected when he was heir to the throne. As a joke people would change the prayer 'Bless the Queen, the Royal Family and Albert Edward, Prince of Wales' to 'Bless the Queen and the Royal Family *all but* Edward, Prince of Wales', but when he died there was a great deal of sorrow in the country for he had been a very likeable man who did not pretend to be any better than he was. His son, King George V, and Queen Mary were approved of because they led good lives almost to the point of being puritanical but were regarded as chilly in comparison to Edward and his beautiful Danish Queen, Alexandra.

I had returned to Scotland feeling like an exile. I thought of nothing but what was going on in London under a new reign, and the constitutional crisis that loomed ever larger as the Liberals launched their attack on the House of Lords. I just wanted to get back to London and spend the rest of my life under the shadow of Big Ben. I followed events with great interest. Asquith called a second election at the end of 1910 that failed to change the composition of the House, and then all through the summer of 1911, the hottest for seventy years with temperatures of 95° F for days on end, the Parliament Bill was debated in both Houses, the temperatures of the MPs and peers rising to match the weather. The climax came in August when the Lords passed the bill rather than have the King create sufficient peers to give the House of Lords a Liberal majority. The Parliament Act meant that the Conservative-dominated House of Lords could now hold up Liberal legislation for only two years.

My great hope and prayer was that my father would be elected for Parliament, and I so wanted him to contest the by-election which came up in the Govan division of Glasgow at the end of 1911. 'Oh no, I would never do that,' he said when the local Liberals asked him to stand. 'I'm interested in education; I'm not a legislator.' They tried to persuade him by saying: 'Oh, Mr Holmes, we don't expect you to win, we just expect you to put up a good show. We don't want this by-election to go by default.'

My father resisted for a while, but one night he came home and said: 'Well, I'm standing for Govan.' I flung my arms around his neck in gratitude. I desperately hoped that we should soon be returning to the exciting atmosphere of Parliament.

My mother was determined that, whatever his personal views, my father should agree to support votes for women. I remember her saying, very seriously: 'Now, Dan, I must just tell you that if you don't see your way to support a cause so near to my heart as that of the enfranchisement of women, I'm very sorry but I can't sit on your platform.' He knew that she meant it; she was a most determined woman. So a painfully written sentence appeared in the last paragraph of his election address: 'I am in favour of votes for women.' For me, that sentence, extracted so unwillingly from my father, was the most important aspect of the by-election.

My father refused to canvass and would have nothing to do with the organisation of the campaign. He spent most of the day at home, writing speeches, until the car which he had insisted on having at his disposal arrived to take him the twelve miles to Glasgow for the evening meetings. He was also provided with a room where he could rest. These requirements had been agreed to, most considerately, by the local party: 'Oh, anything you want, Mr Holmes, anything you want.'

I was thrilled that I was allowed to attend these meetings. My mother and I travelled with him in the car with strict instructions that neither of us should speak during the journey! We sat on the platform and my mother soon found she had to fit in with the requirements of a candidate's wife. On one occasion she was forbidden to wear a handsome hat with a white feather because it carried the suggestion of surrender! My father never spoke for more than an hour, because my mother warned him that she would leave the platform if he exceeded that time.

He was a most eloquent speaker who used his learning to illustrate present-day events. I particularly remember an occasion in Glasgow Town Hall, during one of his election campaigns, when there was standing room only and he held the audience spellbound. He said: 'Now, you have all heard of the great eruption of Vesuvius at the beginning of the Christian era.' 'Oh, aye, Mr Holmes,' came the enthusiastic response. 'Well, do you know what they were doing when Vesuvius erupted? They were having an election.' This was greeted with loud laughter.

'Now, today, we candidates send out election addresses, but in those days the election addresses were written in the form of graffiti on the walls, and, when the lava was cleared away, there they were – we could read them. For instance, one candidate wrote, and I have seen this myself, "If you vote for me I will plant fruit trees and vegetables and you'll live free." This reminds me very much of the election address of the Socialist candidate, Mr McCubban, because he says that if you vote for him you will get a great deal of state aid.' This went down extremely well. He was always drawing from his extensive knowledge, and people used to say: 'Oh, have ye been to hear Mr Holmes? Oh, man; it's a great education.'

He handled questions very well. When asked: 'Mr Holmes, what will be the position of the Vale of Leaven strikers under a Liberal Government?' he replied: 'Oh, the Vale of Leaven, I suppose.' Once, when he thought someone was asking a cheeky question, he reverted to the language of the classroom with: 'I don't answer impertinent questions.'

He had not been expected to win, so the declaration of his victory, on 22 December 1911, was particularly thrilling. The successful outcome was very important because the Liberal Government had lost many seats in the first election of 1910 and had not won them back in the second. This change in my father's fortunes meant that we moved to London, and I felt that my destiny was going to work out.

CHAPTER 2
1912–1919

My father took his seat in January 1912, on the opening day of the new session of Parliament. The gregarious side of his nature, of which we had never seen much at home, found full satisfaction in the library of the House of Commons, where he spent most of the time, between divisions, discussing literature and capping quotations with other studious MPs of various parties. He rated a scholarly level of education very highly and would sometimes dismiss people without it as 'having nothing in them'.

He became known as the 'Poet Laureate of the House of Commons' and filled a notebook with verse about his colleagues, and current issues. In one poem he wrote:

> Though politicians dream of fame
> And hope to win a deathless name
> Time strews upon them when they've gone
> The poppy of oblivion.
> But lo the singer and his lays
> Grow mightier with the lapse of days
> And soar above the wreck of time
> On the immortal wings of rhyme.

Soon after his arrival, he was invited to speak at a dinner at which one of the guests was a very famous journalist, Sir Henry Lucy, the parliamentary correspondent of *Punch*, who reported debates in his own particular manner under the pseudonym 'Toby, MP'. He found my father an unusual and attractive speaker, and asked to be informed when he was to make his maiden speech.

As a consequence, in April 1912, a most amusing article about the member for Govan appeared in *Punch*: 'Members delivering their maiden speech are usually so impressed with importance of occasion as to begin by recommending themselves to merciful consideration of House. Gentleman from Govan had neither necessity nor desire for clemency.' The debate in which my father spoke was the second reading of the Temperance (Scotland) Bill. He entertained the House by saying: 'I do not expect that, in our generation at least, alcohol will ever be out of date and when I look at the history and even the climate of my native country I know quite well that my fellow countrymen will never be sickeningly abstemious or ostentatiously teetotal . . .'

The excellent *Punch* cartoonist E. T. Reed caricatured my father by exaggerating the little wisps of hair that stood up around his otherwise extremely bald head. Reed's skill did not impress my father's mother, who, when shown the drawing, merely remarked: 'It's not a bit like him.' My father said: 'I fear she didn't understand the nature of the paper.'

My father was not really a politician: his great interest in life was education; but on the few occasions when he joined in a debate, the House of Commons filled up and people listened. Although he did not speak very often, and only went to his constituency about twice a year, in those days he was considered a loyal party member and a conscientious constituency MP. Today it is very different, and MPs visit their constituencies frequently and hold weekly 'surgeries'.

Before the outbreak of the First World War we lived in a hotel in Lancaster Gate and at first I attended St Mary's, a nearby school. I did not stay long, because it was a very High Church school and the headmistress was opposed to the Liberal policy of disestablishing the Church of Wales. Although, later, the Archbishop of Wales said that he would not accept re-establishment if it were offered, because the church had done so much better without it, at the time we had to pray every morning in school assembly that 'the attack on the Church in Wales may be frustrated'. I stood there with a scarlet face and my mouth tightly shut, refusing to pray against my father's work. My parents removed me and I then went to a more congenial school in Holland Park.

Taking advantage of living in Lancaster Gate, I began to have riding lessons and, every Sunday morning after church, I joined the inhabitants of the Bayswater Road, and the other fashionable people, whose custom it was to ride in carriages or on horseback in Hyde Park. Unfortunately I could not get a very good riding company and I felt ashamed that the man who came out with me wore a horrible straw hat. One day, in 1912, he insisted on taking me where King George V and Princess Mary used to ride, and, sure enough, we saw the King approaching. The King's grooms grinned for all they were worth at us; I suppose they thought we looked rather comic. The King, however, was most courteous and raised his bowler hat to us. Both Princess Mary and myself were riding side-saddle, as women did in those days. Although I was pleased to have been acknowledged by the King, I had not wanted to intrude upon him in that way and was annoyed with my attendant.

What I particularly enjoyed was going to the House of Commons, to be present at prayers and listen to the debates. If my behaviour was up to standard I was allowed to go on Wednesday, my half-day from school. This made me very vulnerable because, if I had not behaved as my father thought I should have done, he would say: 'You'll not get to the House of Commons for a month.' A funny punishment for a girl in her teens, but he knew I just loved the House of Commons.

In those days there were four parties at work. The Liberal Party, much reduced in size, was still in government under the premiership of the much-venerated leader Asquith, regarded at the time as indispensable and known by his supporters as 'Old Man'. But the reverence he had from us all was not fully justified and he did not prove a strong enough leader during the First World War. Often called 'the last of the Romans', Asquith had a remarkable gift of speech; Ciceronian periods rolled out of his mouth without any apparent effort. Working with great dispatch, he never appeared to be under any strain. Even Queen Victoria admitted, when she had to ask him to dinner because he was her Home Secretary, that he was surprisingly agreeable, sensible, and rather good looking. But he could not really be known from his public appearances. At home at The Wharf, Sutton Courtenay, he was great fun; he liked young people and a good joke. Although he particularly enjoyed talking to young women, he could never envisage them as political colleagues. He had the 'ministering angel' complex about them, which made electioneering difficult for him when women got the vote in 1918 and had to be taken seriously.

Next in importance and seniority stood David Lloyd George, the Chancellor of the Exchequer, about whom there was enthusiasm and doubt in equal measure. His drive and energy in establishing, against Conservative opposition, the foundations of what later became the Welfare State was much admired, but his reputation was damaged in 1913 when it became known that he had been less than frank with Parliament over share dealings in the Marconi Company. This scandal was a blow to the Government because other ministers, including Sir Herbert Samuel, the Postmaster-General, and Rufus Isaacs, the Attorney-General, were implicated. There was such an obvious split between Asquith and Lloyd George that you could not agree with both of them.

The Liberal front bench had a formidable array of statesmen: Edward Grey, the Foreign Secretary; Reginald McKenna, the First Lord of the Admiralty; Sir John Simon, the Home Secretary, whom Mr Asquith privately called 'the impeccable'; Sir Rufus Isaacs; Sir Herbert Samuel; and Mr Churchill, a recent convert of whom we were very proud.

Until 1911 the leader of the Conservative and Unionist Party had been Arthur Balfour. He was the most languid-looking party leader I have ever seen. He used to sit, apparently taking no notice of what was going on for hours at a time. He looked more like a philosopher than a statesman, and indeed I believe he was the only Prime Minister ever invited to give the Gifford Lectures. At the right moment he came out of his apparent dream, got up and delivered a first-rate speech, taking up all the points that had been raised. In 1911, there had been a fierce contest for the leadership of the Conservative and Unionist Party between Austen Chamberlain and Walter Long. In the event a dark horse got in, and so, when my father entered Parliament, the Conservative leader was a little-known Scot, Andrew Bonar Law, who presented an undistinguished appearance. He seemed most uninspiring and was considered a near-nonentity by many people. At Bonar Law's funeral in 1923, I remember Ramsay MacDonald saying to me, rather sourly: 'If they can bury Bonar Law in the Abbey, they can bury anybody in the Abbey.'

The Conservatives were furious that the Government wanted to give Home Rule to Ireland and tried to hold up business as much as they could. The two most disruptive opposition MPs were Lord Hugh and Lord Robert Cecil, the sons of the former Prime Minister, the late Marquess of Salisbury. Sittings of the House were constantly disturbed by their loud cries of 'Divide! Divide!' as they tried to force a vote that they hoped would defeat the Government. They would often leave off the first syllable of 'Divide', and this enabled a paper to pun: 'It is less the caste of "Vere de Vere", than the caste of " 'vide! Divide!" ' Strangely, in the 1920s, Lord Robert, later Viscount Cecil of Chelwood, broke with the Conservatives and worked with the Labour Foreign Secretary, Arthur Henderson, in consolidating the League of Nations.

Before the First World War, the Labour Party was helping to keep the Government in office. Although MPs representing the Labour movement had been elected in the 1890s, the Labour Party as such had been founded only in 1900, so when I first attended debates it was a very new party indeed. Few Liberals realised that it would eventually eclipse their party. The Labour Party was led by James Ramsay MacDonald, a gifted but temperamental Scot who was always deeply conscious of the fact that he was an illegitimate child. As fellow Scots, he and my father, although members of different parties, were warm personal friends. During the war years when Ramsay, as a pacifist, went in fear of attack from the Seamen's Union, he and my father travelled together by tube to Hampstead for Ramsay's protection. On 4 August 1918, the fourth anniversary of the outbreak of war, when victory still seemed uncertain and Ramsay was one of the most hated men in Britain, he came, unexpectedly, to have tea with us. During an hour or two's visit the war was never mentioned. He knew we supported it, but it was touching that in his lonely position he seemed to find some comfort in our friendship.

Among this party but not wholly of it was James Keir Hardie, conspicuous both for his independent attitude and his tweed cap. I remember seeing him many times in the famous headgear that had made such a stir when he first appeared wearing it in the House. It was considered shocking because MPs dressed so formally in those days. When my father became an MP, my mother bought him a frock coat and a top hat or, as it was known in Scotland, from the Scots word for chimney, a 'lum' hat. The Scottish Labour MPs used to very much enjoy teasing my father about his 'lum' hat. I was delighted when, recently, my son, Anthony, was given an armchair that had belonged to Keir Hardie.

While the socialist MPs were very different from the others, it would have been impossible in 1912 to guess to which party members of the two front benches belonged, judging by their appearance and way of life. They dined constantly with each other, weekended together, and appeared to look at life in much the same way. Only when they were taking part in a debate was the difference apparent.

James Maxton, the Independent Labour MP from Clydeside, I particularly remember as a delightful person whom everybody liked for his lovable personality. It was said that he was stopped by the police for speeding but was not arrested when the policemen recognised the much-admired James Maxton. He was a widower and was devoted to his 'wee boy'.

Then there were the eighty or so Irish Nationalist MPs, members of the Irish Parliamentary Party, whom I remember as a great delight. They were reluctant attenders, always thinking of one thing: Home Rule for Ireland. Asquith had to depend on them for a majority after the 1910 elections; so these were very important people, and they knew it. They were most interesting, quite unlike any of the English, Welsh or Scotch MPs. They brought a perceptive wit into the debates which has never been replaced since they ceased attending the House in 1918. It was awfully dull when the Irish left.

The Irish Parliamentary Party contained people of varied opinions. The leader, John Redmond, and his brother, William, belonged to the landlord class and were much more sedate than their followers; they were natural conservatives and felt an affection for the British Empire. When the war broke out, Willie Redmond was one of the first to join the forces and it was poignant that, when he was killed, his body was recovered from the battlefield by members of the Ulster Division, the most bitter opponents of Home Rule.

The great wit of the party was T. P. O'Connor, who, though Irish to the core, sat for the Scotland division of Liverpool. He was known by everyone as 'T.P.', pronounced 'Tay Pay'.

I have an affectionate recollection of another Irish MP, Jeremiah MacVeigh, who used to join us from time to time for that great treat, tea on the terrace. Jerry MacVeigh was very friendly to me and told me that my appearance on the terrace was the greatest blow that Scotland ever struck for freedom. I never dared to tell him that I was implacably opposed to Home Rule for Scotland, because it would mean a Scottish Parliament in Edinburgh and I wanted to stay in London!

Not that I was not proud of my Scottish heritage. Only once was I careless enough to call myself English, and then I was quickly pulled up. It was on a night bus travelling between Delphi, where I had been spending a few days among the 'bright rocks' by the stone of the Sybil, and Levadhia, where I was hoping to get a bus to Athens. When our bus was held up, I asked a fellow passenger, in French, what had happened and whether we were likely to catch our connection, the Olympic *rapide*. He assured me that it was '*rapide*' only by euphemism

and that, however late we might be, it would certainly be later. Then
he added the bad news that I spoke French with a Central European
accent. Where did I come from? he wanted to know. I remarked casually:
'I'm an English tourist.' 'Impossible!' came the reply. 'Madame is, perhaps, Scottish?' Surprised, I said: 'How do you know?' 'Oh,' he said,
'the Scots are a little *drôle*.' Whether he meant funny peculiar or funny
amusing I had not the nerve to ask!

There was tremendous uproar in the House during the years when
the Government was steering through the bill to give Ireland Home
Rule: on one occasion an Ulster Unionist MP threw the Speaker's copy
of Standing Orders at Winston Churchill and hit him on the head. Bonar
Law was encouraging the Ulster Unionists to ignore the bill if it were
passed and it seemed that Ulster was on the brink of insurrection. But
some concessions were made and, after the Conservative-dominated
House of Lords had held it up for two years, the bill was eventually put
on the statute book. It was shelved during the First World War and was
then overtaken by events in Ireland.

I was particularly interested in the attempts that were made to pass
legislation to give women the vote. Although the Prime Minister was
opposed to the enfranchisement of women, a majority of his Cabinet
and of his party were in favour. Responding to this pressure in the
summer of 1912, Asquith announced, when introducing a Franchise and
Registration Bill to abolish plural voting and property qualifications for
voting, that members could amend the bill to include women. I was very
excited, thinking that the vote was at last within our grasp; but great
disappointment was to follow when, six months later, Speaker Lowther
ruled that the amendment would change the nature of the bill too much
and a separate bill would be needed. Asquith was privately relieved, and
although a bill to give women the vote was allowed time for debate by
the Government in 1913, it was defeated, Asquith speaking against it.
The militant suffragettes stepped up their campaign against the Government, and women still had not got the vote on the eve of war.

Although I enjoyed many exciting visits to Parliament during those
last few years of peace, there was one occasion that stands out in my
memory more than all the others. It was at five minutes to three on the
afternoon of 3 April 1912 that I first saw my husband to be. I was in the
gallery with my mother when the door into the lobby opened and a
young-looking, fair-haired man came into the chamber, very alert, his
face illuminated by a shaft of sunlight. When I asked my mother who
he was and why he was counting the MPs on both sides of the House,
she gave me the name that I afterwards shared: 'That is Mr Wedgwood
Benn. He is a Liberal whip and he is responsible for seeing that no
division is allowed unless there are enough Liberals to carry the day.'

The possibility of the Liberals being defeated in a vote and being
forced to call a general election always terrified me as I did not know if

my father had the means to stand again. Lady McCallum, who was sitting with us, said I went as white as a sheet at the thought of the Government's being defeated!

On one occasion the Tories managed to hide a large number of their MPs in various bathrooms in the House of Commons and they suddenly appeared as the vote was being taken. Happily for the Government, there were not quite enough of them. A Liberal MP got up and asked Mr Wedgwood Benn if there had been such an event since the pool of Bethesda. He replied: 'No, in this case no miracle followed!' He constantly delighted the House with his wit.

I saw William Wedgwood Benn on subsequent visits to Parliament, and as I admired him so much, and thought he was charming to look at, I decided to get his photograph. I wrote to Elliot and Fry, the photographers, but I did not want to ask only for Wedgwood Benn's photograph, in case they told him, so I asked for Asquith's and Lloyd George's photographs too. They sent all three, but I kept only William's and returned the others, together with the necessary few shillings from my Post Office account, saying: 'Mr Benn will do for the present.' He became my pin-up boy!

William had entered Parliament in 1906 as member for St George's-in-the-East and Wapping, a very small East London constituency with only three thousand voters. At twenty-eight, he was the youngest MP. His first question was to the War Minister, Richard Haldane, asking if he could get a war pension for one of his constituents: a veteran of the Crimean War!

He became Parliamentary Private Secretary to Reginald McKenna, the First Lord of the Admiralty, and then, after keeping his seat in the election of January 1910, was appointed a junior lord of the Treasury and a junior government whip. The Liberal Chief Whip, Alexander Murray, the Master of Elibank, told William to memorise the names and faces of every MP to make sure there were always enough Liberals and their allies in the House to win every division.

An ardent supporter of social reform, he was delighted to be chosen by the Chancellor of the Exchequer, David Lloyd George, whom at that time he greatly admired, to help steer the National Insurance Bill through the Commons. This bill, which provided unemployment and health insurance for millions of workers, was passed in 1911 and can be regarded as the foundation stone of the Welfare State.

However, William became disillusioned with Lloyd George because of the Marconi scandal, and used to say: 'That man can't be trusted; he doesn't know right from wrong.'

Although I saw him frequently from the Ladies' Gallery, I did not meet my future husband until December 1912, at the wedding of his colleague John Gulland, a fellow Liberal whip. I was fifteen at the time and William was thirty-five. At one point, Mr Gulland came up to my parents and me with Wedgwood Benn and said he wanted us to have a word with his colleague. 'Oh, Miss Holmes,' William said, 'I understand that you quite often go to the Ladies' Gallery.' He accompanied this statement with a very knowing smile because he had been told by our great friend, Sir John McCallum, that I admired him. One day Sir John, my father and Wedgwood Benn were in conversation when Sir John said: 'Did you know that you had an admirer in the Ladies' Gallery?' My father should have said nothing and the incident would have passed, but, embarrassed, he remarked: 'Nonsense! She's only a child,' and Wedgwood Benn saw the truth at once. I think he was quite touched that a schoolgirl admired him.

At fifteen I was now thinking seriously of my future. Did I want a career or a family? In those days hardly any middle-class women contemplated both. It was felt that the two could not be combined without grave risk of strain for a marriage and neglect for the children. While I did not believe that a woman's whole outlook should be entirely bound by home and family, I very much wanted as many children as possible and I could not endure the idea of being away from them for hours every day for any reason. I must therefore marry a man who could support the whole family and myself and I thought it would be very interesting to marry an MP.

When I innocently told my mother about my future plans she was deeply shocked. 'Never tell anyone you would like to marry,' she expostulated, 'and you must not mention children.' Astonished I asked: 'Why? Most women marry. Why mustn't it be mentioned?' 'Oh,' she replied, 'you should never think of marriage until an actual offer comes along, and you must never think of a family: that's most unseemly.' I digested this in surprise. It represented, I think, a very frequently held view in Scotland seventy or eighty years ago, and was part of the belief that women were the inferior sex. Even though my mother was a feminist, when it came to sexual matters she was still influenced by her puritanical upbringing.

William and I did not see each other very often after our initial meeting, and then, in August 1914, war came. For the first two months he was occupied with the Prince of Wales' National Relief Fund, which came about in the following way. In 1912 there had been a great London dock strike and William and the Duke of Atholl had raised, with the help of the *Daily News*, a large sum of money for the relief of the dependants of the strikers. A few days before war was declared, William and some newspaper owners had the idea of setting up a similar fund for the relief of soldiers' dependants, and they were delighted when the Prince of Wales agreed to become President. When war broke out on 4 August, William's name happened to be the only one that occurred in the Court Circular. He went to Buckingham Palace and was asked by King George V to become Chairman of the Committee of the National Relief Fund. By September, two million pounds, of an eventual five million, had been collected and was being put to good use providing separation allowances for the wives of thousands of newly enrolled soldiers. To thank him for his work, the Prince gave William a beautifully inscribed silver cigarette case. I am sorry to say it was stolen.

As soon as he had put the fund on its feet, in October 1914, he joined the Middlesex Yeomanry. Although he was in his late thirties, and as a Member of Parliament was exempt from military service, he felt it was his duty to volunteer. He was sent to Egypt and from there the regiment was drafted, without the horses, to Gallipoli to join the expedition that hoped to advance and take Constantinople.

The Gallipoli campaign was very much mismanaged by the British, while the Turks had a brilliant commander, Mustafa Kemal Pasha, who became known as Atatürk and was later the first Turkish president. In the parliament at Ankara his chair is always left empty so that the Turks' great man can be present in spirit.

William was adjutant for his regiment. A few days after landing, orders were given for an offensive to capture two mountains; the Middlesex Yeomanry were to be the first line of reserve. The attack took place on 21 August 1915. The first advance was unsuccessful and so William's division, under 'Scatters' Wilson, was ordered to march across a salt lake under fierce enemy shelling. The casualties were appalling but eventually the survivors reached a place called Chocolate Hill. Ordered to advance further, they were unable to make progress and went back to camp, but a day later they marched back to Chocolate Hill and held it for several weeks despite constant shelling. Eventually they were moved into trenches. Nothing had been gained: the division had come out to the Gallipoli peninsula over three thousand strong and returned with well under a thousand. William kept a regimental flag, and each year on the anniversary would recall the first day of the battle. It was a truly terrible experience.

Whatever he did he threw his whole heart and soul and spirit into it, and if there was a nasty job to be done, he was always the first to undertake it. A fellow soldier told me that he saw William set off from the regiment's position, to crawl several miles under fire down to the coast with the general's orders. The troops were horrified and thought they would never see him again, but he just smiled and said: 'Well, have a cup of tea ready for me when I come back.' Gallipoli was such a wasteful campaign; so many lives were lost unnecessarily, including William's young brother, Oliver.

The conditions in the trenches were so disgusting, with flies swarming everywhere, that William, like many others, came down with jaundice, and had to convalesce in Malta. He was then sent back to Egypt, where he became an observer attached to the Royal Naval Air Service, East Indies and Egypt Seaplane Squadron, under the command of Colonel L'Estrange Malone. William had as colleagues some remarkable men, including Leonard Woolley, the archaeologist, and Erskine Childers, the author of *The Riddle of the Sands*, who was executed by the Irish Free State during the civil war in the 1920s. The seaplane station was a few wooden huts on a sand island in Port Said harbour and the planes were carried on the *Ben-my-Chree*, a converted passenger ship that had been designed for the Liverpool to Isle of Man run. Little could the shipbuilders have realised her destiny.

William flew on reconnaissance and bombing missions as a military observer. He felt that the work was so valuable that, in September 1916, he declined an offer to return to England to be Parliamentary Secretary at the Ministry of Munitions. In December, Lloyd George became Prime Minister and set up a new Coalition Government. Remaining loyal to the deposed Asquith, William turned down Lloyd George's offer to become a Chief Whip.

In January 1917 the *Ben-my-Chree* sailed to join the French naval forces that were occupying Castelorizo, a small island situated a few miles from Rhodes and a thousand yards from the Turkish coast. Suddenly, there was a terrific explosion as the Turks began to shell the ship. This continued, accurately and remorselessly, until the *Ben-my-Chree* became engulfed in flames and sank. During the successful evacuation, William risked his life searching the ship for missing sailors. Anticipating a Turkish invasion that, thankfully, did not materialise, the French Governor ordered William to defend the town with a small force of British and French sailors. After being in control for over a week, the British and French sailors were safely evacuated. William was awarded the Distinguished Service Order and the French Croix de Guerre and Légion d'honneur.

William felt that everyone who went up in a plane should learn to fly, and so he only agreed to go to Italy and join the Adriatic Barrage, an anti-submarine air defence system, after gaining his wings. I am sorry to say that a few planes were damaged in the process! Unfortunately, he caught malaria, which was to plague him for the rest of his life. It returned times without number, and for the last few years of his life he was never without oxygen in the house. In the end he died at the age of eighty-three from the emphysema it brought about. He bore this with great courage and, if he could possibly help it, never let it stand in the way of what he had set himself to do.

While convalescing in England, William learned that his constituency, St George's-in-the-East, was going to be merged with Whitechapel, whose Liberal MP might well be chosen to contest the enlarged constituency. Although concerned about his political career, he went back to Italy and in the summer of 1918 became an observer with the air force that was supporting the Italians against the Austrians in northern Italy.

Here he experienced his greatest adventure. He arranged with the Italian army to try a daring plan that had never been done before: to drop a spy from a plane behind enemy lines. William chose as his pilot the Canadian air ace Colonel Barker, who later won the VC. They devised a special trap door that would release the agent at the right moment, and, after weeks of careful preparation, set out in pitch darkness with William navigating by means of searchlights and wireless. The brave man who volunteered for the experiment was an Italian called Lieutenant Alessandro Tandura. He was to be dropped over his home town, near Vittorio, in enemy territory from where he would send reports by carrier pigeons and signals. It was an extremely dangerous undertaking because, if caught, he would certainly be shot.

Although Tandura was temporarily stunned when he landed, the operation proved to be a great success. He buried his uniform and parachute in the field, put on peasant's clothing, and was hidden by his sweetheart. During the remaining months of the war, he was able to send valuable information to headquarters. After the war he married his fiancée and they named their son after William: in Italy today there may well be an old man called Wedgwood Benn Tandura! William was awarded the Distinguished Flying Cross, and the Italian Bronze Medal for Military Valour. Tandura won the Gold Medal, Italy's highest military honour.

William decided to return to England in September 1918 to prepare for the forthcoming election. When he came home he wrote modestly about his experiences in a book called *In the Side-Shows*. As well as containing some pretty severe criticism of the military system, it tells a very illuminating story of what four years in the armed forces brought to him and what he learned from it. I took money from my Post Office account and bought a copy.

I was seventeen when the war began and I had just 'come out'. I went to school in the morning with my hair down, and was allowed to go to parties in the evening with my hair up: the traditional sign that a girl was moving into adulthood. I had my first evening dress, a lovely pale pink satin, and my mother and I were anxious to know what my father's response would be because he was very puritanical, and the dress was very low cut. When he saw it, his only words were: 'Child, I see your neck.'

I remember the summer of 1914, that last summer of peace. It was a brilliant Season but, looking back, it had something of the atmosphere of the Duchess of Richmond's Ball, on the eve of Waterloo. The first big event I attended was the India Office party, held annually at the Banqueting Hall in Whitehall. Little did I imagine that I would one day be the hostess, when my husband was Secretary of State for India.

I went to a garden party at Number 10 Downing Street, wearing a cape which was white satin on one side and black satin on the other. All the Cabinet were there and so was Violet Asquith, the daughter of the Prime Minister's first wife, Helen Melland. Violet had been engaged to Lord Archie Gordon – a son of Lord Aberdeen – who had died in a

motor accident. During the war, in December 1915, she married
Asquith's private secretary, Maurice Bonham-Carter, always known as
'Bongie'. The very gorgeous wedding was considered by many people
to be unsuitable for wartime.

There had been a feeling until the last moment that Britain should be
isolationist and should not get involved in a European war. What turned
opinion was the German invasion of Belgium; that was what tipped the
scales as far as my father was concerned. When the declaration of war
was announced in the House of Commons on 4 August 1914, the one
ladies' ticket available went, of course, to my mother. The chamber was
packed to overflowing and seats were put up all along the floor of the
House. I was present a few days later and heard Winston Churchill, the
First Lord of the Admiralty, announce the first naval casualty: the cruiser
Amphion. The occasion was made memorable by Churchill's manner of
delivery with every 's' pronounced as 'sh': 'The House will have read
with sorrow of the loss of the cruiser, *Amphion*. The Germans' mine-
layer was pursued and sunk but the survivors were humanely saved.'

I stayed at school for another year but, like so many people, I wanted
to feel I was doing my bit for the war effort, and I asked to be allowed
to become a temporary civil servant. I took a secretarial course and then
worked, at the newly formed Ministry of Labour, for another temporary
civil servant, Mr Bertrand Christian, who was from Nesbitts the pub-
lishers. I had a room of my own in an office in Tothill Street, just by
St James's Park station, and the work was congenial, but I felt I was not
really doing much to help the war and it would have been very much
better if I had stayed on at school and got some qualifications. I certainly
had more independence as a result of the war and, like so many other
women, was doing a type of job that I would not have done in peace-
time. This was certainly an important factor in the emancipation of
women from traditional roles.

At the beginning of the war we moved to Hampstead Garden Suburb,
but for a period during the war my parents decided to live in Oxford,
from where my father commuted to Parliament. I stayed in Hampstead,
in a block of flats looked after by a housekeeper, and travelled on my
own by tube between St James's Park and Golders Green. It was quite
a long walk from the station and there were, occasionally, air raids from
the huge Zeppelin airships and, later, the big Gotha planes. During the
war, women travelled on their own more than before, but I was really
amazed that my mother allowed me to live by myself and commute in
this way. I stayed in Oxford at weekends.

I used to go to 'bomb parties' in Hampstead, arranged by Scottish
friends, Mr and Mrs Miller-Craig. Whenever there was a bomb alert, I
would hurry into a nice dress and go along to their home for a musical
evening. Mr Miller-Craig, a civil servant at the Scottish Office, sang
beautifully in his lovely baritone voice. When the all-clear sounded I

went home on my own, being too independent to let the Miller-Craigs accompany me. Although the extent of the bombing was nothing like that of the Second World War, there were several thousand casualties and it was an anxious time.

During the war, I joined a very beautiful Hampstead church, St Jude on the Hill, and was confirmed there by Bishop Winnington-Ingram. At this time I developed a great desire to study theology in order to understand my religion as fully as possible. To my surprise this did not commend itself to my vicar, the redoubtable Basil Graham Bourchier – 'B.G.B.' Looking at me coldly he asked: 'Can't you trust your church and your vicar to tell you what you need to know?' I could not!

I went to social meetings every week and I did a lot of work for 'B.G.B.' by distributing the parish papers. He was a cousin of the actor Arthur Bourchier, and had the same histrionic talent and beautiful voice. When he preached there was standing room only. He was kind enough to say that I had helped to build the church, because, when my dear friend St John Harmsworth died, I suggested to his father, Sir Leicester Harmsworth, that he endow a chapel at St Jude's to his son's memory. A newspaper magnate like his brother, Lord Northcliffe, Sir Leicester had the means to provide all the money that was required to build the St John's Chapel.

During the war, the Liberal Associations in the eighty-two London constituencies had become somewhat moribund, as everyone was concentrating on winning the war rather than on party politics. Being known by the Whips' Office, I was asked, just before the war ended, if I would go round and try to waken up the Liberal Associations. Clearly, as soon as victory was achieved, there would be a general election and things must be got into readiness for this test. I had no office facilities or headed notepaper; just a list of names of people who had been active in Liberal politics before the war. With the help of a map of London, I went to each constituency and asked people to arrange meetings for me to address. I explained that now the war was over we must get Liberalism going again. It was interesting but I had been asked to do too much, and after a time my health broke down. My mother took me on a holiday to Cornwall where I recovered.

The war came to an end in November 1918 and the general election, the first for eight years, was held in December. I was delighted that an Act had been passed allowing women to stand for Parliament and giving women over thirty the right to vote, but I was concerned about the contests facing my father, and Captain William Wedgwood Benn.

The Liberal Party had split in 1916 when Lloyd George replaced Asquith as Prime Minister and led the Coalition Government with the Conservatives. Both Wedgwood Benn and my father were against Lloyd George and stood in the 1918 election as Independent Liberals, supporting Asquith. This meant they would have to face candidates endorsed

by – or as it became known, given a 'coupon' by – Lloyd George.
My father defended his seat at Govan, but William had to contest a new
seat.

When he came home, just before the general election, he was disappointed not to have been selected as candidate for the enlarged constituency. Resolving to follow the advice of Augustine Birrell, the former
Chief Secretary of Ireland, to 'do the high sublime', William gave way,
handing over his office and all his files to his rival. This left him, after
four years of war service, completely without hope of being in the new
Parliament. Within days, however, he had an invitation from the constituency of Leith, near Edinburgh, to come and stand as an Independent
Liberal against a Conservative who had the endorsement of Lloyd
George's 'coupon'. To the great surprise of the Government and the
delight of his family, friends, and the Independent Liberals, he won easily,
returning to sit in Parliament for one of the most creative periods of his
life.

Unfortunately, William was one of only twenty-eight supporters of
Asquith to be returned to Parliament at the so-called 'Coupon Election'.
My father at Govan, and over two hundred other Independent Liberals,
including Asquith, were brought down by the Coalition landslide.
Asquith's small band of supporters became known as the 'Wee Frees', a
name chosen by William's father, Sir John Benn. Not many years before,
when a large majority of the Assembly of the Scottish Free Church voted
to join the United Presbyterian Church, a small group refused to accept
this decision and, remaining independent, were consequently nicknamed
the 'Wee Frees'. Contemporaries drew a parallel with the Asquithian
Liberals who would not join Lloyd George's coalition with the Conservatives. William arranged weekly meetings for the Independent Liberals
and organised them in opposition to the Coalition.

In February 1920, for the first time in many years, William and I met
in Paisley, at the by-election caused by the death of my family's great
friend, the Independent Liberal MP Sir John McCallum. This sad event
gave Asquith the opportunity to contest the seat, and to our delight he
won with an increased majority.

The Paisley by-election made the reputation of his daughter Violet
Bonham-Carter. She made a flaming speech in her father's favour and
after that she was a star speaker wherever she went. She used to speak
from memory, with her husband, 'Bongie', sitting in the front row with
her typed-out speech, acting as prompt.

Unfortunately, the return of the leader of the 'Wee Frees' to Parliament did not prove to be the start of the Liberal revival we all longed
to see.

The story got round that William and I had met for the first time in
Paisley and, when we got engaged, the papers, and many people, said:
'They met at the Paisley by-election.'

We were thrilled when, in the spring of 1920, my father was invited to fight a by-election in North Edinburgh. William went to give help to my father and to Walter Runciman, the former Liberal Cabinet minister, who was fighting a by-election in neighbouring South Edinburgh. My mother and I went up to help my father, and William and I met again. He had always remembered me as his schoolgirl fan and now felt a serious attraction of which I was, at first, quite unaware. Sadly, both seats were lost to Liberalism and we all went home much disappointed.

After his defeat at North Edinburgh, my father never stood for Parliament again, and we moved to a lovely architect-designed house called Rowlands, at Seaford on the Sussex coast. At that time I was in very low spirits because, at the age of twenty-three, I knew I had not yet found my place in life. Politics as a career of my own was not attractive; it was too late to go to university for a full degree; and my parents would not hear of my taking a diploma in theology at St Hugh's College, Oxford, although at that time the course was open to non-graduates. I had even thought of becoming a nun. At least, I thought bitterly, I do not need any qualifications except for a right disposition of the heart. Many years later, when I told this to my good friend the late Dr Charlotte Klein of the Sisters of Zion, she retorted somewhat tartly, in her characteristic fashion: 'It wasn't your vocation – you had to produce your family!' I am sure she was right – and so it happened.

Shortly after our move to Seaford, my father had a letter from Captain Wedgwood Benn to say that he and his young nephew would be passing through Seaford on a bicycling tour and might they come to tea? My father was naturally delighted to renew an old parliamentary friendship. They had been on close terms in the House and shared a taste for French literature, meeting once a week in Wedgwood Benn's rooms to read the Funeral Orations of Bossuet. My father, all unsuspecting that anyone but himself was the attraction, replied that the visit would be a great pleasure. He warned me: 'Now, Captain Benn is coming to see us, you'd better keep out of the way.' Well, I had my suspicions, and I was determined not to do that! The two cyclists duly arrived. After tea and a long chat they set off again, William suggesting that perhaps my sister and I might accompany them part of the way to Alfriston, where they were to stay the night. This we duly did, and when we all arrived at Alfriston our two visitors then accompanied us back to Seaford!

Soon Captain Benn appeared again, this time with his elder brother and sister-in-law, Ernest and Gwendolen Benn, and their daughter, Betty, out on half-term leave from Roedean School. Ernest declared afterwards that he thought there was 'nothing in it' because he considered Hermione and me to be only a 'couple of flappers' (this was the uncomplimentary term applied in those days to adolescent girls). But to me it was apparent that something must be afoot.

What of my idea of becoming a nun? During the next few weeks I
thought a great deal about this. It had been a growing hope, fanned by
the recollection of the gracious sisters at the French hospice nearly
twenty years before, and the sense of a presence that had been with me
ever since. Was it all going to vanish now with a proposal, if it came,
and the promise of a home of my own? It was a problem I could not
solve. I must leave it to Fate, but I knew that the hope of fulfilment
based on a secure life's partnership was something that I dared not refuse.
Surely nothing could bring greater blessings on the next stage of my
existence.

We were going to spend a week in London, and William wrote to
my mother, inviting us to tea at the House of Commons. My mother
said to me: 'Now, I don't want you to build on this: I'm sure there's
nothing in it.' I had my own views. He took my sister and me to the
theatre, and then asked if he could take me on my own. My father
became very suspicious.

We went to see a play called *The Grain of Mustard Seed*. It was the first
time we had ever been alone together in our lives, and while we were
in the theatre he suddenly caught hold of my hand. As we walked along
Piccadilly, his proposal was a statement and my acceptance was a question. He said: 'We could live round the corner and you could have a
chop at the House every night.' I hate chops! I said: 'What shall I call
you – Captain Benn?' How ridiculous that was! And he said: 'Call me
William.' It cannot be said that we were in love, but we were strongly
attracted to each other and we felt sure we could fall in love and be
happy together. Indeed, it almost felt like one of those 'sensible' arranged
marriages of long ago. I remember there was a poor man on a bench
nearby and William said: 'I'm so happy,' and put a half-crown in the
man's pocket. Unfortunately, the pocket had a hole in it and it fell with
a clank on the pavement. Arriving at the Forum Club, where I was
staying with my mother, we announced: 'We're engaged.' This was an
awful shock to my mother. When William went away, she said: 'Oh
dear, I wish you wouldn't get married, I'll have to be polite to Sir John
and Lady Benn.' The next morning, William visited my father at his
club, the Reform. Thinking that William wanted a marriage settlement,
my father's response was: 'You'd better see her mother.' After being
assured by William that this was not his intention, all my father said was:
'She's a good girl.'

At forty-three it was at first very difficult for William to think in terms
of two people. I remember he wrote to about fifty friends and acquaintances saying: 'Just to let you know I am going to be married on
November 17th.' He received fifty replies saying: 'Splendid! Many congratulations – who is she?' It took him some time to live that down.
We were married eight weeks after our engagement, at St Margaret's,
Westminster.

CHAPTER 3
1920–1926

After we had announced our engagement, the question soon arose: 'Where should we be married?' At this point a number of groups began to show signs of wanting to 'take over' the event in the interest of some cause or other. The Liberal Association in William's constituency urged us to hold our wedding in Leith in order to encourage the local Liberals. But we both agreed that this would exclude too many friends and that the House of Commons' church, St Margaret's, Westminster, was the correct place. Many Leith people were able to come up for the event, including a local baker who travelled in the guard's van of the overnight express protecting a many-tiered cake of monumental proportions topped with a model aeroplane!

The successful take-over was by the Independent Liberals, the 'Wee Frees'. They wanted the occasion to be an opportunity to publicise the continued existence of an active Asquithian opposition to the Coalition Liberal Prime Minister, Lloyd George. William had no objection to this, and so it was agreed that we would be provided with a 'beauty chorus' of good-looking young Independent Liberal ushers to show people to their seats, and Asquith, Margot and family, would have the seats of honour. Lloyd George was not invited but did send us a beautiful copy of Macaulay's *Essays*, inscribed 'With best wishes from us all'.

As I awoke on 17 November 1920, my glance fell on the white satin wedding dress, softly flushed by a lining of pink silk, that had been carefully hung up the night before. Everything else was there: gloves, handbag, and the beautiful Paisley shawl, given by my mother, that had been skilfully turned into a wrap coat without applying the scissors. My eye travelled contentedly round the room. Then followed a stab of panic. Where were my white satin shoes? They had been bought and, I believed, delivered a month before. After a fruitless search, my young sister, Hermione, postponing her dressing as principal bridesmaid, dashed down to the shop in Regent Street and, fortunately, came back with an identical pair. The situation was saved, and I breathed again. 'Very lucky,' declared my dressmaker, full of words of traditional wisdom for the occasion. 'Very lucky – any incident concerning shoes on a wedding day. You will be very happy.' What nonsense to suppose that would be the reason! But I took everything as it came on that very special day.

Soon, I heard the sound of a familiar voice downstairs, as William called to collect my luggage for the honeymoon. Instinctively I moved towards the door. 'No! No!' cried my dressmaker, putting her arm across my way. 'You mustn't see your bridegroom on your wedding day till you meet at the altar. You'll have very bad luck otherwise.' She was a friendly soul, so I retreated. After all, William had heard from me by the morning's post: I had sent him, in the most appropriate style for a dedicated parliamentarian, a message, underlined in the manner of a three-line whip: 'Wake up, Captain Benn. It's your wedding day!'

I soon discovered that more was missing than my shoes: my mother! As she was very unpredictable and hated big public occasions, we assumed, rightly as it turned out, that she had decided to spend the day somewhere else. For once my dressmaker was silent, having no inkling as to what tradition had to say about an event so unlikely as the disappearance of the bride's mother. Luckily, an aunt agreed to stand in to receive guests.

I joined my father in Reggie and Pamela McKenna's car, lent us in their absence. In this highly polished vehicle, we were driven to St Margaret's by Bruce, their chauffeur, and accompanied by Henry, their butler; two old family retainers who had known William for many years and were delighted to have a share in the wedding arrangements.

Setting out too early, we found it necessary to go round St James's Park twice before arriving at the church. The wedding guests we passed on the way must have thought I had changed my mind at the last minute! My father, unfortunately, was not enjoying himself. This type of occasion was quite new to him and he would rather have been at home with his books. 'I wish it were over,' was his only utterance, many times repeated, on the journey.

It was a beautiful, crisp winter's day and, in the sunshine, everything looked its best. As we reached the church door, Big Ben struck two-fifteen, someone took my Paisley shawl, and my father and I started to walk up the aisle. Suddenly, a voice boomed in my ear: 'The very best of luck.' Startled, but not shaken, I turned to see the redoubtable vicar of St Jude on the Hill, the Reverend Basil Bourchier. 'Bless you,' I heard myself say.

St Margaret's was a dream of beauty, with glorious autumn flowers everywhere and the best blue carpet underfoot. My train was carried by a new nephew, Peter Pain, now a High Court judge, and, bringing up the rear was my new niece, four-year-old Julia Benn, carrying a basket of posies. It had been explained to her by her formidable nanny, 'Nugger', that she was the flower girl and on no account was she to move away from the other bridesmaids until the service was over. But she did not pay any attention. Liking the look of the guest of honour, Asquith, with his pleasant avuncular appearance, she walked up to the front pew and pushed her posy into his face to smell. I doubt whether our former Prime Minister had ever before been picked out so pic-

turesquely for a personal tribute of this kind. It delighted the congregation and, for a few minutes, stole the show. Then Julia moved back to
her place and did not stir again.

Our wedding, conducted by Dr Winnington-Ingram, the Bishop of
London, continued without interruption. I had enjoyed arranging the
service, as far as the Prayer Book allowed me to do so. Clearly, some of
the exchanges belonged to another age. 'Who gives this woman?' suggested a possession passed from one owner to another, and the controversial word 'obey' was not made optional until a few years later.

I wanted the hymns to express the sense of our own happy commitment to a lifelong partnership made in the presence of our friends. I
hoped that an atmosphere of worship would be unmistakable. We began
with the hymn 'Praise my soul the King of Heaven' and ended with the
beautiful Whitsun hymn that I love best of all: 'Come, Holy Ghost, our
souls inspire'. I was born on a Whit Monday and always feel renewed
year by year as Whitsun comes around.

Finally, we were duly married; and then came the Bishop's homily.
Surprisingly, he ignored my husband and addressed himself exclusively to
me. 'My dear child,' he began, 'you are today marrying a public man and
at this moment your life passes into his.' A gentle lisp and an expression
of settled benevolence softened the words, but even in the midst of the
happy preoccupations of the wedding ceremony it was impossible to miss
the urgency, even the fear, that underlay this pronouncement.

In 1920 feminism was well on the march and more women were leaving
the home and entering public life. Women over thirty had the vote;
Nancy Astor had taken her seat in the Commons the year before; and
there was a movement for women's ordination. What indeed would
happen to the country and the Church of England if feminism continued?

My granddaughter told me that she would have walked out if the
Bishop's remarks had been made to her; but, then, she would not have
gone into the church in the first place!

Later, I realised that the Bishop's comments had been prompted by a
particular incident. William told me that when he went to Fulham Palace
to finalise arrangements for the wedding, he had asked Dr Winnington-
Ingram to leave out the word 'obey'. Of course, as a legislator, he should
have known that the service was settled by Act of Parliament and could
not be modified at will. Assuming, wrongly, that I had been refusing to
say the offending word, the Bishop put his hand on William's shoulder
and remarked reassuringly: 'My dear boy, don't worry – they all say it
when it comes to it.' William was furious!

In the vestry many friends crowded round us to join in signing the
marriage certificate. True to his political affiliation, William had picked
out people of congenial views and no one else. All the Independent
Liberal leaders were there: Henry Asquith; Sir Donald Maclean, Chairman of the Parliamentary Party; and the Marquess of Crewe, leader of

the Peers, whom Asquith had described as 'that somewhat inaudible
statesman'. George Barnes represented the Labour Party, and T. P.
O'Connor the Irish MPs. Last of all, a curate approached me with a
dangerously dripping pen. 'If you will just sign here,' he promised, 'it
will release you.' 'You mean, tie me up!' I heard myself reply.

Our wedding had been a big event: many onlookers had gathered
outside to cheer William, who was a very well-known MP; and in
Parliament Square we were greeted by a poster from the famous green-
coloured evening paper, the *Westminster Gazette*, bearing the words,
'Captain Benn's Marriage'. Big Ben struck three, in what seemed a note
of approval, and we were on our way to the Hotel Cecil, where the
splendid Leith wedding cake, having safely survived its long night's journey, awaited the cut I was to give it with my husband's military sword.

'Where are you going now?' Margot Asquith asked me. She was very
amused when I told her how William had faithfully promised that we
should leave politics behind and 'get away from it all', and when I had
asked him what exactly this would mean, he had said, with the well-
known twinkle in his eye: 'Well, I thought we might attend the first
session of the League of Nations in Geneva, and then go on to Rome
for Christmas to have a look at Mussolini's new Fascist movement, and
then down to Sicily to see what the Mafia are up to with their *Omertà*
motto of "silence".' This was a preview of what life was to be like! The
word 'holiday' was not in my husband's vocabulary unless, as I discovered later, it was spent 'messing about in boats'.

Our friends gave us a warm send-off and we soon arrived at St
Margaret's Bay, where we were to spend the first part of our honeymoon.
Despite the wild, rough weather, William, who was a great sailor, wanted
to go out in a boat. I never lived down the reply I made: 'I'll go if we
have a man in the boat!'

For the next stage of our honeymoon, we went over to the Continent,
arriving in Geneva where the new hope of world peace, the League of
Nations, was meeting in an old Hussite hall. It was agreeable to find that
British people were taking a full part. Among the familiar faces were
Lord Robert Cecil, later to be President of the League of Nations Union
for many years, and the future Labour Government minister, Philip
Noel-Baker. After attending several meetings, with Christmas a week
ahead, we decided to cross into Italy. 'Why', asked William, always out
for adventure, 'go by train through a hole in a mountain, when we could
have a glorious day's sunshine and a superb view all the time if we
accompanied the postman in his sleigh?'

It seemed a formidable undertaking, but of course I could not be so
cowardly as to reject it, especially when my husband reminded me that,
being twenty years younger than he, I must be that much stronger! We
left Brig before dawn, wrapped up as well as we could manage, and did
indeed witness the most spectacular views. As we climbed up the Sim-

plon pass, the rising but still hidden sun touched the peaks of the snow-covered mountains with a growing radiance. Soon the whole scene – sky and earth – was aflame. Every few hours we stopped for a change of horses and usually a welcome cup of coffee. All around us was a bird's-eye view of the world that brought a totally new idea of our old earthly home.

At midday we reached the Simplon monastery itself, famed for its life-saving work of training and sending out dogs to find and succour lost pilgrims. The brethren showed us around and welcomed us to a hot lunch, after which we set out on the second part of the journey. Altogether it had been an unforgettable day, and it was nearly dusk when we arrived at the Italian frontier town of Domodossola, twenty minutes away by train from Brig, our starting point. Thankfully we boarded the train for Milan, more tired than we realised.

It was then that we had the first disagreement of our newly married life. It was about – of all unlikely subjects – tariff reform! It is difficult now to convey the depth of feeling aroused during the early part of the century by the issue of whether to impose import taxes on foreign goods or to continue with free trade. The subject cropped up and William, good Liberal that he was, condemned it root and branch. I was incautious enough to remark that it might on occasion be wise to give some early protection to a young industry until it got going. The effect of this statement was catastrophic. William said that his whole political life was founded on a number of deeply held principles; they were his whole stock in trade and could never be abandoned. He added with something like desperation: 'I've always had support for them at home. I must have support . . .!'

I realised that here I had reached one of the turning points of my existence. I had always enjoyed trying to think things out for myself and coming to my own conclusions about them. If contradicting my husband's deeply held political beliefs was going to make him unhappy, then I decided that, where politics was concerned, I would listen with the utmost sympathy, agree where I could, and maintain a friendly silence when I disagreed.

We stayed in Milan for a few days before going on to Rome. A story was making the rounds in Milan that at a cinema show at which Mussolini's health had been pledged, a man who remained seated when everyone else rose, received a warning from a well-wisher behind him: 'I entirely sympathise with your views about Mussolini, but for your own safety I advise you to get up.' To the man's consternation, the seated figure turned out to be Mussolini! He was at this time establishing his position and would shortly take power in Italy.

I had always wished to visit Rome to see whether or not my destiny lay in membership of the Roman Catholic Church. Would I find my true spiritual home there? I could detect a faint anxiety in my new husband lest I should announce my submission there and then to the

Vatican. We arrived in Rome on Christmas Eve in time to go to what I was sure would be a midnight mass at the Sistine Chapel. Alas, there was no such thing. All was closed and dark.

From start to finish, Rome had the opposite effect to the one I had expected, and even half hoped for. While I could worship in Roman Catholic churches – indeed, being deeply ecumenical, I can worship with fellow Christians anywhere – I discovered that Rome was not my spiritual home. Much as I loved the beautiful service with the prayers growing ever more familiar, I could never have lived with the unrelenting atmosphere of authority. Think as much as you like, it seemed to say, as long as you arrive at the necessary conclusions.

William was even more against all this. Indeed, all his life he showed himself to be in a state of active antipathy to the Vatican and its pronouncements. When, much later, we were in Rome during his period in office as President of the Inter-Parliamentary Union, he ignored a hint that an invitation to visit the Vatican would be forthcoming if he wanted one. I much regretted this as I thought an audience with the Pope would have been of the greatest interest. Requests to think it over were turned down with much energy: 'A "political" free churchman does not consort with the Pope.'

As time went on, I began to doubt whether this were really the reason, however much he might think so. Sometimes, quite unintentionally, he would drop remarks that suggested otherwise. Once, when we were discussing the English Civil War, I declared that I was a passionate Cromwellian. Indeed, at the time of the coronation of King George V in 1911, when I was fourteen, I had had a painful time in the front row of the choir at school because I would not sing 'Here's a health unto His Majesty', but stood in silence. Even more than Cromwell, I admired John Hampden, of whom Macaulay said that he had the manners of a courtier and the morals of a Puritan. 'On what side would you have been if you had lived at that time?' I asked William. Without a moment's hesitation, he replied: 'Oh, I would have been a Cavalier.' That came from a long way down, as I saw at once.

Every moment of William's day was planned beforehand and these plans were carried out with meticulous care. Everything he did was done in the light of an overarching political purpose. He saw himself as a public servant sent to the House of Commons to save not only his constituents but the party of which he was a member and, beyond this, the country itself. After soldiering in wartime, which, when it came, meant to him 'personal risk, voluntarily undertaken', he believed that political life offered the highest opportunities of public service.

He was at constant war with much that he liked and exercised an implacable discipline over his daily life. As a child he had been nicknamed 'Billy Dawdle'; as an adult he fought this trait by keeping an account of how he spent every moment of his time. Later, I learned that he had been born left-handed but had been forced to use his right hand. This made him what I believe is called 'shifted sinistral' and it came out in one amusing way: if he ever set a table, it was always for left-handed people. This need to do something against one's inherited nature made very heavy demands.

How does this connect with the Church of Rome? It has sometimes occurred to me that William's great distaste had a surprising cause. It might have arisen from a more or less unconscious desire on his part to participate in some of the things offered by the Church of Rome to its members. All his life he suffered from a perfectionist conscience that gave him no peace. An understanding father confessor might have set William's increasing scrupulosity to rights and released him, by confession and forgiveness, from the torments of a relentless conscience, enabling him to find true peace and self-understanding. He could have enjoyed life more and been delivered from his lot as the pitiless driver of himself that he became down the years. This solace was not to be found in being a ' "political" free churchman'.

William always liked to go where there was trouble, and so we ended our holiday in Sicily, where he hoped to find out as much as he could about the Mafia. But it proved quite impossible to understand and evaluate their system of control. No one would answer any questions or utter a single word about it. *Omertà* was the watchword and no one from outside could break it. After a short and uncomfortable stay on this beautiful island – I had to nurse William through a recurrence of malaria – we turned thankfully towards home and a free society.

I made two discoveries on our honeymoon journey: one was the realisation that I would not become a convert to Roman Catholicism; the other was what a delightful companion marriage had given me. William was in every way the best of company.

Our temperaments and ways of looking at life were different but, most happily, compatible. We were both keen left-of-centre Liberal-radicals, working for a more just society. We liked the same people and activities, and above all, perhaps, we enjoyed the same jokes! William did not tell funny stories but enlivened what was being said by a keen wit that salted every situation as it arose with a spicy new insight into its significance. He could put it all in a sparklingly epigrammatic phrase.

When we moved into our first home, a little flat in London, just opposite Church House, William encouraged me to adopt the system he employed for using every hour of the day profitably; his great desire being that I should share fully in his marvellously organised life in all its ramifications. I had already come across this method because, independently of William, I too had read the recently published book that had inspired him: Arnold Bennett's *How to Live on 24 Hours a Day*. In William's case the system had been brought to perfection, thus illustrating what happens when seed falls on good ground; in my case, I fear, it fell on thorns. 'Never mind,' he would say, when I expressed regret at my incompetence, 'I reckon it will take me two years to teach you!'

The essence of the system was that every minute of each day was accounted for under three headings: 'work', 'rest' and 'waste of time'. Work was 'the job' in one or other of many forms. 'Job first!' was William's lifelong motto. 'But,' I protested, 'what about the time we spend together?' 'Oh,' he said, 'that's easy. If we're happy, it's rest; and if not, it's a waste of time and isn't recorded.' At the end of each day the amount of time spent on 'work' and 'rest' was calculated and entered on to a chart.

While he was a bachelor, this revealing object had been pinned to a large cork notice board that stood on the mantelpiece of his bedroom. Like a temperature chart, a line of red ink straggled over the graph paper, showing the intensity of each year's fight to do better than the year before. My earliest success in married life was to persuade William that his study would be a more suitable place for the display of the chart than our bedroom.

In his breast pocket, William carried, till the day of his death, a sacred 'job list'. Every night, he carefully wrote out all the work contemplated for the next day. At the end of each day he surveyed this programme in retrospect and noted how much of it had been faithfully carried out.

William used a complicated system of numbering to organise his papers, newspaper cuttings and correspondence. He offered me my own private number: 101. This would mean that everything I wished to keep hold of would be filed under the care of a secretary. Alas! I did not always keep to the rules and, on seeing some unmarked papers floating about loose on my desk, he would say, in not wholly assumed disgust: 'What is this private muck heap?' Looking back over the years, I feel sure that it was here that I made one of the biggest of my lesser mistakes in life; had I adopted a more systematic and organised approach to the use of my time, I might have achieved more.

At the time of our engagement, William assumed that I did not indulge in alcoholic drinks. He had had a Congregationalist upbringing and, like all his family, was a staunch teetotaller. One day he happened to remark: 'You and I are teetotallers.' 'I'm not,' I replied. He was quite distressed and asked me to become teetotal, which annoyed me a little as I thought it was an interference.

'Give me a good reason,' I said. He answered: 'Well, it would upset my mother terribly.' I told him he would have to think of a different reason because I was not accepting that. 'Well,' he said, 'if we have a family, which I hope we will, I should like them to be brought up as teetotallers – what they do after that is their own affair – and you cannot bring up a teetotaller if you aren't one.' I said that was a reason, and I would accept it. On reflection, he felt that he had put undue pressure on me and presently he said: 'I'm going to let you off that promise; I won't ask you to be a teetotaller,' but I decided to keep to it and have been one ever since. Our children have all been teetotallers, and I think that is especially surprising in Anthony's case, as Members of Parliament are under a lot of strain and many of them drink. It is interesting that my husband's influence on our sons should have been so strong without any pressure being put on them at all.

For some time we did not have any alcohol in the house. I said: 'Look here, if I went to someone's house and they wouldn't give me a cup of tea because they thought it was bad for me, I would be very annoyed.' I told William that I would not entertain people unless I could give them a drop of what they liked to drink. It took him a long time to change his mind, but being persuaded of the justice of my case, and deciding, eventually, that he wanted a wider choice of guests than such well-known teetotallers as the Bishop of London, Dr Winnington-Ingram, and the MP, Leif Jones, he agreed to our giving dinner parties with wine and spirits like everyone else.

I was somewhat anxious as to how I would be received by my in-laws. My mother, who never said anything very good about her children, had not helped matters by remarking to William's mother: 'She's got no business to be married at all; she knows nothing about running a house.'

What sort of family was I marrying into? William's father, Sir John Benn, nearly seventy at the time of our marriage, had been a publisher and politician and had been given a baronetcy in recognition of his political work. The eldest son of the Reverend Julius Benn, a Congregationalist minister, he had known real hardship in his youth. His education had ended at the age of eleven when he had become an office boy, walking the two miles to work in his mother's boots because his one pair of shoes was not sturdy enough.

He eventually prospered and became a furniture designer and editor of his own magazine, *The Cabinet Maker*, a venture that was the beginning of the publishing house Benn Brothers. He married Elizabeth Pickstone, and William, their second son, was born on 10 May 1877. He was given the name Wedgwood, because Elizabeth was a distant relative of the pottery family. In later years many people thought William must have a stake in the famous firm and therefore be a millionaire. Nothing could have been further from the truth.

William's father had political ambitions and in 1889 was elected to the newly formed London County Council as a member of the Progressive Party, an alliance of radical Liberals and the Labour movement, becoming Chairman in 1904. He was responsible, among many other measures, for introducing electric trams. In 1892 he was elected as Liberal MP for St George's-in-the-East and Wapping, later to be William's first constituency.

For a time the family lived in a house in Cable Street which they renamed Gladstone House, after their great Liberal hero, and William and his elder brother, Ernest, attended what is now the Central Foundation School for Boys. When the family moved to Upminster and

Ernest left school to start work at Benn Brothers, William lived in Gladstone House on his own.

Given the way William drove himself from his teens onwards, this was the worst possible arrangement. He used to come home from school and work for half the night, without eating properly. I feel sure it retarded his growth. Fortunately, he was very successful academically and won a scholarship to London University where, like my father, he obtained the best degree. William joined the family firm and then decided to follow his father into politics. John Benn lost his seat and William was selected as candidate for St George's. His brother continued to build up Benn Brothers, which he did most successfully.

As a father-in-law, Sir John Benn was delightful. He was the most outward-looking member of the family and was very kind, welcoming and uncritical. But marriage brought me an ambiguous relationship with William's devoted mother, Elizabeth Benn. My brother-in-law's wife, Gwen, had already, sadly, come to grief over her relationship with 'Grandma Benn' and she was exceedingly sympathetic and cautionary about what I was going to suffer. She and Ernest had been married for seventeen years so everyone concerned was well acquainted with the situation.

A clue to its nature came to light only recently when it was discovered that the family Bible chronicled the date of Ernest's marriage without a mention of Gwen! This went to the root of the matter. Grandma Benn never thought anyone was good enough to marry one of her children. For her, life was divided into 'the Benn Family' and the vastly inferior 'Outside World'. In-laws were, of course, of the latter class and could never be accepted as really worthy of joining the former. It almost seemed that 'the Outside World' existed to admire, praise and indeed serve the Benns. When Sir John Benn was on his deathbed, Grandma Benn refused to allow any enquiries about his condition to be answered, on the grounds that she did not want 'the Outside World' to know anything about it.

She had ambivalent feelings towards me. First, of course, as an inexperienced little girl from 'outside' who could never be adequate as a wife for her beloved and brilliant 'Billy', as she called William. When this view was uppermost she would sigh and say: 'Do look after that boy for me!' But alongside this image of me grew a different one of a likeable, and then lovable, young human being to be classed as almost a granddaughter not a daughter-in-law.

When, later, we left the flat and settled in our minute house – one room on each of four floors – my mother-in-law was our first visitor. Anxious to do her proud, I took some money from my Post Office account and bought flowers for our sitting room. On leaving, she glanced critically round the room, looking hard at the parquet floor that had not yet come up to scratch, and remarked: 'What a difference you could make to that with a little polish,' and then uttered her final judgement:

'You know, darling, a few flowers don't deceive an old housekeeper!'
Determined at all costs to remain friendly, I said, with some effort: 'The
flowers were not intended to deceive you, they were intended to welcome you, Mother.'

When I thought it all over, I came to the conclusion that a good
relationship, if achieved, would have to arise from my initiative, not hers.
It was certainly a case for trying to 'get understanding'. To discover how
I could achieve this, there was only one thing to do – to listen. This
strategy worked like magic. No one had ever listened to her before with
their full attention in a desire to learn about her thoughts, feelings and
experience of life. Of one near in-law she said significantly: 'My dear,
she always brings her knitting so as not to waste the time completely!'

I enjoyed our talks. From them I learned a great deal I would never
otherwise have known, not only about her own personality, but about
William and the family in which he had grown up.

Elizabeth Benn's story of her own early life carried me into a world
of which I had hitherto had no inkling. Her father had been a well-to-do
wholesale chemist in Cheshire. He and his family lived in a large house
and were the centre of voluntary welfare work in the district. Undertaken in active partnership with the local Congregational church, this
consisted in carrying necessary comforts to all those members of the
congregation who were in need. All the household arts and skills were
taught and learned at home as soon as schooling was over. This last
apparently went on well into the upper teens, for my mother-in-law
recalled going, by stagecoach at the age of eighteen, to a 'finishing
school' in Stockport.

The turning point in her life came one Sunday evening, on her return
home from church, when she met John Benn, a young furniture designer
who had family connections with the church and had come to spend a
holiday in the town.

In those far-off days, a century or more ago, it was not the custom
for young middle-class women to take decisions on their own as to
whom they would marry; everything was in the hands of the parents. It
was a year later, on his next holiday, that John Benn ventured to make
his feelings known; longer still before he obtained parental approval for
an engagement; years longer before he could marry his sweetheart and
take her to the little London home that he had acquired and furnished
in accordance with her wishes and his own inspiration. She told me with
what thrilling excitement, joy and fulfilment she first entered the long-
hoped-for little house. Everything was perfect, and open on the piano,
all ready to play, lay a piece of music: 'Home Sweet Home'.

Six children were born to her in the next thirteen years. Nowadays
fathers are usually present at the birth of their children, but then this
was ruled out in most families as a matter of course, being considered
too painful for them, and generally unsuitable. Grandma Benn told me

how when her first child was coming she felt she could no longer control the expression of her distress and asked the doctor: 'Is my husband nearby?' 'Oh, we can't have him here!' said the doctor, misunderstanding. She had only wanted to be sure that he was far away!

Alas! he was in the next room, sitting with her mother, and when her cries reached him he asked in disbelief: 'Is that my little girl?' 'Yes, John, it is indeed,' answered her mother, who was not averse to fathers realising what new life cost the mother. Elizabeth Benn thought her mother had been very cruel to impose that on her son-in-law!

Of her six children, the eldest occupied a special place in his mother's life. Over the others she exercised a protective care, but to Ernest she looked for support. 'If it weren't for Ernest I should fade away,' she confessed to me once, in widowhood, near the end of her life. All the surviving four showed her great love and kindness but Ernest surpassed them all. He kept in daily touch and, every night after dinner, even if he had seen his mother shortly before, went straight to the telephone for twenty minutes' leisured, interested chat on the day's events and his own work.

Ernest's political views began to diverge from those held by the rest of the family. His highly successful book, *The Confessions of a Capitalist*, followed later by the foundation of the Society of Individualists, highlighted the coming split in the Liberal Party between the Radical left wing and the monetarists. Ernest would have delighted in Mrs Thatcher's policies; though it is doubtful if he would have approved of their being carried out by a woman Prime Minister.

Grandma Benn's own personal reaction to the loss of her husband in 1922 was characteristically heroic. Almost immediately after his death she presided at the breakfast table and poured out tea and coffee for the whole assembled family as though nothing had happened. Her bearing on the day of his funeral was even more memorable. Dressed in a quiet grey silk frock – Benns on principle do not wear mourning – she waited among the family for the moment when they would leave the house together for the funeral service. Her last farewell had been said. Only at one sound did she turn pale, when sudden loud knocks announced that 'the Outside World' was knocking the nails into his coffin.

At the funeral in the beautiful and peaceful Limpsfield parish churchyard she was herself again. Standing by the grave of her life's partner she gently dropped into it, one by one, a bunch of red roses. Her whole bearing was one of deep unshakeable faith. She had been tried and tested to the utmost and come through.

Mothers-in-law, I believe, often need to be listened to with the utmost sympathy and with a resolute ignoring of all setbacks. Although her ambiguous attitude towards me was never completely absent, William's mother became more and more affectionate when she realised that I was always ready for a friendly talk. The most outstanding evidence of this arose just after Sir John Benn's death. Only once did her courage break. Leaning on my shoulder, she shed bitter tears. 'I wanted so much to go with him – we've never been apart,' she sobbed; 'but I know that's wrong of me. I must be left something; but what can it be? I look round the family – they're all settled, they're all happy.' And then leaning again on my shoulder she cried out: 'It must be because of Billy that I'm left.'

The fact that she had no idea what a devastating criticism her remark implied of me as a wife, and yet at the same time was turning to me for solace, showed the confusing dichotomy in which her relationship to me was embedded. She was quite unaware of this herself, so I did not think it necessary to allow the matter to disturb me overmuch.

Our friendship proceeded quite happily, but tact was really necessary when the children arrived. Elizabeth Benn's settled opinion on how children should be handled was poles apart from mine. In her system, for example, cold compresses were considered the right treatment for every ill; I believed, on the contrary, that only bone-dry garments should be put on children whether they were up or in bed. Water was for washing in; not therapy. Grandma Benn could not but lose here and she had to accept it. Very soon she came to understand that there must be give and take in this relationship, even more than most.

Soon after our return to London from our honeymoon, my mother-in-law raised the question of weekends in the country. We must, 'for everyone's sake', spend every one of these with them. I soon found that William was not opposed to this idea, for his parents were old and getting frail.

The combination of living in a flat and spending every weekend in Oxted with William's parents meant that I had to part with my little dog, Dugald. My in-laws did not like dogs; and my parents could not keep him, as they were always moving about and now spent an increasing amount of time abroad. We gave Dugald to neighbours, and when we spent next summer in Seaford I saw him and called: 'Dugald! Dugald!' and he went down on his tummy. I never saw him again and I was heartbroken.

After living in the flat for two or three months, we moved to a little house at 15 Cowley Street, a few minutes from the House of Commons. William's father had lived out at Blackheath when he was an MP and getting the last train home had been a nightmare for him. The years 1921–5 passed happily by for us, bringing our two eldest sons, Michael and Anthony, and with them much new experience and rare delight. It is my belief that nothing in life can bring a greater joy and fulfilment than the gift of children to a husband and wife already happy in each other's society.

Michael's arrival, on 5 September 1921, was a great joy for both of us. He was christened in the crypt chapel of the House of Commons by the rector of St Margaret's, and had as godparents Mr Speaker Whitley,

Reggie McKenna, and my sister-in-law Irene Pain. From the first he was a lovely child, beautiful to look at and exceptionally trusting and friendly to those around him, whether his own family or strangers. My parents were now living entirely abroad, except for a very occasional visit home, and I came more and more to find family friendship and support from William's two sisters, Margaret Hughes and Irene Pain; and from his brother and sister-in-law, Ernest and Gwendolen Benn. All three families had country homes to which we made delightful visits from time to time.

I also enjoyed meeting William's cousin, Margaret Rutherford. Peggy had always wanted to be an actress from childhood and eventually became very well known for her comedy roles in plays and films, including her portrayal of Agatha Christie's detective Miss Marple. She was a natural eccentric and was the same person in real life as on the stage. At a fancy dress party on one occasion she was wearing a most peculiar outfit. I congratulated her on this, saying: 'Oh, Peggy, my dear, now how did you manage to think up that dress?' 'Oh, this was my best dress for last summer,' was the reply. She really was very quaint.

William was a wonderful father and had an 'alongside' attitude to our sons that did not interfere in the slightest with his authority as a parent. He taught them to sail, at which he was an adept, and it fostered in them an understanding of the times when complete obedience was necessary: there could be only one captain in a boat.

He did not ask them to follow all his habits, such as charting their time, but he insisted that they keep an account of their pocket money. Here I doubt if he was always very successful – judging by the laughter I heard as they meaningfully asked each other: 'Have you "made up" your accounts for Dad?'

We decided that our children should have a good education so they would be able to 'deal with the Tories'. This was of course long before the days of the comprehensive schools, and what difference they would have made to our plans I cannot say. As things were in the 1920s and 1930s, we always made the boys' education our first priority, whatever the cost. Not being in favour of boarding, we sent them to Westminster School, where they were happy despite the dress regulations. The local workmen were provided with a great source of amusement as Michael and Anthony walked to school wearing top hats, morning coats and carrying rolled umbrellas!

The house was so small that we could not get furniture up the stairs. One day my cook rushed out and said to me: 'Don't look! Don't look!' Of course I did look and was horrified because there was William, with a nursery table strapped round his waist, climbing up the fire escape to Michael's room on the top floor. I scolded him and said it was very dangerous. 'Oh,' he said, 'I've never heard such nonsense: builders do it every day.'

There was hardly any room for resident helpers, so apart from Michael's nurse, we relied on daily help. We discovered that our cook was addicted to gambling and was pawning the silver. I had to go round all the local pawnbrokers' shops to get it out. We paid her debts and gave her a second chance, but it began all over again and so, unfortunately, we had to dismiss her.

The street was so close to Parliament that, inevitably, many of our neighbours were involved in politics. At the end of the street lived Walter Runciman, later Lord Runciman, who had been President of the Board of Trade during the First World War. He was rather pious and very different from his old father, Sir Walter Runciman, a cheerful, jolly man. People used to say: 'Now, Sir Walter, you wouldn't like your son hearing you make that joke.' Walter Runciman's son, the future historian Sir Steven Runciman, was clever but rather eccentric. The Runcimans used to give parties and dances. Steven, then a Cambridge undergraduate, did not dance but used to give me supper. On one occasion he asked: 'What time would you like your second supper tonight?' I said: 'Oh, about midnight.' His reply was: 'Oh, Mother's hoping everyone will have gone by then.' When I told this story to his father, Walter Runciman said: 'Steven has no morals at all!'

In those days, the older generation of women still paid afternoon calls, a custom that was dying out among the younger generation. These unannounced visits could be quite trying. On one afternoon, Mrs Runciman, a most dominating woman, called. The visit got off to an inauspicious start as, the minute she put her finger on the front door bell, all the lights fused! Finding the tea too strong for her liking, she looked round the table and said: 'I should like some hot water, please.' She wanted to let me know that the table was not set properly, but I do not think she should have embarrassed a young bride.

On another occasion, an old lady called while I was putting Michael to bed and insisted on coming up to the nursery and giving me a lot of unwanted advice on how to bring up babies. But my particular memory is of a Conservative MP's wife who called in a carriage and pair, with her coachman sporting a cockade in his hat. What a different era that was!

We were very happy in Cowley Street, but the imminent arrival of our second child required a move to somewhere larger. Our new home was 40 Grosvenor Road, later renamed Millbank; a tall, narrow, five-storey house built in the 1880s on the site of the old Millbank prison. We bought it on a thirty-three-year lease for £2,000 and lived there, except for the war years, until our lease expired in 1958. There was no question of extending the lease, and the houses were pulled down to make way for the present Millbank Tower.

Our second son was born on 3 April 1925 and we decided to call him Anthony. I said: 'Well, you know, I'm afraid it will degenerate into "Tony".' And so it did. I do not care for the short name, but I have to settle down to accept the fact that Tony is what he is called. I never use that name myself, but I sometimes call him 'James'. We used to nickname him and his elder brother 'Bill' and 'Jim', and 'Jim' got lengthened to 'James'.

Both my parents expressed their surprise that after one experience of childbirth I should have ventured so soon on a second. My father never asked: 'When is the happy event?' but: 'When is your ordeal?' In vain I pointed out that this was not how I looked on the experience at all: birth was as natural as marriage and death. I believed that one's own attitude to it was vital and likely to colour what in fact happened. This I have always found to be the case. A cheerful, relaxed expectation of a good result was all-important.

Socially we very much enjoyed the company of the Independent Liberals – a very friendly body of people. The Asquiths and well-to-do members of the party like Sir John Simon and Walter Runciman entertained both at their London and country homes. Sir John had a chauffeur with an unusual name and it was a little disconcerting when a maid announced the arrival of the car with: 'Excuse me, sir, but Kingdom's come.' Sir Archie and Marigold Sinclair were delightful members of the circle, and later Sir Oswald and Lady Cynthia Mosley became unofficially attached to all our activities. Asquith and Margot were exceedingly anxious that they should become Liberals just as, a little later on, the Labour Party pressed them to become members, with more success.

Looking back on Asquith from a time lapse of over sixty years, it becomes more, and not less, difficult to understand him as a human being. His great gift was a crystal-clear brain and the facility of a great lawyer to see immediately everything that was at stake in any situation and put the issue in a minimum of forceful and luminous phrases. Not a word too few; not a word too many. It was a delight to listen to him. He and Margot entertained in London and at The Wharf, their country home at Sutton Courtenay, near Oxford, and as a host he was agreeable, witty and amusing. 'Nothing but a good joke from Mr Asquith,' William used to say. And yet there was something missing; he never appeared to me to be a fully integrated personality.

Asquith was fond of a drink and there were jokes about this. If he were noticeably the worse for wear, people would sing, with a slurred accent, the words of a song from *The Bing Boys*, a very popular musical of the period: 'Another little drink, another little drink, another little drink wouldn't do us any harm!' William once met Asquith in a very unsteady state walking through the lobby of the House of Commons and said to him: 'Shall I take you to your room, sir?' Asquith replied, simply: 'I wish you would.'

In private, Asquith was quite different from his public image. The aloof intellectual had quite disappeared. Rumours, occasionally mooted, that he had a liking for young women contemporary in age with his daughter Violet became credible. Among the inner circle there was much speculation as to the exact nature of these romantic attachments, but I shall never believe that he was an unfaithful husband in a divorceable sense. I considered him to be much too fastidious a man for such a lapse to be conceivable. But letters of his to these younger women, published in full after his death, do show beyond doubt that his marriage to Margot was not as emotionally satisfying as his first marriage to Helen Melland, with its quiet home life at Hampstead, had been.

Asquith and Margot were a case of the wrong labels getting tied around the wrong necks. People used to say: 'Oh, that magnanimous old man married to that giddy wife,' but in fact it was a giddy husband married to a magnanimous wife. Margot provided him with a lot of money, firstly from her father, Sir Charles Tennant, who said of Asquith: 'Oh, Henry Asquith hasn't got enough money to buy his own golf clubs,' and then through her writing.

Margot's income and her generous disposition of it undoubtedly made a great difference to Asquith's career. Margot frequently said that she considered money to be the least important thing in life, and she certainly acted accordingly. Keeping in view, however, that she might be much in need of it later on, she had kept a full and accurate account in diary form of her whole life. Sure enough, just after the First World War, the time came for this to be sold on the best possible terms. When she told her husband that she had disposed of the first volume for £13,000, a great deal in those days, he merely made the dry rejoinder: 'I hope it's not worth it!'

Margot told me that the first eleven years of her married life were full of severe ill health. She bore five children, but three of them died and she very nearly died each time. Finally, the doctor said: 'Now look, if you have any more you will die, and you mustn't even risk having any more.' It was accepted by Asquith and Margot that from then on marriage must be on different lines. Margot, who adored her husband and thought him the greatest man alive, showed no signs of realising what this new turn of events would mean to him. It was quite obvious from her conversation and diaries that she was of a very different temperament from her husband: marital relations were apparently never important in her life.

But after this Asquith appeared more and more to need some much younger woman to whom he could pour out his heart. The best-known of these women was Venetia Stanley, who eventually found the strain too much and married Edwin Montagu, a Cabinet minister. It is almost incredible to learn, from the published letters, that during the First World War when, as Prime Minister, he led the nation in a desperate fight for its life, he was writing romantic letters to Venetia Stanley, sometimes from the Cabinet Room. Had we, his ardent supporters, known this we would surely have supported Lloyd George for the premiership.

When Asquith was MP for Paisley, my native town, he and his family

stayed in a Glasgow hotel when campaigning, but made their daily headquarters at Scotscraig, the home of my uncle John Scott Eadie and his wife.
Naturally over the years they became very intimate. Margot told my aunt
that after Asquith's death, one of his women correspondents, Hilda Harris-
son, offered her all the letters she had received from Asquith for a large
sum. Margot had not got the money, but it is doubtful if she would have
handed it over anyway. She replied, stingingly: 'Publish and be damned!'
The letters duly appeared under the title *H.H.A.: Letters to a Friend*, the
initials standing for Herbert Henry Asquith. Margot's only request was that
Desmond MacCarthy should edit them; which he did.

At 10 Downing Street and later in Bedford Square Margot played her
part as a political wife in her own brilliant and erratic way. Her friendships were of all political parties and none. They stretched far and wide
in the world of art, literature and fashion. Innumerable Tories were
included. I can recall lunch parties where one might meet a famous
literary critic, such as Desmond MacCarthy; a Tory marchioness; and a
duchess who, unexpectedly, happened to look in. The fact that Margot
was hostess never seemed to put any particular responsibility on her to
stay to the end of her own parties. At one lunch at the Asquiths' house
in Bedford Square, she had to go to another engagement before the end
of lunch so she said: 'I have to leave you now; Clouder will look after
you.' 'Very characteristic,' remarked the Marchioness of Salisbury as
Margot hurried away. She knew that their butler, Clouder, would see
that all went well as regards food and drink, and make sure that the
guests' cars – Margot herself always called for 'my carriage', as a good
Victorian should – would line up at the right time.

We had been rather surprised when the Asquiths, on leaving Downing
Street, had moved, after a short stay in Cavendish Square, to the somewhat gloomy Bedford Square; but it turned out that this was at the wish
of the indispensable Clouder, who organised their lives and without
whom existence would have been impossible. He knew exactly what
every member of the family ought to be doing and when. He and his
wife had a boarding house in Bloomsbury and so the Asquiths' move to
Bedford Square enabled Clouder to keep an eye on his business and
return there late at night.

Elizabeth Asquith, Margot's daughter, used to say: 'Clouder makes
perfect ladies of us all,' and if you met Clouder in Sutton Courtenay
you stopped and had a very friendly talk with him. Margot's great
relaxation was bridge, at which she hoped to make some much-needed
money. Clouder knew whom to invite for lunch and weekends to try
and settle the bridge debts. The weekend guests all settled down soon
after breakfast, and again after lunch and tea. On these occasions Mr
Asquith betook himself to his library in the garden. It was rumoured
that he could never remember what was 'out', and as the stakes were
high all players must be expert.

William and I were not attracted to card games and we had taken care
never to learn bridge. This liberated us to spend a delightful weekend
doing whatever we enjoyed. The Wharf was short of sitting rooms but
the weather was fine and the garden beautiful. A river ran through it and
there were always rowing boats moored alongside the actual wharf itself.

Margot did not join the general breakfast party at The Wharf. Here
Asquith presided and Clouder hovered over us all. Taking what we
wanted from the wide selection of hot and cold food, we sat down, but
Asquith, for some reason, began his breakfast in peripatetic fashion.
Helping himself to porridge and milk or cream, he walked round the
long table as he ate. When he passed each of the guests, he threw us our
correct conversational gambit, picking up the conversation as he came
to each of us again. It was like Señor Capablanca playing sixteen games
of chess simultaneously; an odd performance. Asquith's memory was
similar to Gladstone's. (My headmistress told me that she had two
meetings with Gladstone, separated by an interval of about ten years. On
the second occasion, he carried on the conversation as if there had been
no time lapse.)

William and I were guests of the Asquiths because we were members
of the Independent Liberal Party and William was one of its best-known
MPs. One afternoon, Margot, evidently fearing that I might be feeling
neglected, invited me to come out to her suite of rooms on the top floor
of Asquith's garden library.

When we arrived, Margot explained that she practically lived there.
The large bed-sitting room was tastefully furnished; and she especially
drew my attention to a beautifully carved antique cradle, saying nostal-
gically, 'Both my children lay in this.' Of her five children only Elizabeth
and Anthony, known as 'Puffin', survived. Elizabeth married Prince
Bibesco and went to live in Romania, and Anthony became a film
director.

'I always sleep here,' Margot said, 'and tea trays begin to come along
from six o'clock onwards. I have written all my books here and always
start early and go on till 1 pm, satisfied that I've done enough for the
day.' Before we left, she kissed me, saying: 'Do call me Margot.' I had
then not long been married and took this as a sort of initiation into the
family circle of front bench Liberal wives. I responded warmly.

In one of her books, written many years later, when William had
joined the Labour Party, Margot wrote that the only Labour leader she
could abide was 'that erstwhile Liberal, Wedgwood Benn', adding that
he had a 'delightful, even noble side' to his nature. For this I gave her
full marks, although I would not have called it just a 'side'!

Our social circle was wider than 'Wee Free' Liberals, and among those
of my husband's friends with whom I became acquainted on my marriage
in 1920 were the Tories Waldorf and Nancy Astor. Waldorf had been
Conservative MP for Plymouth; but in 1919, his father, the elderly

Viscount Astor, an American who had taken British citizenship, died, and Waldorf found himself in the same predicament as my son Anthony did forty-one years later. Unable to change the law, Waldorf had to accept the fact that he was now a lord and, with great reluctance, gave up his seat. Rumours spread that his American wife, Nancy, who had always shared in the work of the constituency, was being suggested by her husband as the new candidate. This would certainly mean that, at last, the House of Commons would have a woman MP, and the election was followed throughout the country with great interest. She was duly returned at the by-election and took her seat, sponsored by Lloyd George and Balfour.

She was not, in fact, the first woman to be elected. Countess Markievicz had been successful in the general election of 1918, but neither she nor any of her Sinn Fein colleagues actually took their seats. Defying the British Government, they set up their own Parliament in Dublin.

Of course, Nancy's presence gave great encouragement and delight to women anxious to see their sex make their way in public life. Her correspondence was monumental; and she once said to me that if her husband had not been a rich man she could never have coped with it and all she had to do. My husband privately disagreed with this; in his opinion, women's oganisations in the country would have come more than adequately to her aid. It was not, however, necessary and she certainly coped magnificently and showed herself a devoted feminist.

She gave support to the small number of women MPs, whatever their political persuasion, who were elected during the succeeding years. Nancy was very hospitable to Ellen Wilkinson, the Labour MP for Jarrow, who became famous for her support of the unemployed on the 'Jarrow March' in 1936, and was subsequently Education Minister in Attlee's government. 'Red Ellen', as she was known, was writing a book and had not the means to support herself, so Nancy Astor invited her to be her guest at her country house, Cliveden. She used to tease Ellen by saying: 'You red-hot Socialist!'

Nancy's exposed position meant that everything she did and said received special attention, and of course it could not fail to be noticed that she had everything to learn about parliamentary custom and protocol. Years later the press said she never grasped how to formulate a question to ministers.

Unfortunately, Waldorf Astor did a silly thing. He put in *Who's Who* that Nancy was a widow when he married her, when in fact she had been divorced. This was attacked by an odious character, an MP and journalist called Horatio Bottomley, who ran a mean little paper called *John Bull*. He had already maliciously attacked Ramsay MacDonald for his pacifism and illegitimacy, and was later exposed as a swindler and sent to prison.

When Nancy came into the House after Bottomley's abuse, my husband led the cries of 'Hear! Hear!' She never forgot this and used to refer to it with gratitude. When a painting was commissioned of Nancy taking her seat, she asked that my husband should be in the picture, on the front bench. On my marriage to William, she sent a beautiful silver gilt ornament and extended a warm friendship to me. When my son Michael was born she sent bunches and bunches of pink carnations to my bedroom.

Waldorf, in contrast to Nancy's great animation, was a very quiet man but, surprisingly, William and I both got the impression that he was the boss of the show. Later, when he did not want her to stand for Parliament again, although she was very annoyed because she had enjoyed being an MP she had to accept.

Nancy and Waldorf gave glittering dinner parties in their town house in St James's Square, but it was on our visits to their magnificent home, Cliveden, on the Thames, that I really got to know her. The first time we stayed at Cliveden we had a beautiful ground-floor suite overlooking the splendid garden. A strange feature was that the windows seemed to have a life of their own. When the maid brought in early morning tea, the vibrations sent the window up.

I was amused that Nancy, a staunch teetotaller, used to drink cider at lunch and dinner, presumably thinking that cider was not alcoholic. She gave her guests what they wanted at meals but did not encourage drinking at other times. On one occasion some peeresses stayed up until Nancy had gone to bed and then ordered whiskies.

She would say when we arrived: 'Now, you are not going to be entertained – just be at home and do what you like. There's the garden to walk and sit in and the river to go on if you wish.' But it was very noticeable that she always spent some hours each day conversing with visitors. She once said: 'I never have anyone I don't want to stay.' During these talks, she revealed that the mainspring of her being and the source of all her energy and enthusiasm for life, public and private, was Christian Science. As she described her initiation into this it was evident that she had had an unforgettably mystic experience, which overcame her again as she spoke of it.

Her earlier adult life, in America, had been deeply unhappy in a first marriage with the father of her son, Bobby Shaw. 'But at least', she said, 'I always had Bobby.' Finally she was able to divorce her husband and then she met and married Waldorf Astor. Coming to live in England, she took part in his parliamentary and social life to the full; but she was unsettled and, though her marriage was a success, not happy in herself. She felt constantly ill and never could achieve good health. Then suddenly she heard of Christian Science and took up an intensive study of it. She followed the daily lessons sent out from headquarters in Boston and read all the prescribed passages from the book *Science and Health with Key to the Scriptures*, by Mary Baker Eddy. In addition she attended meetings and studied the Christian Science magazine with its articles and testimonies of the cures people had experienced.

I remember how her face lit up when she told us: 'Then one day when here upstairs looking out over the park and the river, I had an unforgettable vision of what life should be like. We are the children of God. He made us and all his ideas are perfect. It is for us to reach out, claim and appropriate our freedom as the children of God; to go always onwards into a fuller life and a deeper knowledge of what it means to be whole here and now.' Then she fell silent, immersed again in what it had meant to her at the time.

Since that day, many years before, she had never taken a pill or a potion and she had never been ill. It was an impressive testimony to her deepest convictions; accepted and lived out in complete consistency.

While we were very content with our family and social life, politically the scene was less happy. After the overwhelming victory of Lloyd George's Coalition in the general election of 1918, the Conservative Party began to find itself saddled with a Liberal Prime Minister on whom it could not always rely.

Rumours were rife of the existence of a personal fund of a million pounds in Lloyd George's own private bank account, believed to have been collected by the sale of honours. This did the Government as a whole no good and caused much indignation in many quarters.

Finally, Stanley Baldwin, the much-respected Conservative frontbencher, an iron-master renowned for his wide views on the necessity for good relations in industry, took upon himself, at great personal risk, to free the Conservative Party once and for all of the incubus of Lloyd George and his domination. The main difficulty was that the leader of the Conservative Party, Austen Chamberlain, who had succeeded Bonar Law, wanted to support Lloyd George. At the Carlton Club in 1922, a famous meeting took place at which Baldwin backed Bonar Law, now returned to the fray, against Chamberlain. Bonar Law became leader once more, withdrew the Conservatives from the Coalition, and ousted Lloyd George as Prime Minister.

A general election followed in November 1922 and we all took to our constituencies. On my humble level this gave me the first opportunity of fighting as a member's wife. I used to tease my husband by saying he only married me because he had a Scottish constituency, and I was a Scot! It was a hard test that began every morning with canvassing and making calls; sometimes women's afternoon meetings; and always big meetings at night. My husband and I began at different ends of the constituency and often did not meet till the end of the evening.

I am not a trained politician nor a political thinker and I made no attempt at grandiose speaking. I find that it is always best to speak quite simply and unassumingly on what has come within one's own experience and on what therefore interests one most. Plainly, we do not yet live in a just society and seventy years ago it was even less just. Any meeting was willing to listen with patience, if not with complete agreement, to anything put forward in this spirit. Indeed, the great respect and affection in which my husband was held as a dedicated constituency member assured this result. He had a wonderful platform manner. Questions were always welcome and he would identify himself with the questioner, especially if the meeting tended to be hostile.

We were pleased with the result because, although the Conservatives formed a government, the Independent Liberals nearly doubled their seats, and William was returned for Leith with an increased majority. The National Liberals, so called, under Lloyd George saw their representation halved.

After the election, there were moves afoot to reunite the Liberal Party. William was unhappy about this as he feared Lloyd George would make a bid for the leadership; but the Independent Liberals insisted that if the Party were to reunite, Lloyd George had to provide the money.

The 1922 Parliament proved to be of short duration. Bonar Law retired because of ill health and was succeeded by Stanley Baldwin in May 1923. He decided that import duties were necessary to reduce unemployment, and when another election followed in December 1923, the Liberals fought as a united body, with funds provided by Lloyd George, on their traditional platform of free trade. Although the combined Liberals won 159 seats and William once again increased his majority at Leith, it was the Labour Party that came second behind the much depleted Conservatives.

When Ramsay MacDonald returned to Parliament out of the wilderness of post-war defeat, the Labour Party began to take on a more impressive image. MacDonald had a certain style all his own that put other leaders, especially the previous one, Clynes, in the shade. Philip Snowden and Arthur Henderson were also greatly respected. It began to look as though a Labour Government might not be as impossible as many people thought.

In 1924, it happened. A minority Labour Government, supported by the Liberals, moved into Downing Street. But the Government was very weak and, after it lost a vote of censure, there followed, in October 1924, the third election in three years. The Conservatives, dropping their policy of protection, did extremely well and returned to power, partly because a forged letter, allegedly written by Zinoviev of the Communist International, enabled the Conservatives to suggest that the Labour Party had close links with the Communists. The number of Liberal seats fell to forty and William's majority was reduced. Following Asquith's defeat at Paisley, there was a move to make Lloyd George leader of the party – a state of affairs that William would not accept. In November he sent a letter to the *Daily News* saying he could not support Lloyd George as leader.

In order to oppose Lloyd George, William set up a Radical Group, consisting of about a quarter of the Liberal MPs, under the nominal leadership of Walter Runciman. As part of the activities of the Radical

Group, William organised, during the parliamentary session, weekly lunch parties that were held in a large private room on the terrace floor of the House of Commons. These were always addressed by some well-known figure outside Parliament, such as William Beveridge, later famous for his Report that was the basis of the post-1945 Welfare State. I was particularly interested to hear Sir Ronald Storrs, the Military Governor of Jerusalem under the British mandate, who described himself as 'the British successor to Pontius Pilate'. He whetted my appetite for a visit.

My husband was extremely anxious that the Radical Group should take a prominent part in Liberal policy, especially when Asquith, knowing that he did not have the energy to fight another seat, went to the Lords in 1925. Unable to take the name Earl of Oxford, because of objections from the family who had originally held the title, he had to be satisfied with the clumsy 'Earl of Oxford and Asquith', which was rather unfortunate because some people referred to him as 'Ox and Ass'. Realising that Asquith's elevation would give increased power to Lloyd George, who still had a large private fund, William said to me: 'I will not put my conscience in pawn to that man.'

As the most enthusiastic and active member of the Independent or 'Wee Free' Liberals, and later of the Radical Group, William was the driving force behind the Liberal opposition to Lloyd George. My husband was a great fighter and this period was, in some ways, the happiest of his parliamentary life. He never wanted power or office for its own sake but only so that he could help solve the country's problems. He enjoyed being in opposition far more than being in government.

He was appalled by the 'Honours Scandal' and also very much disapproved of the Coalition Government's policy against unrest in Ireland, particularly the use of the notorious Black and Tans. William made several visits to Ireland, where he was very well known and liked, to see what was happening at first hand. On one occasion, when he was wearing a black raincoat and a black felt hat, an Irish irregular soldier came up to him and, mistaking him for a priest, whispered: 'Would you like to see where the boys are drilling tonight, Father?' He used to enjoy telling that story!

After the 1918 election, the Independent Liberal organisation gave William a set of basement offices in Parliament Street, near the House of Commons, that became the centre of the 'Wee Free' campaign in Parliament. Every day by lunch time, an exhaustive digest of the coming day's questions and debates had been skilfully constructed, together with a complete briefing, for MPs taking part in debates, on each of the topics concerned. This was all supplied by my husband from his own reading of The Times for that day, backed up by his elaborate system of filing that had covered each of the issues over a period of years. William, on finding that two important stories would often back on to each other, had written to the editor of The Times asking him to make a better distribution of the news. The editor wrote back, suggesting that he buy two copies!

A vital part of the system was its complicated pattern of numbers. Every subject had its number and, daily, two copies of the Royal Edition of *The Times*, printed on rag paper guaranteed to put out any fire, were marked with classification numbers by William, and chopped up and pasted in the appropriate files by secretaries. My husband would then dictate the daily bulletin that enabled Independent Liberal MPs to make devastatingly accurate speeches, based on well-evidenced facts. The reputation of the Party grew out of all proportion to their numbers, much to the annoyance of Lloyd George and his Coalition Liberals and, later, the Conservative Government. William carried on his filing system from the time he returned to Parliament at the end of the First World War until the day before his death in November 1960. The daily bulletins ended when he joined the Labour Party, as his offer to provide them was declined. A complete set of these files is in the possession of the House of Lords.

I often used to go along to William's office, and on one occasion I was there when he had an interesting conversation with one of his senior helpers, Victor Gollancz, who at that time had parliamentary ambitions and was 'learning the ropes'. Mr Gollancz, it appeared, had now come to a difficult decision; his family was increasing and he must set about earning a living. Had my husband any ideas? William considered this question for a moment and then asked: 'Have you ever thought of publishing?' As a result, my husband gave Victor a letter of introduction to his brother, Ernest Benn. After doing extremely well at Benn Brothers, Victor asked if he could be a partner. On Ernest's refusal, he set up his own publishing house, which became quite a rival.

At first, William organised the Radical Group from the offices in Parliament Street, along the same lines as he had organised the 'Wee Frees', but by 1925 money was in such short supply that the offices had to be given up. My husband was in no doubt: our new home must house the office and the staff, as well as our growing family. 'But where?' I asked woefully. 'Well, what about the ground floor?' This consisted of a dining room, pantry, and an office with cloakrooms.

Fortunately, we came to a compromise that saved the dining room and pantry. My husband took the ground-floor office, the sitting room, a half-landing above, and, making a hole through the ground floor, annexed a large basement room in addition. This was reached by a rough and ready ladder and presented a somewhat daunting appearance. In fact, the approach was so narrow that one rather plump secretary, whom my husband was interviewing, declined to accept the post because she feared she would not 'fit the job'. After this, personal statistics had to be recognised as literally vital!

I think we must have been the only married couple living together to whom three copies of *The Times* were delivered: the Royal Editions for William's files, and an ordinary copy for me. William's office was not large enough to house everything he wished to keep, the result being that we slept with Hansard for twenty years! In the end, teething troubles were overcome and home and political office settled down for a partnership that lasted, apart from the interruption of the war years, from 1925 to 1958.

When we settled down into our houses in Cowley Street, and later Grosvenor Road, and life organised itself into the departmental activities of family and politics, I began to think again of my own interests that lay outside of these. Anxious to earn enough money to buy a pram for Michael, I wrote articles for *Good Housekeeping* and a short story for the *Daily News*. I enjoyed writing and was able to buy a very beautiful Dunkley pram.

My main interest was, and is, theology. I wanted to study and learn, and also give my children a clear idea of what the Christian religion was about. I greatly hoped that my teaching, even if woefully incomplete, would at least give them nothing to unlearn when they left my care and grew up to think for themselves.

I taught them about the Prophets of the Old Testament, with their emphasis on justice, and encouraged them to understand the Jewishness of Jesus. On Sundays I took the boys to St John's, Smith Square, where the rector, Canon Woodward, afterwards Bishop of Bristol, held an afternoon children's service. I believe I achieved what I set out to do, and I am always pleased when I hear Anthony say in interviews: 'I was brought up on the Old Testament.'

I discovered that King's College in the Strand welcomed external students for various biblical and theological courses. I had an interview with the Tutor to Women Students, Evelyn Hippisley, who became a lifelong friend, and explained to her that while my intention was to study seriously, with an already busy daily life I did not contemplate sitting for any examinations. Nowadays young wives and mothers have no difficulty in taking all this in their stride, but sixty-five years ago such was not considered a possibility.

Every Tuesday, I attended the graduate class taken by the Regius Professor, Dr William Oesterley. I was very pleased when he gave me the task of delivering one of his lectures when he had to be absent. I loved the classes, as I learned to read the New Testament in Greek and the Old Testament in Hebrew. Hebrew is such a lovely language. I do not believe you can get into the spirit of the Old Testament if you do not know a little Hebrew. In the Authorised Version of the Bible there is a translation of a phrase about Elijah in the desert: 'and after the fire a still, small voice'. Well, the literal translation from the Hebrew is: 'and there came to him the sound of a thin silence'. I think that is a wonderful phrase.

Of all religious debates, I was particularly interested in an issue that at the time was considered by many people to be so shocking as to be almost unmentionable: the ordination of women into the Anglican priesthood. This interest arose quite spontaneously in my own mind about the years 1916/17, when I was myself confirmed. Soon after, I heard of two events which showed that it was indeed a live issue and one destined to grow in importance. In 1917, the head of Mansfield College, the Congregational foundation in Oxford, ordained the first woman, Constance Coltman, to the Congregational ministry in Britain.

Many years later, she told me how it came about. After taking her MA degree at Oxford, she began to feel herself called to the ministry. She turned this over in her mind for some time and then approached the head of the College. He listened with surprise and interest and finally said: 'If you are aware of a call, who am I to deny it? You must be allowed to test it out to the full, as would any man in the same circumstances.' The result was her ordination and the beginning of the movement for the ordination of women in this country. Since then many women have been ordained, but not yet in the Anglican community in this country.

The second event took place at the Congregational City Temple, one of the leading churches of the Congregational Union of England and Wales. A well-known American preacher, Dr Fort Newton, accepted an invitation to be the minister, on condition that he was assisted by a colleague who would preach on Sunday evenings. To the general surprise, an Anglican woman, Maude Royden, was appointed to fill the place and became an instant success.

She had been active in the suffrage society that my mother and I supported, the National Union of Women's Suffrage Societies, and had edited the journal, Common Cause. In the 1920s she was the main driving force for the ordination of women.

Maude had a genius for making religion relevant to the issues of the day. A well-furnished mind enabled her to bring out illustrations with a bearing on all she said and she was a beautiful speaker, easy and, indeed, delightful to listen to. The City Temple was crowded on Sunday nights and the world sat up and took notice, particularly the Anglican world.

The strength of its opposition was massive when it was known that Hudson Shaw, the Rector of St Botolph's, Bishopsgate – who later married Maude, just before his death – had invited her to take the Three Hours' Service in his church on Good Friday, 1919. The Bishop of London forbade Maude to take the service and so it was held in the parish hall. In the Liberal press a well-known commentator, A. G. Gardiner, the editor of the Daily News, wrote: 'Maude Royden is more than a preacher: she is a portent.'

She did not leave the Church of England but set up the Guild House in Eccleston Square and ministered there, as well as preaching at St Botolph's. I used to go regularly to the Guild House to hear Maude preach. Guest speakers were invited to give series of lectures, and Gandhi spoke there when he visited England in 1931. Much educational and

charitable work was undertaken, especially in connection with Dr
Schweitzer's hospital at Lambarene. Maude told me that once when the
great man was her guest for a few days, she got up early on the morning
after his arrival and came into her sitting room to make sure the housemaid was lighting the fire to greet Dr Schweitzer when he came down
later. To her surprise, she found him on his knees before the grate
showing the housemaid how to light a fire that would burn to Maude's
satisfaction. I immediately thought of my father's ineptitude with coal
fires and found the comparison very amusing. I was delighted when
Maude was made a Companion of Honour on Ramsay MacDonald's
recommendation.

By remaining an Anglican, she was restricted in the practice of her
vocation. She said to me: 'What a monstrous thing it is that as minister
here, I preach to the congregation; I give pastoral counselling; I do
everything; but I am not allowed to celebrate the sacrament.'

The main objections to the ordination of women were that women
were not only inferior to men but unclean. One bishop remarked that
he was against women priests because 'woman was created second, and
fell first', and Maude explained to me: 'There is something very unpleas-
ant and slimy about the objection to the ordination of women: it is to
do with the ancient idea that women are unclean.' This was confirmed
when a clergyman said to me: 'I would have no objection to women
being ordained if they would absent themselves at certain times of the
month.'

By dint of searching for like-minded people who would support the
cause, I found that a little society was already in existence, not, I thought,
too happily named: the League of the Church Militant. It had notepaper
and a few pamphlets, but no office and no funds to speak of. I became
a member of the committee, and it was agreed that all our committee
meetings would be held in my house at Cowley Street and, later, at
Grosvenor Road. The committee members brought sandwiches and I
provided a hot drink. At the regular meetings of the League of the
Church Militant, women preached sermons.

The membership of the Society was small but impressive. Maude
Royden was President; and great support was given by Mr and Mrs
Marston Acres. There were social workers of great dedication; teachers,
especially those who worked with handicapped children; and church
workers who had little recognition or encouragement. There was also
one deaconess who had been appointed under the new rules set forth
by the Lambeth Conference of 1920. Deaconess Belfield hoped and
believed she was set for eventual ordination as a deacon and sent an
annual report of her work to the Archbishop of Canterbury.

We looked around for useful things to do that would reach the general
public. I recall that just at that time Dorothy Maude, a daughter of the
Bishop of Kensington, had decided to enter the mission field and we

arranged a meeting in a room at Church House at which she would be given a warm send-off. We hoped she would give us a lot of publicity during the course of her speech but, presumably not wishing to embarrass her father, she merely alluded, somewhat cryptically, to 'those who had really planned this meeting', adding: 'If anybody is interested in the ordination of women there is a book stall near the door.' I do not think we gained any new members on this occasion and we soon looked around for other opportunities. One soon arose.

In 1925, I dined one evening at Nancy and Waldorf Astor's to meet Queen Marie of Romania. Among the guests present at this characteristically glittering occasion were Archbishop Randall Davidson of Canterbury, and Mrs Davidson. After dinner, as the ladies had coffee together, I found myself in conversation with Mrs Davidson. On an impulse I said to her: 'I wonder if I might speak to you about something I have much at heart, of which I think you probably won't approve: the ordination of women.' Although startled, she encouraged me to go on. When I had done so, she said in the most friendly way: 'You must come and talk to the Archbishop about it.'

That spring, when Anthony was just a month old, the invitation duly came for my husband and myself to dine at Lambeth Palace. It was a splendid occasion. After a service in the beautiful chapel, we gathered in the dining room round a long table, decorated with flowers and glittering with glass and silver. I was placed on one side of the Archbishop's Chaplain, Dr Mervyn Haigh, later Bishop of Winchester. He treated me, I thought, with what felt like a distinctly cool suspicion; there was little doubt that I had been put beside him for observation.

After a wonderful dinner, we adjourned to the drawing room and then the real business of the evening began. Dr Randall Davidson seated himself in an imposing archiepiscopal chair and, one by one, those guests who had got to be put right were led up to sit beside him for a few minutes, sometimes longer, of conversation. I discovered that this was the Archbishop's regular way of dealing with dissidents.

Over eighty years of age, Dr Davidson had been Archbishop of Canterbury for many years. No other person had a greater experience of public life, nor indeed a longer memory of significant events. As Dean of Windsor and then Bishop of Winchester, he had ministered to Queen Victoria in her old age, and would relate how, on many occasions, he had had an audience with her, sitting in the Prince Consort's dressing room, watching the steam rise from the jug of hot water, brought in every evening by a servant, for the Prince's pre-dinner ablutions. Although Albert had been dead for almost forty years, the Queen had never had the heart to cancel this ritual, and so it continued until her own death.

The Archbishop was a Scot and a convert from Presbyterianism. It so happened that at that time the Archbishop of York, Dr Cosmo Gordon Lang, was also a Scot who had been born into the Presbyterian Church of Scotland. Dr Davidson, who enjoyed a joke, used to relate how he and Dr Lang had once met a Scottish minister operating in London and on asking what ministry he was exercising, received the reply: 'Oh, I'm looking out for stray Presbyterians.'

Being very well briefed, Dr Davidson asked me in a forthright way: 'Do you want to be a priest?' I was able to say that the issue was not, at that time anyway, a personal one. 'That is not my present ambition,' I said. 'Why are you interested in this movement then?' I explained: 'I have two little boys, and I want them to be brought up in a world in which the Church gives equal spiritual status to women. I believe that will make a great difference to their attitude to women, collectively and individually.'

At this the Archbishop launched into a long account of his own views. He had always been a convinced feminist and had always supported the franchise for women. Beyond that, he had always believed that all the professions should be open to women; but, at last homing in on the issue, he raised his voice and pronounced with an implacably dismissive emphasis: 'This is different. It cannot be. It goes against the Catholic tradition of two millennia. You must stop working for the ordination of women.' I said: 'Well, Archbishop, I do not think you can make that distinction and I shall be very sorry if the Church commits itself to that. Because I think it is right, I can't stop; and I must keep working for it.' I cannot recall that he advanced any argument. He just said there never had been women priests and there never could be. Presently, after a few kindly personal words of advice on how to view this matter in the future, I was led away to make room for the next interviewee.

It was interesting that the Archbishop had thought it worthwhile to try and nip in the bud any such views when he came across them. Needless to say the whole incident and his words had the opposite effect. That evening I felt for the first time the full weight of the opposition ranged against the ordination of women.

A year or so later, I had another idea for publicising the cause. With the assistance of William, I arranged and chaired a meeting in the large Harcourt dining room on the terrace level of the House of Commons. I invited Dr Maude Royden, the doyenne of this Cinderella of causes, to come and address a large group of women who had been successful in entering their respective professions and making good there, in the hope that she would interest them in the cause of the ordination of women.

People seem always to enjoy coming to a function at the House of Commons, and nearly everyone accepted. Among them were MPs, doctors, business executives and lawyers. The arts were represented by actresses and, most notably, by the singer Clara Butt, whose deep voice seemed to make the teacups rattle when she spoke in the discussion that followed Maude's talk. The audience itself made a most unusual gathering. Sixty years ago women were in a very different position from now and, looking back over two generations, it is gratifying to see what immense progress has been made; though not in everything.

After the meeting, I asked Susan Lawrence, the Labour MP who later became a junior health minister, what she had thought of the talk. I was most disappointed to hear her say: 'Well, today I'm an agnostic and take no interest in the matter, but if I think myself back into my Anglican past, well, I don't like it!' Some of the other women felt the same way. How strangely binding and blinding a gut reaction can be!

We persisted in our own work, taking every opportunity that presented itself of making our cause known. Women finally obtained the vote on equal terms to men in 1928 and the League of the Church Militant, which had originally been set up as part of the suffrage movement, was disbanded. I became a founder member of its inter-denominational replacement, the Society for the Ministry of Women in the Church. Maude Royden was the Anglican President. When, after the Second World War, I left the Church of England and became a Congregationalist, I was the Free Church President of this body for many years.

Gradually more and more influential Anglican women took up the cudgels and now the Movement for the Ordination of Women has a status and influence that no one would dispute. Today the movement has wide support within the Church of England, and even some support within the Roman Catholic Church; sixty years ago, the subject was barely mentionable in Anglican circles. There are now hundreds of women ordained in Anglican churches abroad and I hope that, given the strong support of the Archbishop of Canterbury, Dr George Carey, an Anglican woman will soon be ordained in Britain.

By early 1926, William was becoming more and more uncomfortable in the Liberal Party, feeling that it was no longer truly radical, and began to consider joining the Labour Party. I knew Ethel Snowden, wife of Philip Snowden, who had been Chancellor of the Exchequer in Ramsay Mac-Donald's 1924 Cabinet, and on one occasion, when I was talking to her in the Ladies' Gallery, she said: 'Your husband's so much wanted in the Labour Party. Don't you think he could take just that small step and join?'

Ernest Benn was shocked that William was contemplating leaving the Liberal Party. It suggested that William was under so much strain from overwork that he might not be able to make a rational decision. From Ernest's point of view, anyone who wanted to join the Labour Party must be ill! He felt that his brother should recuperate on holiday before taking a decision which Ernest was sure William would regret. Consequently, in February 1926, after insisting that he and Gwen look after Michael and Anthony, Ernest generously sent us on a Mediterranean cruise. Apart from working holidays in skiing resorts where William had lectured on Parliament, this would be the first trip abroad since our honeymoon. But what was meant to be a holiday of a few weeks, turned into a three-month journey that took us as far as the Soviet Union.

CHAPTER 4

JOURNEY TO THE MIDDLE EAST, 1926

We set out from Waterloo Station on the morning of 19 February 1926, a cold, wet, dreary day. It felt very strange to be leaving the country at the beginning of a parliamentary session. Early the day before, I had left the children in the safekeeping of Ernest and Gwen; but it had not been easy watching Michael wave me goodbye from the doorstep. Baby Anthony was unconscious of our departure.

The journey from London to Paris was uneventful and at three o'clock we caught the Mentone train which carried us south in great comfort. With only two suitcases and a hat-box we were setting out for the freest sort of holiday. We were 'ghosts', in the sense that no one knew us, and we did not drag with us one single 'chain' in the shape of a cabin trunk.

The next morning I woke to my first sight of the Riviera: a paradise of blue sea, mimosa and carnations. Antibes, Nice, Cannes all flashed by and at eleven o'clock the train drew up at Mentone where my parents were living. On the platform my father almost smothered me with the warmth of his welcome, for William had omitted my name in the telegram he had sent. As we left the station my father pointed to the top floor of a high building where my mother stood at a window. 'Oh, my daughter's with him! My daughter's with him!' she cried as we waved our greeting.

For some years my parents had been living abroad to satisfy my mother's love of sunshine; but she continued to be impulsive, and found it hard to remain in one place. On one occasion she was out walking in the town, noticed the Golden Arrow train, and thought: 'If I caught that, I could see my girls in London.' When my mother, who I thought was in Mentone, arrived on my doorstep, I said: 'But, Mother, what about Father?' 'Oh,' she replied, 'I sent him a telegram from Paris.' Once when staying with me she decided she would like to go back to see my father in Mentone, and so left without telling anybody.

It was delightful seeing my parents again and I particularly enjoyed a day in Monte Carlo. On hiring a car, we discovered that the driver had been an officer in General Wrangel's White Russian army. It was only six years since the triumph of the Soviet Red Army, and, unfortunately, our driver found the subject too painful to talk about.

Monte Carlo was exquisite. The streets were white and spotless and even the leaves of the trees looked as if they were dusted each morning. The air was clear and invigorating, the view superb; and the display of flowers, fashionable clothes and jewels was dazzling. The wealth of Monte Carlo came, of course, from the gambling losses of foreigners, and we felt it would be impossible to visit the town without looking in at the famous Casino. After a few formalities with passports, we were admitted into the Rooms. Deciding to try my hand at the roulette wheel, I soon lost my small stake. I was none too pleased, but William was thrilled, fearing that a win might have turned me into a regular gambler.

After spending a few days with my parents we set out for Venice. We were scheduled to arrive early in the morning, have a bath and breakfast on our boat, the *Praga*, spend the day sightseeing, and then begin the cruise that was supposed to stop William joining the Labour Party.

Arriving in Venice at 6 am, we found the station heavily decorated with flags to welcome Count Volpi, the former Governor of Tripoli, who was then Mussolini's Finance Minister, coming in triumph to receive the congratulations of his native city for his services in Washington and London. Mussolini's 'March on Rome' had taken place in 1922 and Italy was now under Fascist rule.

I shall never forget my first impression of the Grand Canal just before sunrise: the soft light of the lamps, the plash of the water against the steps, the high-prowed, graceful gondolas; all enchantingly mysterious. It was intensely cold during the half-hour or so that we went in and out of the winding waterways, and the warning cries of our gondolier, perched in the stern, were the only sounds we heard all the way. As dawn broke we reached the quay – to find no *Praga*. Our gondolier was anxious to leave us to sit on our luggage until such time as the boat appeared; but this seemed too great a risk and, fortunately, we did not take it, for the *Praga* was nine hours late.

We spent the day sightseeing. We were amused at the way the gondoliers pursued the American tourists, knowing they always had the most money to spend. 'Gondola! Gondola take you to the islands,' they would call out, pronouncing the word in the American way with 'dola' rhyming with 'cola'. The beauty of the city was spoiled only by the hideously stencilled portraits of Mussolini surmounted by the words *Il Duce* ('The Leader') and *V V Mussolini* ('Long live Mussolini') on the bases of statues.

The quietness of Venice compared with London was extraordinary. There were no motors, no horses; only the gondolas gliding along. The sun had risen above the mists as we reached the Great Arcade and I saw for the first time the Piazza, almost empty apart from the pigeons that clustered on the ground in front of the tall posts that symbolised the proud Venetian conquests of other nations. Behind stood the Cathedral of San Marco, glittering in the sun; rich in design, in sculpture and in age.

We spent a little time by the Doge's Palace, stood by the Bridge of Sighs, and took lunch at a charming Venetian restaurant off the Piazza. In the afternoon we sailed up and down the Grand Canal. I was fascinated by the many-coloured striped poles sticking out of the water – mooring posts for the gondolas of local families. Like other famous streets of the world, the Grand Canal turns and sweeps, so that every bend brings a new vista. By the Rialto we passed a funeral barge, all black and silver, with liveried gondoliers.

Four o'clock found us once more in the Piazza, drinking tea and watching the world of Venice talking, laughing and walking up and down – up and down. The children's nannies were entrancing: almost all were bare-headed, with long, braided hair; immense drop-earrings shaped like the balls from a Christmas tree; bright-coloured dresses in green crêpe de Chine or cherry silk, bunched out over innumerable petticoats; and starched, frilly aprons, white shawls, white stockings and black patent shoes.

That evening, at dusk, we sighted the *Praga* in the harbour. She proved to be a most comfortable and spotlessly clean ship, and was officered by native Italians, with the exception of the Captain. A Slovene from Trieste, he had found himself, in 1918, when the city changed hands at the end of the First World War, transformed overnight from a subject of the Austro-Hungarian Empire to an Italian national. At first silent on politics he melted, as so many people did, under William's sympathy and charm. 'Everywhere,' he confided to us, 'the people of Trieste say: "A thousand times give us the Austrians." ' Then, afraid that he had gone too far, he caught William's arm and said, with the frightened look we were to see all too often in undemocratic countries: 'But, Mister . . . you won't say anything . . . for, of course, now I'm an Italian.'

We sailed calmly down the Adriatic until we entered the Ionian Sea, when the blue skies vanished with the onset of a great storm of sleet and snow. All night, with the Captain unable to leave the bridge, the ship staggered through the blizzard at a snail's pace, and it was not until 9 am that we saw the Gulf of Corinth.

The canal is so narrow that it seemed as if we should scrape the sides of the high, brown, stony cliffs on which the men of Corinth had carved their names in Greek. It was very strange to step suddenly out of the familiar world of Latin letters. At the end of the canal, we sailed suddenly into the glorious panorama of the Bay of Salamis. To the right of us were the rugged mountains of the Peloponnese; to the left, the mountains of the mainland, all the high peaks aglitter with sun and snow.

The cold that attacked us was cruel. We were told that such weather was quite abnormal, the Purser assuring us that in December he had slept on deck through the whole voyage. Unable to visit Athens, because of mining activity, it was with much sorrow and despair that we watched the city draw away from us in a glorious sunset. Perhaps Athene had

refused us permission to insult her city with the casual visit of an hour
or two!

In the open sea the storm was worse than ever and it seemed that we
would be unable to land in Crete. Would Knossos go the way of Athens?
Fortunately, the Captain was able to put us ashore in a lifeboat. Everything we saw delighted us: the quaint streets; pepper trees; donkey carts;
the Venetian palaces; the winged lion of St Mark on the harbour forti-
fications; the minaret of a mosque. In our sense of deliverance from the
sea and the storm, we thought it the loveliest country in the world. We
drove over the hill among the blossoms and wild flowers to Knossos. An
hour or so, no more, was spent in the ancient palace of King Minos,
then being excavated by Sir Arthur Evans. We wandered as we pleased,
seeing and imagining much.

The storm took us again, and two days later we awoke to see the flat,
brown shores of Egypt with the palm trees bent by the strong wind
which followed us all the way. Many hours were wasted on tiresome
formalities, but, very luckily for us, one of the officials knew William
as a sympathetic friend of Egypt and this enabled us to save much time
and trouble. We were given some valuable tips about trains and hotels;
most useful at a time when American millionaires were booking up all
the accommodation!

After a short stay in Alexandria, we set out at sunset for Cairo. Beside
our train ran long canals bearing unfamiliar boats; on the banks walked
white-robed people, leading or, sometimes, riding camels up to houses
made of baked clay.

Egypt at that time was officially independent and ruled by King Fuad
and an elected assembly; but, in reality, Britain was still in control, as
she had been since 1882. There was a nationalist movement demanding
genuine independence, and on the morning of our first full day in Cairo,
William, an ardent believer in self-determination for all peoples, went
to see the nationalist leader, Zaghlul Pasha.

I spent the morning in the museum among the marvellous relics of
ancient Egypt. A few years before, the archaeologist Howard Carter had
caused a sensation with the discovery of the tomb of the boy King
Tutankhamen; and I was thrilled to have the chance to see the much-
talked-of treasures, particularly the stupendous gold sarcophagus. I was
fascinated to think that artefacts which were already in the tomb before
one word of the Old Testament had been written had all the brilliance
of the latest workmanship. Tutankhamen's mummy had been left at
Luxor but there were many others, with heads and shoulders unwrapped,
in the Hall of the Kings; the most lifelike being that of Rameses II –
the Pharaoh of the Exodus.

That afternoon we rode out to the Pyramids in a sunless haze which
before long melted in depressing drizzle. At Mena House, the gateway
to the desert, we fought our way through the clamorous masses of

donkey and camel boys, more troublesome even than the rain which
pelted hard, while the rugged height of the Great Pyramid towered
above us. Shouts, cries, entreaties echoed in our ears all the way – even
William suggested I should take a camel to quieten them. The rain and
mud-storm, the stinging of the wind and sand, and above all, the cries
of the crowd that followed us, made it more like Election Day in Leith
than a restful holiday in Egypt!

At a turn of the track we found ourselves before the figure of
the Sphinx, which still had vestiges of red paint visible on its face. My
first feeling was of surprise at its apparent smallness. Scaffolding up
its back was aiding the work of restoration and, all round its body, the
sand of ages was being cleared away to reveal again its lion paws. I
thought of the legend that said that Mary had laid the infant Jesus
between them.

That night we dined with the High Commissioner, Lord Lloyd, and
Lady Lloyd. An aide-de-camp waited for us in the hall of the Residency,
a beautiful palace on the Nile, and we passed by rows of native servants,
impressively dressed in scarlet, gold and white, into the richly furnished
drawing room. I had an impression of pale green brocade, logs burning
in a marble grate, and exotic snapdragons of every hue massed in giant
glass bowls. All the guests assembled to await presentation, for the Lloyds
kept up a semi-royal state greater even than the Governors-General and
the Viceroys. An awed silence fell upon the room as the aide-de-camp
ushered them in. Lord Lloyd, then in his mid-forties, was short with jet
black hair, determined on being the 'strong man'. Lady Lloyd was less
stiff than he, but they were both markedly remote.

In the drawing room afterwards the ladies took out their quilting and
tapestry work and the evening passed for most of us in pleasant small-talk,
except for William and Lord Lloyd, who were discussing Egyptian
politics in a corner. Their views on the British Empire could not have
been more different and we were not surprised when, a few months
later, Lord Lloyd ordered a gunboat to Alexandria to stop Zaghlul
becoming Prime Minister after his Wafd Party had gained a majority in
the Assembly. At eleven o'clock we were bidden goodnight in the royal
fashion: 'It's been very nice to see you – goodbye!'

Before leaving Cairo we visited the great Mosque University of Al
Azhar. Wearing slippers, and accompanied by guides, we went into the
great courtyard of this important political centre. Round its cloisters
students of all ages and nationalities, with open Korans before them,
crooned and swayed on their mats. The course of study, which involved
learning the whole Koran by heart, lasted seventeen years and began,
sometimes, when the student was as young as four.

We climbed up to the citadel and visited the Mosque of Mehemet Ali,
the Albanian who ruled Egypt in the nineteenth century. It was a
splendid building with many windows, Turkey carpets and fine glass

chandeliers. From the walled terrace, with its commanding views of the city and the desert, we bade farewell to Cairo.

The charmingly named 'Milk and Honey' express train ran nightly from Cairo to Jerusalem. I thought, as we boarded, how it would have saved Moses forty years! It was one of our most thrilling journeys. The train was alive with pilgrims. There were Jewish settlers with their few bundles going to the Promised Land; Christians visiting the Holy Places; and British soldiers going back to duty in the desert camps. At midnight, in order to change trains, we crossed the Suez Canal in a little ferry boat. We had to wait a few minutes while a ship came up from the southern hemisphere. The soldiers told us that homesick Tommies often lined up on the banks to see the P & O passengers making their way home to England.

At the setting of the moon, in the reddening east we saw the land we were about to enter. Our first stop was Ashkelon, and thenceforward every name had a link or association with the Old or New Testament. The little villages that we passed were rich in sheep and goats, and full of apple, peach and plum orchards. The white and pink blossom against the delicate spring green was exquisite. The whole land was carpeted with deep crimson anemones and 'lilies of the field', growing in their thousands. As we drew nearer to Jerusalem, where the country grew wilder, rising to rocky heights and falling downwards in deep ravines, wild lilies still grew wherever a footing was afforded among the stones.

At the end of our journey we passed the cave where Samson hid from his pursuers; and at nine o'clock on the morning of 11 March we drove into the walled city of Jerusalem through the Jaffa Gate by which General Allenby had entered, as conqueror, after defeating the Turks in 1917. Once inside, our guide beckoned us to leave the car and follow him through the narrow bazaars, down slippery steps, round and along, until at last he brought us to the St John's Hotel, set on the site of the old hospital of the Knights Templar. The hotel and our room delighted us. From our balcony, set on a corner of the first floor, we had a beautiful view of the Mount of Olives down to the Garden of Gethsemane and the country around. A few yards to our left stood the Church of the Holy Sepulchre.

We lost no time in going out and visiting the native bazaar with its high vaulted roof, sheltering every imaginable type of merchandise. The vegetable market alone was a wonder with its row upon row of cauliflowers as large as footballs. On all sides we tripped over squatting figures who were preparing and consuming meals. In unceasing accompaniment to the buying, selling and small talk of the people came weird tunes from a score of gramophones, drifting round the corners and echoing from the roof. In all the bazaars of the East we heard that noise, and, everywhere, it might have been the same record playing.

Choosing a quiet hour just before dusk, we paid our first visit to the Church of the Holy Sepulchre. It chanced to be the hour for Muslim prayers and we approached it to the sound of the muezzin-call from a minaret close by. We made our way through the gloom to the Chapel of St Helena where, on the walls and pillars, the Crusaders in their thousands had cut the sign of the cross with their swords. We saw Christians of many denominations, but we were particularly aware of the presence of the Franciscans, whose special charge was the Holy Sepulchre and who lived in the church.

We dined one night with the Governor of Jerusalem, Sir Ronald Storrs, whom I had met at one of William's Radical Group lunches. He had a very deep sense of his responsibilities towards the Holy City and would not, for example, allow dancing within the walls. Britain had been given the Palestine mandate by the League of Nations in 1922, and Sir Ronald showed us the great schemes that were in progress for developing Jerusalem and Palestine, including a new water supply for the city and the extraction of potassium from the Dead Sea. Jewish immigration was being encouraged in accordance with the mandate, and in 1925, the year before our visit, the Hebrew University had been opened by Balfour, a committed supporter of the Jewish cause.

Everything was done to facilitate contact between the British officials and the local population. I was amused by a conversation manual, painstakingly compiled, and published to this end. On one side of the page was English and, on the other, Hebrew. One request was 'Make me an evening jacket at your lowest price,' followed, in expectation of an unsatisfactory result, by 'Lo! It is too straight and narrow'!

Sir Ronald gave me one of Allenby's proclamations: it was written in Arabic, Hebrew and English, as were all subsequent edicts. William and I were fortunate to meet Field Marshal Lord Allenby on our next visit to Jerusalem, in 1934, when we lunched with the High Commissioner and Commander-in-Chief, Sir Arthur Wauchope, at Government House, a residence set high on the hills above the old city and the Garden of Gethsemane with a superb view of the desert and the mountains. Finding myself placed next to the great man, I ventured the question: 'Oh, Lord Allenby, do tell me how you took Jerusalem.' The effect was electric. Springing immediately to life, he started to talk very loudly and, twisting round the knives and forks and the plates and glasses, gave a graphic demonstration of the campaign: 'I put the guns here, and the cavalry there.' When fellow guests discovered what was going on, conversation stopped and we were all taken on a verbal conducted tour of the historic operations. Unfortunately, I was so excited to be talking to the man who was the most recent conqueror of Jerusalem that I was unable to remember the details!

There was a rumour that Allenby had been given the keys of Jerusalem in a most unorthodox fashion by his valet, who woke him with the announcement: 'Your early tea, sir, and the keys of Jerusalem.' Summoning up my courage, I asked: 'Is that true?' Allenby replied: 'No, it's a damned lie!' He had had them presented in the correct manner.

Before leaving Jerusalem on our first trip, we very much wanted to see the Temple; but the only day we had available was a Friday, the Muslim equivalent of the Christian Sunday. Fortunately, the omnipotent Sir Ronald Storrs arranged for us to be specially admitted and shown round by a very informed guide, Rudi Bey. The Temple area is sacred to Judaism, Christianity and Islam, and one Holy Place has succeeded another with the changes and chances of the centuries.

Shoes in hand, we entered the mosque and, through the great grille-screen put up by the Crusaders, saw the traditional rock on which Abraham had prepared to sacrifice Isaac. When we reached the Wailing Wall, Rudi Bey's lip curled at the sight and mention of the Jews. His attitude was typical of the other Arabs we met.

When we had bidden goodbye to our guide we drove out by the Damascus Gate to the Garden of Gethsemane, only a small portion of which remained as such, for a great new church had been built over the stone on which our Lord is believed to have prayed.

That afternoon we drove out to Bethlehem and visited the Church of the Nativity. On our return to Jerusalem we drove to the Mount of Olives. The rocky grandeur of Palestine surrounded us. To our right lay the Holy City within its ancient walls, temples and towers silhouetted black against the blazing sunset; while far below on the left stretched the whole valley of the river Jordan as far as the eye could see. The silvery river wound its way towards the great expanse of the Dead Sea, blue as a turquoise, and in the distance stood the white roofs of Jericho. An unforgettable experience.

On the next day we said farewell to Jerusalem, grateful for the glimpse afforded us and the memories we took away. We set out for Haifa in a Ford motor car that carried ourselves and an 'Auld Kirk' minister, Mr Milligan, and his wife. They were excellent company, being well supplied with guidebooks which made every point of interest on the way – especially the place where Jesus was missed by his parents – easy to identify. We visited Nazareth but were far more interested in contemplating the unchanged background of the hills of Galilee than the various places of doubtful authenticity such as the Madonna's kitchen and Joseph's workshop.

At Haifa a car was waiting to take us on to Beirut, where we were supposed to rejoin the *Praga* and continue to Constantinople; but William had had more than enough of a pleasure cruise and was considering journeying across the desert to Baghdad. Travelling along the northern coasts of Palestine, we were sometimes at sea level and sometimes at a height. Finally, at the summit of a long winding hill, was a pavilion, flying the Union Jack, with PALESTINE written on a frieze. We passed through the British Customs and after a mile or so of neutral ground entered Syria, which then included Lebanon and was under the French mandate.

William lunched in Beirut, the French administrative centre, with the High Commissioner, Henri de Jouvenal. He was not happy with William's idea of crossing the desert, as the nationalist Druse rebellion was still in progress in Syria. If William was determined to go, then I should stay in the Residency.

That evening we dined with Norman Mayers, the British Consul. The 'abnormal' weather that had accompanied us throughout our trip held for the moment in Beirut and we shivered round the oil stove that moved from room to room with us. Telling us about affairs in Syria, he explained how foreigners were secretly sympathetic to the Druse rebellion as it was felt that the French administration was very heavy-handed. Like de Jouvenal, however, he was against our crossing the desert: people did so against advice and at their own risk.

This made William more desirous to go and more determined to leave me. With the aid of the Consul he even found a mission at which to deposit me! I visited it, not because I had any intention of staying there, but in order to see if it was the one at which my grandfather Eadie had met Aunt Emily. Sadly, I discovered that Aunt Emily's mission had been in ruins since the First World War.

Refusing to be left behind in Beirut, I went with William to make arrangements for travelling to Baghdad by the 'Desert Mail', an enterprise recently started by a young New Zealander, Norman Nairne. We were greeted in his drawing room by a warm fire burning in one of the few open fireplaces in Beirut, and a delicious tea of Scotch scones and pancakes! Nairne was to travel with us in a convoy of three cars. Starting at the same time, another convoy was to carry a League of Nations commission on their way to Persia to suggest crops that could take the place of opium.

The route was through Tripoli, Homs and the marvellous old desert city of Palmyra. The French High Commissioner had arranged an armoured car and aeroplane patrol on the desert stretch from Homs to Palmyra, the centre of the nationalist unrest, and an hour or so from Damascus.

We left Beirut in the afternoon in a powerful touring Cadillac well equipped for all emergencies. 'What are the ropes and spades for?' we asked. 'And surely there's too much to eat?' 'Wait till you see the mud,' Nairne replied. 'Convoy last week was bogged down for six days. After the first three we begin to ration the food.' He went off to ensure that the mails were properly strapped round the first car. The government of Iraq allowed sixty hours for transit from Haifa to Baghdad, and Nairne was fined for every hour beyond that time.

On the first short stage of our journey we travelled along the coast and were soon in Tripoli. A notice in the hotel informed us that we were not to lock our door as this would prevent the management letting the other beds in the room. Next morning, fortunately, we were still alone! At supper we had our first sight of the League of Nations commission. The most colourful member was an Italian naturalist professor, wearing a type of flying uniform, who, during the course of the journey, whenever a halt was made, frequently wandered off and was usually found absent-mindedly absorbed in catching butterflies.

We set off early the next morning, and there is nothing more thrilling than a journey begun before sunrise through new and sometimes trackless countryside. I sat in the front seat next to Nairne and was filled with admiration at the dexterity with which he opened and consumed packets of chewing gum, and smoked cigarette after cigarette, while driving the car at top speed over almost non-existent roads. All the time he kept up a running conversation about his vision of owning a great fleet of cars and a string of rest houses along the desert route.

The heat of the engine and the rising sun made me very drowsy after an hour or two, and I began to appreciate fully that sleep was thirty hours away. It was impossible to keep one's head still for an instant; wherever one placed it, an immense jolt dislodged it. The passengers in the back, William and a young English couple, had an even rougher ride and several times there was a bang as a head hit the roof.

About noon we drove into Homs. This was the last town on our journey and the country began to change rapidly. Soon we ran straight into a bog – and stuck fast. Fortunately, the other cars came back to help and with the aid of the ropes our vehicle was released. All went well for a short while until we were suddenly stopped by a barrier, bristling with machine guns, right across the road. We certainly thought our fate had come upon us! But Nairne was out in an instant and we realised that these were de Jouvenal's friendly patrols. A great deal of saluting and voluble talk went on, and the report of 'All quiet' was given. The road to Damascus branched off at this point and a body of Druse rebels had been seen two days before; but nothing since. The French were especially anxious that no incident should take place on this particular occasion when representatives of the League of Nations were passing through their mandated territory.

Continuing on our way, we approached a range of hills that an hour before had appeared on the edge of the horizon; a medieval castle, that might have been hewn out of the rock, was distinguishable perched above a precipitous height. This was an old Turkish stronghold that commanded a wide view over the desert on all sides, and stood sentinel over Palmyra. Driving through a gap in the hills, we found ourselves in the midst of noble columns, temples, and steps: the classical remains of a great city of antiquity. As we were taking note of all this a man came up to us and announced that he was the Governor of Palmyra and would show us round.

As we progressed, all the Arabs who were sitting on the walls rose instantly; with a wave of his hand the Governor indicated that they might sit down again. He arranged that a mosque should be opened for us, laughing as we removed our shoes. Insisting that it was quite unnecessary to pander to the native races, he tramped through the mosque with his dirty boots, oblivious to the glowering glances that followed him. On our return journey we were not surprised to learn that while he was on a visit to headquarters in Beirut his wife had been murdered by rebels.

After leaving Palmyra the convoy proceeded at a much faster speed as we had many hundreds of miles to cover before crossing the Euphrates next morning. Occasionally we flew past broken-down cars and camel bones, but for the most part we saw no signs of life, past or present. I obtained great pleasure from the company of an old friend, for I had borrowed a copy of the works of the ancient Athenian, Xenophon, from the American University in Beirut. It was fascinating to discover that in 2,400 years the face of the desert had changed little. The unbroken terrain was there, flat as the sea, and covered with the absinthe plant. Later we crossed the track Xenophon had taken alongside the river Euphrates.

At eight in the evening we ate a most welcome picnic. The subtle smell of the desert rose like honey round us and, dimly, in the darkness, we saw minute wild flowers of many shapes beside the camel thorn. At the hooting of the cars we climbed in, regretfully, and settled down for a sleepless night's drive.

After resting and washing at the Royal Air Force camp at Fellujah, we finally crossed the Euphrates and entered the ancient land of Mesopotamia – renamed Iraq at the end of the First World War. Our convoy ignored the track and drove at an immense speed on the sand. A flying cloud was all that appeared of the other cars as we followed them faster and faster. Sometimes the triangular sail of the muheilah barges travelled with us for a minute or two; sometimes we lost sight of the river altogether. For an hour or two we drove across the unbroken plain of Iraq and then, on the farthest edge of the world, a bright ball of fire leapt into sight: the golden dome of Khazimain. In a few minutes, houses, mosques and minarets took shape out of the sand as Baghdad lay before us. We crossed the Tigris and realised that the journey was over.

After sleeping for many hours in our room at the Maude Hotel, we awoke in the cool of the evening feeling refreshed. We had dinner and then talked to the many Iraqi politicians who used the hotel. Their country, ruled by the Ottoman Empire until the end of the First World War, had been placed under the British mandate in 1920 without any consultation with the people. Although an Iraqi Parliament and Cabinet had been set up, Britain was still in ultimate control and had made Feisal, a son of King Hussein of the Hejaz, King of Iraq. A treaty, signed in 1922, regularising the relationship between Britain and Iraq, had done nothing to satisfy the nationalists.

The Iraqi politicians were delighted to meet a British MP who had opposed the mandate treaty and was on their side. 'You must have been with Captain Benn, then?' said Muzahim Bey, the MP for Babylon, who had been in the Iraqi Cabinet. When he realised who he was talking to he could not do enough for us. We found that he studied *The Times* as closely as William, and was familiar with every detail and every personality in British public life. His colleague Kisbany Bey was MP for Nineveh, and I thought how delightful it must be to represent such historic constituencies.

The next day, 21 March, we decided to call on Gertrude Bell, the city's most famous British resident. William and I knew her father, Sir Hugh Bell, who was a strong admirer of Ernest Benn's political views. Gertrude Bell was a remarkable woman who had lived and travelled in Mesopotamia for the last thirty years and was a fine Arabic scholar. But, although she had been Oriental Secretary to the High Commissioner, and was then the only woman to have written a White Paper, she was not a feminist and had little time for other women. Her devotion to King Feisal was thought to be excessive by some of the other British advisers, one of whom produced this limerick:

> There was an old girl of Iraq
> Who of loyal respect had no lack,
> As thin as an easel,
> She'd curtsy to Feisal,
> And when she got up she would crack.

At the time of our visit she was Director of Archaeology and had been responsible for creating the Baghdad Museum, which contained finds from excavations carried out by herself and others. Her determination had kept many treasures in Iraq that might otherwise have been taken out of the country. We easily found Gertrude Bell's house, for 'The Hatoun' – 'The Lady' – was so well known that everybody we asked gave us exact directions. Unfortunately, she was out when we called, but her faithful and celebrated manservant took our coats and we lingered for a few minutes in the garden she had built for herself, shut in by a high wall and a gate from the nearby road.

Deciding to set out in search of Khazimain and its golden domes, we found a very rickety victoria, a four-wheeled carriage with an open top, and, by means of signs, were able to come to terms for the journey. With the river and the hidden bazaars on our left we drove past shops, dwellings, and listless British soldiers on duty outside their barracks, until we came to the Tigris, which we crossed by a pontoon bridge.

A charming scene greeted us: something approaching a children's fair was in progress. On gaily decorated wooden scaffolding a large number of swings and swinging boats were suspended, and the youth of Baghdad were spending an exciting Sunday morning, shouting and waving paper windmills of many colours. At this point our driver told us that he could take his horse no farther, and as usual many people detached themselves from the crowd and offered to act as our guide. We agreed to let one man take us through the bazaar to Khazimain. We found ourselves very much strangers here and were looked at much more than had been the case in Jerusalem. Emerging, we found ourselves outside the great mosque but were disappointed to be told that only Muslims could enter.

We walked back through the crowds and thought that the people did not look very robust or healthy. Nearly all the children, and many of the adults, had sore eyes; and the prevalence of a complaint called 'Baghdad boil', which chiefly affected the face, was most distressing. I was told that the High Commissioner had had one for a year and would not set foot outside the Residency for months.

While resting after lunch, we received a phone call from Gertrude Bell. She wanted to know 'which Benns' we were, and though obviously disappointed to find that we were not the capitalist Sir Ernest Benn and his wife, invited us, nevertheless, to go along there and then and pay her a visit. She sped a parting guest at our arrival and we sat round an open English fire. Volunteering to give us any help we needed and offering to show us round the Baghdad Museum, she then asked us to dine one day and lunch another.

The next day, as we were drinking our coffee after lunch, a card was brought to us from a Mr Eastwood, a representative of the British Cotton Growers' Asociation. He had seen our names on the list of arrivals and offered his help to take us sightseeing. When I said how much I wanted to visit Babylon he exclaimed: 'Babylon!' and added that it reminded him of a 'slag heap up at Wigan'. At this point William was called to the telephone and came back announcing that the Air Force had arranged for him to fly the following morning to Mosul, where he would remain until the next day. Mosul, rich in oil deposits, was in the north of Iraq, where a border dispute with Turkey was in process of being resolved in Iraq's favour. Immediately, Mr Eastwood offered to show me around while William was away.

On the morning of 23 March William left for the RAF station at Hinaidi whence he was to fly to Mosul. Soon afterwards Mr Eastwood turned up, arrayed in grey flannels, trilby hat and wash-leather gloves, bringing with him a car and a servant. After a short drive we left the car and plunged into the native quarter. As we approached the docks the air rang with cries that might have been the 'Fore!' of agitated golfers, as heavily laden Kurdish porters came at us at a run, their backs bent almost at right angles with impossible loads. 'There's a proverb in Baghdad,' said Mr Eastwood, 'that when the Kurds go home there will be a heavy mortality among the donkeys.' Denied their national aspirations at the end of the First World War, the Kurds were ruled in the 1920s, as they are today, by the Turkish and Iraqi governments.

After visiting the docks we turned into the bazaars. They were the usual familiar narrow alleys, roofed over, thronged with all the different peoples of the Middle East: Arabs, Persians and Jews mingling together, distinguished by their clothes. Emerging, at the end of an hour, into the strange coolness and quiet of the Serai – the official headquarters of the Government Administration – we visited an excellent bookshop kept by a Scotsman, Mr Mackenzie. It was replete with literature on every sort of subject and I bought a Home University Library volume on Muhammad. In the courtyard outside we met Muzahim, the MP for Babylon, wearing the smart velvet cap – like the crown of a trilby – popularised by the King and called, after him, the Feisali.

Declining his kind offer of a lift we lunched at the Carlton and then visited Mr Eastwood's house on the opposite bank of the river. It was built, attractively, round a courtyard, and two tame gazelles followed us about upstairs and through the gardens. The house was in an old part of the town, reached through narrow streets, much overshadowed by the protruding windows specially built to give the ladies of the harem some little glimpse of the world. Underneath his windows and balconies the Tigris flowed past in a thick yellow flood, straining the pontoons.

Leaving the house we set out for the famous ziggurat – a stepped tower surmounted by a temple – of the Aga Khuf that stands on the skyline of the desert. These structures, peculiar to ancient Mesopotamia, are believed to have given rise to the legend of the Tower of Babel. I was interested to see that the ziggurat was built of layer after layer of sun-dried bricks – obviously the scriptural bricks that could not be built without straw, as bits stuck out all over the tower!

After visiting Mr Eastwood's cotton ginneries I was home in time to dress for dinner at Gertrude Bell's house. The party consisted of a member of the High Commissioner's staff; William's old sea-plane colleague, Leonard Woolley, just back from excavating Ur of the Chaldees; and Mrs Keeling, an elegant widow whom Woolley later married. I sensed a certain tension between the two women and was not surprised when Gertrude Bell informed me, in her characteristically direct manner, that Mrs Keeling knew nothing about excavating but did it to amuse herself.

We dined in the charming little hall on excellent native dishes, discreetly Europeanised; and nibbled, between times, the rich sweetmeats of Damascus. Gertrude Bell's talk ranged over the desert from Aleppo to Basra, from Beirut to Baghdad; and, without ascertaining how much we might already know, she advised me, and the absent William, to study the mandate in Syria.

Giving judgement on the various Arab sheikhs, she dubbed one a rogue, another a fine fellow. She described a characteristic scene in the palace: King Feisal in his white robes, seated in the midst of the sheikhs, chaffing the chief rogue, Nuri Shalaan, the Emir of Jauf, for seeking

French protection by obtaining a French passport; the delight of the
other sheikhs, and Nuri's sullen silence. She made fun of the English
officers' bad French. Above all she satirised the absurdity of casual
English visitors who thought themselves adventurous in crossing the
desert with Nairne! I found out later that she had told her father: 'Every
Desert Mail brings silly females, all with letters of introduction to me.'
Leonard Woolley joined weightily in the conversation, and Mrs Keeling
kept her end up, although she confessed on the way home that she had
taken two aspirin and felt very stupid.

In the drawing room the English Administrator gave me a full description of Mosul and the Turkish hinterland, while Gertrude Bell and
Leonard Woolley, with Mrs Keeling a shadowy third, discussed the
Baghdad Museum. At eleven we rose, decorously, to go; the evening
reminding me of the line "Igh class music is a little melan-chol-y, but
it's so refined!' As it happened, I was one of the last British visitors to
see Gertrude Bell, for she died that summer. William and I visited her
father and were impressed by how philosophically Sir Hugh took her
death. 'Life would inevitably have brought her downhill, but death
stayed her at the summit,' he said.

During the days we spent in Baghdad, William and I often visited a
colony of silversmiths who lived near our hotel. As we walked along
River Street, eager, smiling men would hail us, gesturing invitingly at
the tables loaded with glittering silver. We stopped at each in turn, joking
and bargaining. There were coffee pots around which were engraved
enchanting scenes of desert and river life: sometimes camels, palm
trees and minarets rose from the polished surface; sometimes it was the
graceful muheilah sailing along a silver-streaked Euphrates. There were
cigarette cases, matchboxes, wine goblets, powder boxes, sweetmeat
dishes, salt-cellars in the form of mosques, and tall, slim pepper-pots
shaped like minarets. We visited the street a great many times and I was
able to find out a little about the history, religion and habits of these
desert silversmiths.

They were known by various names: Sabaeans, Subbis, and John the
Baptist Christians. I thought it doubtful how far they could be called
Christians except for their three orders of bishop, priest and deacon. I
was interested to learn that they had women priests. They believe John
the Baptist to be the true prophet and their chief, and often repeated,
rite is baptism. Believing that running water is the great cleansing force,
they always live close to it, and associate all their great ceremonials with
it. Their marriages take place in water, and they read their sacred books
over running water in order to carry off all impurities. Shaving is not
allowed and their soft, hazy beards gave an unworldly, mystical look to
their faces. What exactly they worshipped they were reticent in saying,
but I was told that the Neo-Platonism that once shone from Alexandria
was kept alight by them.

Buyer and seller confronted each other directly in this centre of industry and the price was fought out between them in no hasty manner. Being very practical mystics, they replied, unyieldingly, to our protests, in their soft guttural accent: 'But, memsahib, this is good work! The silver is heavy – feel. Look! It has no join.' And the chief spokesmen would open the lid to reveal the convincing interior of a coffee pot, perfectly fashioned, beak and all, from one piece of silver. He drove a hard bargain but enjoyed a joke and loved to be told that he was a rich man while you were poor, and that the price, therefore, should be 100 rupees at the most, and not 130.

On our last day we bought a beautiful coffee service with exquisite little silver cups and saucers: the work of an artist-craftsman. I hoped that when I looked at them at home, I should be able to cross, in my mind, the desert and rivers of Mesopotamia once more.

Leaving, with much regret, the fascinating city of Baghdad, we set out to make the return journey to Beirut. Once again we travelled with Nairne's 'Desert Mail', but this time the mails were strapped on all round the outside, making exit difficult. Inside we carried the water supply. The convoy consisted of only two cars; in the other were RAF officers returning home.

Saying goodbye to 'civilisation' as we rose from lunch in the RAF camp at Fellujah, we spent the afternoon and evening racing the sun to the distant horizon; and when at last it beat us, we put on a tremendous spurt – sixty miles an hour, Nairne said – and the ground passed by us like a grey mist, on which no object was discernible, till we reached our camping place. Then, as before, out jumped Nairne, and soon flames were leaping from under the giant kettle, and arc lights shone on our supper.

The next day at dawn the convoy leader took a wrong turning that brought us within sight of the temples of Palmyra – but at the edge of treacherous salt-marshes that cut it off on one side. Nairne surveyed the surface of the marshes, which looked exceptionally dry, and gave orders to the first car that an attempt should be made to rush across; the alternative being a detour of a hundred miles. We got out of the car and were soon up to our ankles in the marsh.

We watched breathlessly as Nairne started the motor and drove the car at tremendous speed. A few seconds later, through a storm of scurrying mud, we saw the car sink. This was the beginning of four hours of strenuous labour. During the course of the morning an Arab armed with a revolver and riding an ancient camel came to our rescue; as did two others who came up at different times on donkeys: an excellent example of the fellowship of the desert. Sitting on the unopened provisions while drying my shoes and stockings in the rising sun, I watched a remarkable scene. Nairne sat at the wheel and, as he reversed, the whole party violently tugged on the rope. There was William; the

RAF officers; two men from the Anglo-Persian Oil Company (the future British Petroleum); the three Arabs; and, at the end of the rope, the camel and one of the donkeys.

A weird variety of noises filled the air: shouts from Nairne; wild invectives from the Arabs; braying from the donkey; and furious bubble-bubbling from the camel. To loud exclamations of 'Allah! Allah!' the car was successfully pulled out of the marsh.

We arrived, eventually, at the inn at Palmyra, and in the afternoon set off again on the Homs road. We fell in with a party of Americans who tacked themselves on to our convoy. They were agents of the Studebaker Motor Company and were on their way home after selling cars in Persia and Iraq. They gave us tea from the largest vacuum flask ever made and told us a blood-curdling tale of their adventures on the way out, among a hostile band of Arabs. We approached Homs at dusk through the graveyards thronged with mourning relatives. A few houses lay outside and about the town, which had nothing to suggest that it had once been the great Roman city of Emesa.

After Nairne had taken a meal of meat, olives and rice, from a native stall, we set off for Tripoli, leaving the desert behind. All around us were apple, peach and pear trees, heavy with blossom, growing luxuriantly in an undulating country. We were approaching the sea again. At Tripoli everything was in darkness. Hotel after hotel could not take us in, but at last an inn, smaller than the rest, opened its doors and the manager prepared a hot meal. It was too dark to inspect the bedroom very carefully – for which, in the morning, I was not sorry!

William, who had thoroughly enjoyed being abroad, had now given up all idea of returning home in the immediately foreseeable future. He disclosed a wonderful new plan: when we got to Constantinople he would telegraph the Soviet Embassy in London for permission to go home through Moscow. We could then sail up the Black Sea and enter the USSR by Odessa and reach Moscow after several days of travel by train. I was stunned. 'But the children?' I asked in distress. 'We left them for a three weeks' cruise on Ernest's insistence. That was February – it's already April. When can we hope to get back if we take this detour?'

William was quite oblivious to any such pleas. 'Ernest and Gwen will look after them. We must make use of a wonderful opportunity of getting to know parts of the world we may never be near again.'

The last lap of our journey was the two-hour run along the coast to Beirut, where we said goodbye to Nairne and boarded another Il Triestino boat, the *Abbazia*, for the Aegean and Constantinople. Sailing up the coast of Asia Minor, one day succeeded another in a dream of blue and gold. I was particularly interested to see the rocky island of Castelorizo where William had commanded the detachment of English and French troops.

Through the morning haze we saw the magnificent round medieval towers of the Crusaders' island of Rhodes, then under Italian rule. We landed and walked through the narrow streets, thronged at that hour with peasants. The most noticeable was a woman of Castelorizo who wore a many-coloured costume to which her dowry was sewn in the form of a multitude of gold coins which tinkled out a tune as she walked.

On our way to the famous priories we passed through some delightful streets containing half shops, half bazaars, covered over with a delicate trellis of vines. Turning into the renowned Street of the Cavaliers, we saw the carved stone lodges on which are emblazoned, in turn, the coats of arms of every nation that went to the Crusades.

Walking through the great cloistered galleries and halls of the museum, we came on a small formal garden, fragrant with every sort of flower, in which worked the Director of Antiquities. An earnest young Italian, full of the archaeologist's fire, he came up to us and, for the next two hours, made himself our guide. At his word keys appeared for every locked door, and indeed, in one case, so great was his enthusiasm that he ordered one – fortunately modern – to be splintered in! As a result of his kindness we were able to crowd much into a small space of time.

The rest of the day we spent at sea. A gradual passage brought us to the broad bay of Ephesus with the hills behind it. As usual we were beset with swarms of boatmen anxious to drive a good bargain and take us ashore. William was deeply disappointed when he realised that, being a Friday, all the shops would be closed and he would be unable to get *The Times*.

We walked, in blazing sun, up the steep hill in search of places associated with the early Christian martyr Polycarp, Bishop of Smyrna, but they remained always just out of reach. We approached two youths who were standing by their doorway, for guidance, but, alas, they did not understand a word we said.

The following day, 3 April, was my Anthony's first birthday. I had had no news from home, not even a telegram, for three weeks. Our wanderings had cut us off completely; but we felt that our precious boys were safe, and did not worry.

The next day would see our arrival in Constantinople – then often called Cospoli, and eventually known as Istanbul – and the end of a restful, happy interlude in our journey. We had enjoyed the company of our fellow passengers, most of whom were Americans. We made friends with the Soap and Pumicestone King of America and his wife: Elmer R. Murphey and Luella Murphey. Soap and pumicestone had supplied them with their millions and a reason for a business journey round the world every two years, but although these commodities still provided the money, they 'ran' themselves. Mr Murphey's latest venture was a 'Quick-Lite' lamp, and, whenever the boat stopped, a specimen of this wonderful invention was shown to everyone. They were recording their trip with a movie camera.

We had counted on entering the Dardanelles by daylight, as our schedule promised, but the Captain told us that we were ahead of time and we would reach the Straits at 1 am. In deep disappointment we retired to our cabins. But since leaving Smyrna we had been buffeted by one of those sudden storms, so well known to the poets, and as it became more furious the Captain's plans were dashed. The ship moved slower and slower and then stopped altogether.

Above the noise of the waves, we heard loud shoutings and saw, tossing about in the seas below, a tiny boat with shipwrecked mariners clinging to it. A rope ladder was lowered and, holding our breath, we saw them reach it and clamber aboard. Their boat was hauled up after them but they had lost all their possessions. A collection was made for them among the passengers, and everyone who could gave garments. The check suits and pinstripes must have been quite intriguing to the people of Asia Minor in the following months if the sailors continued to wear them!

The delay of the storm, followed by the rescue, meant that it was not until dawn on Easter Day that we entered the Dardanelles, the setting for much epic poetry and prose. On the left was Gallipoli, with Cape Helles at its foot. Stern and forbidding, the land seemed to rise, without foothold, from the grey waters to the top of Achi Baba. On the right, above a marshy plain, was the hill of Troy where signs of successive excavations could be clearly seen. So fast is the current that sweeps down the Straits from the Sea of Marmara that these scenes remained long in sight as we battled our way up.

Cold seemed to attack us in every fibre. After only a short time on deck we would rush in to the warmth before venturing out again to observe the many villages that lay behind their austere battlements, bristling with guns, on either side of the Straits. William saw again a village that he had set out to take eleven years before. In the Sea of Marmara it was rough again and, twenty-four hours late, we sailed past St Sophia and up to the Golden Horn.

After a lengthy argument with the Turkish boatmen who came to take us ashore, an agreed price was reached and our luggage and ourselves were deposited in a doubtful-looking boat. While we tossed about violently, with the boat still attached to the painter of the liner, the men demanded a higher fare and immediate payment. Only by complete nonchalance, and the fact that they were losing other business, did we defeat them. Our two cases and a hat-box were soon out of the clutches of the Customs but, as we left, I saw, piled up, the immense cabin trunks of our American friends and, beside them, the ever hopeful and ebullient Mr Murphey, demonstrating his 'Quick-Lite' lamp to bemused Customs officials.

Turkey was a fascinating country to visit at that time. The President of the Republic, and victor of Gallipoli, Mustafa Kemal Pasha, had overthrown the government of the Sultan of Turkey, driven out the Greeks, and was in the process of revolutionising the state. Known as 'The Ghazi', which means leader and warrior, and later as 'Atatürk' – 'Father of the Turks' – he was determined that Turkey should be a modern country. It was no longer ruled by Islamic law: the Caliphate was abolished; religious courts and schools were closed; marriage had become a civil contract, and it was illegal to have more than one wife. Law codes modelled on those of Europe, including the Swiss Civil Code, had been introduced.

The most visible reforms were those concerning dress. In 1925, Mustafa Kemal had banned the traditional hat, the fez, and did everything he could to encourage the wearing of European clothes. Consignments of new and second-hand clothes and hats were arriving by the boatload from Europe. He wanted women to have more freedom and was particularly against the wearing of the veil. When we arrived, we were struck by its absence. In the Pera quarter of Constantinople where we stayed, sophisticated shops and Parisian fashions were everywhere, and from my window I might have been looking down on a scene in a French boulevard.

The day after our arrival our long-expected letters arrived and, after telegraphing our address, we went for the first of many visits to St Sophia. The great Christian church of Constantine and Justinian stands in a glorious position on the shores of the Sea of Marmara. Orientated to Jerusalem, it was, for eleven hundred years, the centre of Christian worship in the New Rome until the Turks conquered Constantinople in 1453. For six centuries it had been a mosque.

On 7 April, William went off to Ankara, then known as Angora, the new capital recently established by Mustafa Kemal. I joined the Murpheys at the Pera Palace Hotel, and spent some amusing hours visiting the bazaars with people who never returned without a Christmas post of parcels. The bazaars of Constantinople were very fine indeed. Along their tortuous, winding alleys, we passed wonderful displays of silk garments embroidered in gold and silver; red Turkish slippers; metalwork of all kinds; coffee services – not as well made as my Baghdad set; and all manner of precious stones and pearls. A number of White Russian refugees had set up stalls, and several beautiful icons were bought by my American friends.

In one of the bazaars were rows of shops with plate-glass windows where we were invited in to drink as much coffee and smoke as many cigarettes as we pleased while making our selection. In the sharp air of Constantinople, so noticeable after the warmth of the Mediterranean countries, we were often glad to step into a cosy bazaar, sit by a charcoal brazier, and drink the delicious, hot black coffee. The people looked a little more healthy than in Cairo or Baghdad, but in the crowd I saw evidence of terrible sickness.

On Fridays many inhabitants of Constantinople spent the afternoon by the sea. From the Galata Bridge, the little black-funnelled river craft – the buses of the Bosphorus – made, at short intervals, for the cool resorts that lie on both banks of the Straits between Constantinople and the Black Sea. The landing place hummed with life as the Murpheys and I set off for the little resort of Babek, half-way up the Straits. On the steamer over we were disappointed to find that our view was much limited because the passengers were enclosed below. Evening papers were hawked round, and coffee served to those who wished it. Finding a little bit of open deck, I stood with Mr Murphey as he filmed the mosques, minarets and fine houses that cluster right to the water's edge. We sailed along the Bosphorus, admiring the wooded hills and castles on each bank, and relishing the quaint experience of seeing Europe on one side, Asia on the other, and yet being in neither. Every turn brought something new and, after a little under an hour, we arrived at Babek.

With the disappearance of the distinctive fez and veil, the Turks on holiday looked very much like French and English families, and those sitting around us, enjoying the shower of pear blossom and the delicate scent of the japonica, talked over the week's doings and laughed at the antics of their offspring in the way of parents and holiday-makers the world over. We were obliged to leave earlier than I should have wished, for that evening I was dining with Sir Ronald Lindsay, the British Ambassador, and Lady Lindsay, after which we were to go on to the 'Night of Power' service at St Sophia.

I was shown into a lovely white and green room full of spring flowers, and greeted by the immensely tall figure of the Ambassador, a perfect example of the upper-class Conservative abroad! Sir Ronald was full of annoyance at the necessity of being based permanently in Ankara as it had become impossible to conduct relations from Constantinople. After enduring great discomfort in the local hotel, he and his wife had at last got a house; but Ankara, he told me, was without a single one of the things that made life worth living. The only point he would concede was the bracing atmosphere.

Of the new regime he had no better to say. The Turks were trying to ape the system of a widely removed civilisation: the Swiss Civil Code in Turkey, indeed! Education was muddled: it was almost impossible to get teachers, who were badly paid and treated. Although in theory the position of women had greatly improved, outside Constantinople there was, in practice, very little change. He instanced a case at Ankara, a short time before, when a banquet had been given to the foreign members of one of the League of Nations' commissions. A member of the Commission had brought his wife and the Turkish Government decided that this would be a good opportunity to put into practice their new ideas. Accordingly, the part of hostess was to be taken by the wife of one of the ministers. When all was in readiness, the Government, remembering how far it was from European Turkey, dared not make such a break with tradition, and the wife of the Second Secretary of a Balkan legation presided instead.

Of the personality of the President, Sir Ronald had a lot to say, describing him as the son of an Albanian timber-merchant's clerk, brought up by a Turkish stepfather. Mustafa Kemal played down his Albanian origins and put much stress on his mother and stepfather. He went into the army and proved a first-class soldier. Whenever he had been in a position of authority, or his advice had been taken, success had followed the Turkish army. After many adventures (many of which I was able to read in the daily 'Souvenirs du Ghazi' published by him in the papers) he had come to the top through sheer force of character. He was very much the strong man and aroused much hope.

Shut away from Turkey in Europe, which he had not visited since becoming head of state, he would see few visitors. A stern glare from thousands of photographs was all his people were able to see of their 'warrior-saviour' President. Mustafa Kemal's personality, so powerful, so remote and so omnipresent, had become wrapped up in almost legendary glamour. 'Muhammad is our prophet for the next life,' a Turkish official said to William and me, 'and Mustafa Kemal is our prophet for this one.'

The Ambassador hinted at dark stories of nightly orgies of un-Islamic drinking by Mustafa Kemal, and his amazing powers of pulling himself together again on the instant. He lived modestly in a small house near his model farm and had recently divorced his wife for failing to produce an heir. Sir Ronald summed up the President as 'going the way of the Sultans', despite the fervour of the new regime.

Whatever the true feelings of the people, no Turk would say an unfavourable word about Mustafa Kemal. The press was extravagantly eulogistic. I bought half a dozen copies of a bi-monthly journal, the *Echo of Turkey*, published in English in Ankara, which gave, with much other interesting writing, a biographical sketch of the national hero: 'One of those geniuses who periodically appear on the earth. This time given to Turkey.'

After dinner, we drove to St Sophia. Every minaret was dazzlingly illuminated, and round the domes of the mosques lighted texts from the Koran swayed in the breeze. The waters of the Golden Horn were bright with the reflection. At St Sophia, we entered by the Great Door and walked along the incline which Justinian used to ride up in his chariot. Before Mustafa Kemal abolished the Caliphate in 1924, the Caliph used to ride up on the 'Night of Power' on his white charger.

From the gallery, we looked down on a marvellous scene. The mosque was dimly illuminated by thousands of little oil lights, each floating in a glass bowl. Turned towards Mecca, thousands of the faithful were making their supplications; towards the west end of the mosque, the women knelt. This great service takes place two days before the feast of Beiram, which marks the close of the fast of Ramadan and might be likened to Easter following on Lent. The 'Night of Power' commemorates the delivery of his mission to Muhammad. It is similar to the giving of the Tablets of Stone to Moses in the Jewish and Christian religions.

Later that night we drove to the Mosque of Selim in order to look through the carved stonework of the outer wall into the exquisite courtyard. Two tall cypress trees rose to a great height and seemed almost to touch the waving Koranic texts above.

Among the people we met in Constantinople, I remember three men especially: two were typical, and one unique. Ali Bey, a Turkish member of Parliament, called and took tea with us one afternoon. He was a highly-bred, polished young man in his early thirties, well acquainted with European life, and most enthusiastically anxious to show us that Turkey was now up to date and civilised.

A year or so before when his wife – his only wife, he stressed – was visiting Paris, she was asked her nationality. Her reply was greeted with cries of incredulity because she was wearing the latest European fashions. Ali's nostrils quivered as he said: 'I suppose they thought her husband wore enormous trousers with a scimitar stuck in the belt.' He proudly told us that Europeans would soon realise how modern Turkey was becoming.

Having cleared the ground of illusory differences between Turkey and Europe in secular matters, Ali proceeded to show the similarity that existed in religious beliefs and customs. He pointed out that it was now illegal to marry more than one wife and that having more than one had never been sanctioned by Muhammad anyway.

We also met Zia Bey, the Thomas Cook of Turkey. As soon as William and I had set foot in our hotel we found a letter from this gentleman. It did not contain anything to suggest that it was a business communication but merely said that he had heard of our impending arrival and would think it a great honour if he might help to make our stay in the country interesting, amusing and instructive. In due course he arrived and there was nothing he would not, or could not, do. With a bustling manner, he showed us a sheaf of typed itineraries. He made suggestions for a fortnight's tour, a week's tour, a few days' sightseeing. Eventually he did get some custom as he helped William to arrange his trip to Ankara.

Zia was constantly asking us to attend one function or another. We went to a *thé dansant* held at our hotel, the Pera Palace, which we found was being given for a tourist cruise of English, mostly Oxford, professors and scholars, including the editor of *The Times*, Geoffrey Dawson, and a pioneer of women's education, Emily Penrose, the Principal of Somerville College. I danced with a jovial elderly pasha who came no higher than my shoulder.

The Turkish women, of whom there were many present, appeared to be enjoying themselves thoroughly. They did not seem to regret the absence of the veil. Instead of hats, they were wearing attractively draped scarves of soft material that matched their gowns. Zia introduced us to many people, among whom were a young Turkish woman, the daughter of the Chief of Police, and her husband, Ali Idhilmi Bey. He was a tall, slender young man who spoke English remarkably well.

He offered to take us sightseeing and show us the Golden Gate and the walls of old Byzantium. The next day he drove us over the Galata Bridge and along to the Marmora Walls. We crossed the ancient harbour to the fortress, of which only the ruined courtyards remained. Climbing up a dark, crumbling spiral stairway, we came out onto a ledge and saw a wonderful panorama of the city.

The keeper of the courtyard then led us into those appalling dungeons called the Ambassadors' Prison. Until two hundred or so years ago the representatives of foreign powers were thrown in on the outbreak of war. Our gaoler fetched some other keys and we found ourselves standing knee deep in grass and wild flowers, and facing us, the precious propped-up arches of the triumphal Golden Gate, through which the victorious Emperors passed.

Ali Idhilmi took us through to look at the other side, which marks the extreme boundary of the city. Immediately beyond, there was what might be the dry bed of an ancient moat, running along to the right under the Walls of Theodosius. Here we turned our back on the Caesars and devoted the rest of the afternoon to the work of the Sultans and visited the Mosque of Suleiman the Magnificent. No attendants were at the door and we took off our shoes in peace and walked in carrying them.

Ali Idhilmi, although so much at home in our company, told us nothing about himself, but it had long been obvious to us that he was an Englishman. At the Pera Palace, he refused to come in and have tea, and we last saw him, looking rather wistfully at us, as he drove off to enjoy the festivities of Beiram. As we sat, a few minutes later, in the cheerful bay window of the lounge, an attaché of the British Embassy saw us and was able to explain that Ali Idhilmi was an Eton and New College man who, three years before, on a visit to Turkey after leaving Oxford, had fallen in love with the Chief of Police's daughter. For her he became a Muslim, changed his name, and settled down in Cospoli; a strange repetition of Pierre Loti's 'Désenchanté'.

When William returned from Ankara we enjoyed a last afternoon's ramble through the ancient city. We visited the great underground cisterns, the Yeri Batain Serai, that had supplied water to Constantinople since the sixth century. Its hundreds of giant columns, rising from the water, were richly and wonderfully carved. At the foot of some steps, a few small skiffs were tied up, and a boatman asked us to cross with him.

The giant columns, the awful gloom barely relieved by the dim light struggling through here and there, and, above all, the presence of the boatman, so like Charon, the ferryman of the ancient Greek underworld, made it a veritable Styx.

We strolled for a little in the sunshine, along the majestic Seraglio peninsula to the museum, where the wonderful Alexander sarcophagus was to be seen with much else of interest. Here, we again met Geoffrey Dawson, much exercised at the cavalier expulsion of a *Times* correspondent in a Bulgarian cattle-ship. We then went on to the Church of Divine Peace – St Irene – which by a stroke of irony was the Military Museum. It was crowded with old guns, cannons, arms, and uniforms of every variety but we were most interested in relics of the 'Glorious Victory of Gallipoli'. In a glass case a representation was made of the battle at the height of the action. It was well staged and lighted, showing the Turkish guns hard at work, and battleships blowing up, right and left, in the Straits.

We walked on and sat in the Forum of Theodosius, which had been turned into gardens. In it stood a monument that is the most wonderful of all the treasures of the city: the green fragment of the Serpentine Column taken by Constantine from the Temple of Apollo at Delphi, where it was already old. It was the monument built by the united Greek city-states to celebrate their victory over the Persians at Plataea.

Finally we visited the Mosque of Sultan Ahmed, which stands across the square from St Sophia, on the glorious Seraglio peninsula. It was more magnificent than any other we saw, and the brilliant sunlight falling on its green and blue Turkey carpets lit up the austere grey of the inside.

Although we had received no word of permission from the Soviet Embassy in London concerning our desire to travel to Moscow, William and I were both enthusiastic about trying our luck and so, leaving Constantinople behind, we set off up the Black Sea to Odessa.

CHAPTER 5
JOURNEY TO RUSSIA, 1926

As we passed up the Bosphorus and into the Black Sea the cold intensified. An icy wind, blowing straight from the snow-covered steppes ahead, sent us below to make what we could of the gloomy company of Turkish and Levantine merchants compelled to embark on the dark and difficult adventure of Russian travel for the sake of business. When they learned that nothing but interest was driving us there, they appeared more than ever convinced that the British were an incomprehensible race.

After a journey of a few days, we looked out of our portholes at eight o'clock in the morning and saw a great deserted harbour looming through mist and rain. It was our first view of the Soviet Union.

As we neared the harbour I went to our cabin to make sure everything was ready for departure. Soon after we docked, William came running down, in great delight, to ask me to come up at once as our visas had arrived, and we were going to be given an address of welcome by an official deputation from the local soviet. They were in the dining room waiting to greet us with outstretched hands, and an interpreter to make communication possible.

Soon we were driving with them through the streets of Odessa to a local hotel that was to be our headquarters till leaving that night for the long journey to Moscow. The Russian Revolution was only eight and a half years old and on every hand there were signs of the upheaval it had brought. I noted especially the empty spaces where statues of former Tsars and Tsarist officials had been pulled down and the bases wrecked, leaving desolate patches of ruin around them. Churches had lost the crosses that had surmounted them for centuries. 'Change and decay in all around I see' might have been the impression given to a Christian visitor, but our hosts were anxious that we should not come to this conclusion. They pointed out, on every side, the new life that they believed to be springing up through the old. New industries were to be seen everywhere; indeed, they were often to be found in derelict church buildings.

After leaving our luggage at the hotel, we were taken to visit the local soviet, where we first made acquaintance with the ever-welcome Russian tea with lemon. It is an interesting fact I have noticed on subsequent visits to the USSR that once on Russian soil the notion of tea with milk becomes quite unthinkable.

Our hosts were delighted to have the chance to entertain visitors from far-away Britain, and explained that during the course of one brief day they would have to keep us busy. Before lunch we had a drive round the city and its environs with full explanations of all the benefits they believed Soviet rule had brought the town in under nine years.

Lunch was a meal of quite unbelievable opulence, with endless courses of every kind of food traditional to the country: beetroot soup; fish from the Black Sea; chicken Kiev. The zest with which the officials ate the meal suggested to me that they did not have food like that very often. They had probably been instructed to do the British visitors proud.

Taken on an arduous round of visits to factories, we sensed the great local pride in their existence. After seeing a crèche, and the newly renovated opera house, we wanted to pause and look at some beautiful old church buildings, but our hosts had no sympathy with that wish. It was quite evident that the factory chimney had taken the place of the church spire as the symbol of present interest and future hope.

When the question of getting tickets for Moscow arose, our first consideration was how we should travel. First, second and third class having been abolished on the railways since the Revolution, the alternatives were 'hard' or 'soft'. As most people travelled 'hard', from sheer necessity, William, always wanting to travel with the majority, plumped immediately for that category. 'After all,' he reasoned, 'it's only going to be a two and a half days' journey.' But here, alas, my courage failed me. The seats were of remorselessly hard wood, absolutely rectangular, and allowed for no relaxation whatsoever, by day or night. I did not think I could make it. Even if I did, I knew I would not be in a state to take in this wonderful new adventure of making a journey across the Soviet Union. The 'soft' category, although austere enough, did promise cushioned seats. Reluctantly, William gave in. On shorter trips during our stay we travelled 'hard'.

At six o'clock the Odessa soviet sent us on our way with warm thanks and farewells, and a large supply of long, pale-beige Russian cigarettes. I found these most welcome as, in those days, I smoked like a chimney.

The journey was quite comfortable, our carriage being something like the third-class accommodation that existed on British trains of the period, and we were entitled to a whole seat which we slept on at night. Although there was no restaurant car on the train, we fed well on provisions bought at stations on the way. There were pickled cucumbers, delicious bread, half-stewed apples and hard-boiled eggs.

At every station we were out almost before the train stopped; taking a walk in the town if time permitted, as we did at Kiev; or at least walking about the station talking to the peasants in the universal language of signs and smiles. The arrival of the Moscow train, which ran three times a week from Odessa, was a great event and people crowded on the platform at every stop to beg for alms. Some, seeing us to be

Westerners, and judging us to be Christians, made the sign of the cross before holding out entreating palms. I was deeply moved to find that a sign
which in long-past days had made members of a persecuted society known
to each other had returned to some semblance of its earliest use.

I had my camera and many films on me and began taking a long series
of photographs. Unfortunately, at the end of our visit, the films were
taken by Customs officials who assured me they would develop them
and send them to England. I was disappointed, but not really surprised,
when the photographs failed to arrive.

The whole journey was crowded with interest and we were able to
find some fellow passengers who could speak a language known to us –
French or, occasionally, English – and so tell us much. One old lady
who had visited England twenty-five years before told us that her English
friends had kept her alive with their help during the years of hardship
that followed the Revolution. She had stayed near Port Sunlight, a
model community designed to improve the conditions of working
people, and thought that its founder, the soap manufacturer William
Lever, was a saint: 'There would have been no revolution had there been
people like him in Russia.'

We had an interesting conversation with a woman engineer. Working
in the same town as her husband and separated from her child by many
days' journey, she was a characteristic citizen of the USSR, where everybody, men and women, worked, and motherhood was regarded as an
incident rather than a calling. She told me that provision was made for
four months' rest at the time of childbirth; after that the young were looked
after by grandparents or left in crèches. When a pregnant woman could
prove to the satisfaction of the authorities that the coming child was more
than she could support, or for some other reason was undesirable or
unwanted, she would be admitted to the abortion ward of a state hospital.

There was little, if any, place for family life in the Soviet scheme. She
described to us her life with her husband in one small room, where they
lived and did all their work, going out every morning to their respective
offices. Divorce was also extremely easy to obtain. Indeed, we came
across a contemporary joke: the wedding was 'Workers of the world
unite', and the divorce 'You have nothing to lose but your chains.'

During the two-day journey we talked incessantly to the editor of a
Soviet newspaper in Tashkent and learnt much from this enthusiastic
Communist about Soviet forms of government. 'Russia', we realised
more and more, had passed out of the vocabulary of Communists. They
spoke only of the Union of Soviet Socialist Republics.

We assumed that everybody would be a member of the Communist
Party, but the editor explained to us that it was very difficult to gain
membership, and months, if not years, of instruction were required to
gain admittance. To get to any position of authority it was essential for
a man or woman to be a member of the Party.

We thus arrived in Moscow having cleared a little of the fog from our minds, and with a vague idea of the system. The editor insisted on taking us on a round of hotels until he had settled us in a satisfactory one, the Savoy.

Staying there was a very interesting Norwegian, Jonas Lied, who had business interests in Siberia. He had become a Soviet citizen but had been assured by the Norwegian Government that should he be in any kind of danger he could regain his original citizenship. Life under Lenin's rule had suited him quite well, but the growing power of Stalin was obviously making him uneasy. We enjoyed our talks with him, though at times he would make some disturbing observations. Looking round the dining room at the Savoy Hotel, in which there might be twenty-five people, he would say: 'I can see fifteen agents of the GPU' – the political police – 'here now.' Sometimes in the evening he would take us to nightclubs where performances were given, he told us, by near-destitute members of the old aristocracy. These he would pick out by name.

The day we arrived in Moscow we were received by George Chicherin, the People's Commissar for Foreign Affairs, the equivalent of the British Foreign Secretary. He was a diplomat of the old school who had started his career serving the Tsar. We got the impression that he was not a convinced Communist but that he knew the outside world well and had patriotically put his experience at the service of his country.

As always, William's approach to people of other countries opened doors in a notable fashion. He always made it plain that, without necessarily agreeing with the dominant ideas of the system, he had not come with prejudged views but to see and understand the problems with which the country was faced.

The Soviet system at that time was in a state of transition with Stalin, the General Secretary of the Communist Party, who had been sharing power since the death of Lenin two years before, poised to take supreme control. A few months after our visit he expelled his rivals, Trotsky, Kamenev and Zinoviev, from the Politburo. Lenin's New Economic Policy, which allowed a limited amount of private enterprise and had been in operation since 1921, was under attack and would be ended by Stalin the next year.

One bone of contention between Britain and the Soviet Union, and a major reason for diplomatic links between the two countries being so strained, was the existence in Moscow of the Communist International, which openly preached world revolution. Chicherin, jokingly, said: 'We'd be only too delighted if we could get rid of the Communist International and remove it to London!'

An early engagement was tea with Chicherin's deputy, Maxim Litvinov, and his English wife, Ivy Low, both of whom we had met a few years before in London. They had met when he had been an exile in England before the Revolution. In Moscow they were living in a flat near the Kremlin, in what had been the mansion of a rich sugar merchant and was then mainly used to house foreign delegations. We were interested that they appeared to have only the same allotment of cubic space as everybody else, and used the common kitchen. I gained the impression that Ivy Low, who was working as a translator, was not really happy with her life in the Soviet Union, and both the Litvinovs seemed very English.

We saw them again, in 1934, during our second visit to the Soviet Union. By this time Maxim was Commissar for Foreign Affairs and had been allocated one of the country homes that the Government provided for top politicians. We spent a pleasant day with them in their dacha outside Moscow but sensed that Stalin's regime did not suit them. Ivy Low's mother, who was visiting them, seemed very nervous and uneasy and, when the big gates opened to the outside world, shrank back as if she thought they might be invaded by enemies. I was not surprised when Ivy Low eventually settled in England in the 1970s.

We endeavoured to see all we could and actually managed to travel out on our own to the country by carrying slips of paper in which instructions were asked for in Russian, such as: 'These comrades wish to be shown the way to Tsarskoye Selo, please.' This beautiful old palace was eventually reached by means of kind passers-by who directed us to the right railway station.

Our first walk through the streets of Moscow, the heart of Red Russia, was a fascinating experience. We were free to walk where we pleased, hampered only by our ignorance of the Russian language. The spring warmth − it was nearly the end of April − was turning the winter's snow to slush, and there was a dismal drizzle. We made our way through the armies of street vendors who clustered on the kerbs shouting out their wares and entreating us to buy. Every kind of merchandise was displayed on barrows and trays. We found them still there in great numbers at night: some still shouting; others huddled in sleep across the pavements. They were dressed in a queer jumble of shreds and patches: shawls, tattered leather jackets, bits of mangy fur.

Every type of worker was represented. There were sailors of the Red Fleet; soldiers of the Red Army in spiked caps, and long, trailing coats; young Communist women and girls whose heads were bound in the Red Handkerchief of the Revolution; others in green, decorated with the ubiquitous hammer and sickle. Here and there the private trader under the New Economic Policy was to be guessed at where some slight prosperity was evident. Then there were clerks and their wives; both workers, carrying attaché cases with their lunches wrapped up in newspaper. These were the most characteristic of all for, in Soviet Russia, everyone worked except the very young and the very old.

With salaries in industry averaging £4–£10 a month − about half the British level of those days − it was necessary for everyone to pull their weight. Thousands of people eked out a livelihood with odd jobs of every sort in the evening as well. We often conversed in French, or even in English, with men and woman selling newspapers and programmes at the doors of theatres and cinemas.

Jumbled together with all these workers of the Soviet Republic of Russia were the picturesque natives of the Allied Soviet Republics. There were traders from Uzbekistan selling leather straps; bearded peasants from the Caucasus; and Tartars in long robes and white turbans from Turkestan and Azerbaijan. Now and then a face stood out vividly from the throng: some wearer of ancient sealskins, wistful-eyed and underfed.

Mingling with the workers were the beggars. Of course, the existence of beggars is contrary to the principles of Communism. The State is the guardian of those who for some reason are unable to look after themselves. But every official or statesman to whom we talked said that the Soviet Union was far from the ideal of Communism. 'We are a poor country' was the phrase on every lip. The poor were legally entitled to aid, but there was not enough money to provide it. They appeared to have fallen between two stools: State aid was unavailable; private aid was ideologically unacceptable.

We were anxious to see as much of the working of the system as possible and we were given every assistance by Madame Olga Kamenev, the head of the Bureau for Cultural Relations with Foreigners. She was the sister of Trotsky and the wife of Kamenev, the politician who would, eventually, be the victim of one of Stalin's show trials. Adopting his usual approach, William said to Madame Kamenev: 'Now, tell us what your problems are.' She was very surprised that an Englishman should adopt such an uncritical approach and told us about one of their most serious problems.

The upheavals resulting from the First World War and the Revolution had led to bands of homeless children roaming the streets of Moscow. They had survived, somehow, after the death of their parents, or in some cases after they had been abandoned. We had already noticed these children during our walks. Their ages were anything from eight to sixteen, with the average about twelve. They slept under bridges, or in doorways; begged for money; and descended suddenly on costers' barrows when they were desperate for food. They wandered round the country terrifying and robbing passengers in trains.

Madame Kamenev explained the situation to us: 'We tried putting them in institutions but they kept running away. So we have called in the help of our splendid League of Godless Youth.' This turned out to be the Young Men's Christian Association – without religion. 'How did one join this League?' we asked. She showed us, pinned to her wall, pictures of what had to be given up: a glass of vodka, a pack of cards, young women. In addition, complete atheism had to be declared and several nights a week had to be given to welfare work. 'Our youth are absolutely godless,' she often repeated. These young people did all they could to help the homeless children by befriending them.

We were interested that this emphasis on the desirability of atheism was accompanied by a certain amount of religious toleration. Street shrines abounded and people crossed themselves as they passed them. There being no attempt by the authorities to prevent people, other than soldiers, sailors and members of the Party, from worshipping, the churches were full. As a result of the Revolution, all the churches belonged to the State, and every sacred vessel had a State inventory ticket on it, but the churches were let rent-free to the priests for services. Although no police protection was afforded for religious services, which were sometimes disturbed by mockers, there seemed to be more Christians than Communists in the Soviet Union.

But there was no doubt that this was considered a temporary state of affairs that would change as more and more children went through the Soviet school system. We asked in high quarters about State policy and received the reply: 'We teach atheism.'

How did the name of God come into such disrepute? A visit to the anti-religious museums gave some indication. Objects taken from churches under the Tsarist regime included the 'Tears of the Madonna' sold at 50 kopeks a bottle. There were tracts declaring as Christian doctrine that Christ was sent to teach and enforce the doctrine of the Trinity and literal belief in the creation of the world in six days.

By talking to Madame Kamenev and others we realised that the Orthodox Church had been so closely allied with the Tsar that it had come to look like an enemy to many Russian people. We were told that, before the Revolution, the parish priests had been spies for the Tsar's secret police, and in times of great famine and trouble had refused to sell the church jewels to help the people.

Knowing we were anxious to get some insight into the domestic life of the people, Madame Kamenev sent us, accompanied by an interpreter, to visit the home of one of her secretaries. We were surprised to be taken, not to a showplace, but to a grimy and dilapidated apartment house. Before the Revolution the flat had belonged to the woman and her husband, but, no houses having been built in Moscow for years, six families were now using the kitchen. Everyone in the Soviet Union was allocated so many cubic feet, and if people had too much space then others would be billeted on them. The tenement was managed by a committee, and we spent the afternoon going round with the director, who promised to introduce us to 'happy Russian families'. I found these rather unconvincing, especially when one woman said to her husband, in French: 'What are we supposed to say? What's this all about?' Knowing that our interpreter did not understand French, I was tempted to communicate with the 'happy family' in that language, but refrained for fear of putting them under suspicion.

Having been made aware of the overcrowding in Moscow, we were able to appreciate, on a later visit to the three Law Courts, why so many of the cases being tried concerned disputes in the kitchen, especially the flinging about of pots and pans! Every division of each of the courts was presided over by a judge and three assessors: all strictly Communist. On the wall was a slogan: 'The Law is an instrument of the Soviet State.'

We followed our visit to the Law Courts by a long afternoon in a proletarian prison, containing murderers, thieves, and all sorts of non-political disturbers of the peace. Shuddering as we heard the gates of a Bolshevik prison clang behind us, we stepped into a courtyard full of men smoking cigarettes and reading newspapers. In one room we saw other prisoners receiving their friends and were told they had three visits a week. From the Governor we learned that the prisoners had a week's holiday at Christmas. Proletarians are not supposed to commit crimes under a Communist system but, until the ideal could be achieved, any proletarian committing a crime was sent to prison to be reformed. It was impossible to know how much of this to believe.

'Can we see some political prisoners?' I asked. The Governor, looking at me in astonishment, replied: 'But we have no political prisoners in the Soviet Union.' The Lubianka was where the political prisoners were kept, but its function was never admitted and we were not taken there.

The scene as we entered the great ballroom of the Kremlin, where the People's Parliament held its meetings, was one of the most astounding and piquant contrasts on which it was possible to set eyes. The room, lofty and immense, resembling the interior of the Palace of Versailles, was glittering with gilded mirrors and cut-glass chandeliers. In the midst of all the splendour sat the workers and peasants in their poor clothes.

We were particularly struck by a woman delegate with a thunderous voice, wearing a red handkerchief and a red shawl. With impassioned gestures she complained bitterly that in her part of Siberia the school-children spent the winter in stone-cold classrooms. From this and other speeches it was clear that, while delegates felt able to make criticisms about the operation of the system, no criticism could be made about the Communist system as such. We fully realised the limits on people's freedom.

We were most careful not to get in touch with enemies of the Government as we might have been the means of getting them into trouble after we had left, but we were told that arrests were constant and that, during the last week of our stay in Moscow, a thousand people vanished from their homes. We saw none of this, because the political police – the GPU – entered people's houses in the small hours of the morning.

The climate of fear was illustrated by the behaviour of our guide when, on one occasion, she saw me throw into a waste basket a piece of paper containing information about the time of trains. Immediately, she took out the paper and burnt it with a match. Such was the atmosphere of anxiety that even the most routine notes were burnt for fear of their being used by the political police.

Our visit to Moscow coincided with two interesting anniversaries: that of May Day and the Russian Orthodox Easter. Maxim Litvinov obtained tickets for us for the May Day procession but strongly advised us against attending the Easter Eve service in the cathedral in Red Square. 'You realise you won't get any police protection,' he warned.

I was thrilled to be spending May Day in Moscow. Celebrated as Labour Day, it was the occasion for displays and speeches and for a spectacular military review. For five hours we stood in Red Square by Lenin's Mausoleum under the ancient walls of the Kremlin. The Government gave us a place on the diplomatic part of the pavement and we had the added fascination of watching the effect of the parade on the representatives of the world. We were much taken by the Italian Military Attaché. Above his glittering brass helmet a snowy plume seemed to wave a Fascist challenge to Communism.

We watched the Red Legions go by – their appearance both uncouth and menacing. I was told the equipment was poor, but I thought they gained an impressiveness by the complete absence of parade ground paraphernalia. There was a grim reality about the whole proceeding. Presently the drums began to roll and cheers greeted the appearance of the leaders on the flat top of the Lenin Mausoleum. It was like the last act of a Shakespeare play as all the characters of the great drama filled the stage together. There were Stalin, and the Prime Minister, Aleksei Rykov, on whom jointly the divided mantle of Lenin had fallen. Stalin was impressive in figure and grim in countenance. Beside them stood Chicherin, the People's Commissar for Foreign Affairs, and 'Iron Felix' Dzerzhinsky, the head of the political police, whose statue would be unceremoniously pulled down sixty-five years later.

Not far away from us were a few Conservative MPs who had come to Moscow, quite unofficially, to see the new Communist system of government in action. We were both amused to see one of them, Robert Boothby, raise his hat, very slowly, to the strains of the Communist 'Internationale'. William teased him about that when he next saw him in the House of Commons!

After the parade we went to the Meyerhold theatre, where special performances were being given on May Day to celebrate the Revolution. The very construction and decoration of the auditorium appeared to be a challenge. It was blankly whitewashed like a workhouse. There was no curtain, and the backcloth consisted of a number of bamboo rods hung close together. There were no footlights: the limelight was worked from the gallery. The orchestra was led by a black man, who was assisted by a musician playing a grand piano in a niche high up in the cornice.

It was difficult to know exactly when the performance started, as the actors wore ordinary working clothes and could not be distinguished by their dress either from the audience or from the scene-shifters. We learnt that action was about to begin from the flicker of the lights and the blowing of a factory steam whistle. At this point the spotlight was turned on a group of people who were engaged in some revolutionary conversation. On them, accordingly, attention was centred and with-drawn from the scene-shifters, who were rattling the backcloth as they passed to and fro about their work. Suddenly the light was switched on to another group of actors, who carried the plot forward a further stage. In this particular scene there was a great deal of shooting. At one point a man fired his revolver point-blank into the audience.

The performance was advertised to start at six-thirty, but we were in ample time at seven and were able to wander about the foyer, in which country cousins of many races were having an evening out. When at last we sat down in our places, our neighbour, after many friendly but fruitless conversational overtures, made a final onslaught as, with beaming smiles, he turned to us and said: 'Workers of the world, unite!' To this union of hearts language could add nothing. We were later told that the perfor-mance had lasted until five in the morning, but we left long before then.

Despite the warnings of Litvinov, we were determined to attend the Orthodox Easter Eve service at St Saviour's Cathedral in Red Square. When we arrived the building was still locked. It was dark and intensely cold, with snow lying unmelted on the ground. A large number of people sat on the steps and stamped about from time to time to keep warm. After an hour the doors swung slowly open and the crowd rushed in thankfully; we found ourselves inside with them and slightly breathless from the experience. The unheated cathedral was lighted by thousands of flickering candles, many of which hung high on the walls and hardly served to do more than show up the darkness. The only sound was that of hurrying people, and very soon the vast building seemed to be filled to overflowing.

All this time the doors of the high altar had remained closed; but we were aware of a service going on behind them, for the sound of chanting rose and fell. About midnight a steady move towards the sanctuary began and many members of the congregation paused, with unlighted candle in hand, to kiss and salute icons on the way. Once the heavy red curtain before the high altar rolled back; inner doors opened for an instant, and before they closed again we had a vision of many priests in gorgeous vestments. The atmosphere was now so charged with emotion that we ceased to feel any chill in the cathedral; indeed, it seemed to us to be growing hotter and hotter.

At a given moment the chanting grew suddenly louder; the doors and gates opened to their fullest extent and a great procession of dignitaries came down the steps and into the body of the cathedral, advancing slowly between two lines of deeply bowing people. As they passed by, the glittering round-topped mitres of the Patriarch and the other bishops moved high above the heads of the worshippers. From the instant of their coming the Holy Fire had leapt from candle to candle in the hands of the people, with cries of 'Christ is risen! Christ is risen!' Many exchanged kisses; most crossed themselves; and some attempted to pray, but the surging crowd was too great, the movement too constant and conflicting to allow of kneeling. A nun at a stall sold us two candles and we lit them and joined in the throng. When the crowd pressed thickly in upon us we blew them out, as did everyone else, and then, a moment or two later, lighted them at someone else's candle.

At about about half past midnight, as we tried to get out, the crisis of the evening came quite without warning. Everyone in the cathedral had become urgently possessed of the same idea of leaving it; an uncomfortable jostling began behind; we were carried without our volition towards the great west doors; and there, at that precise moment, we came face to face with a solid phalanx of shouting men and women – militant atheists – forcing their way in. The result was chaos. More and more candles were blown out with every instant and soon there was almost complete darkness.

I was pushed this way and that, and felt sure my ribs would break. But, just as I thought I might be suffocated and crushed to death, the pressure of the crowd pushed me on to the street. To my horror there was no sign of William. Fearing for his life, I called out: 'William! William!' and to my surprise, a reassuring voice answered, in broken English: 'Do not be alarmed! He will surely come.' After what seemed like an eternity we found each other again and walked back, shaking and thankful, along the side of the Moskva River, under the ghostly towers of the Kremlin, through the silent Red Square; away from the rows of jeerers, perched on walls and balustrades, who had pursued us with howls and mock chants in falsetto voices. Only then did we fully understand why we had been warned of the absence of police protection for religious services.

Throughout the whole Easter week we caught a sense of the subdued but unmistakable rejoicing that ran like an unseen current through the city. We heard from foreigners we met whispered stories of the courage of crowds that had stood by at past Easters, hissing and jeering, while soldiers of the Red Army had sacked and looted churches. We saw in the dainty and inviting patisseries of the town all the homely and familiar emblems of the festival – beribboned eggs, silver-papered fish, and chocolate hens. We saw a village church carry out its celebrations, and ate in a hospitable Communist home all the seasonable fare of an old Russian Easter. This was the great feast of the year, beloved of the people; its traditional accompaniments, above all that marvellous tall cake, the *kulitch*, made, if possible, with a hundred eggs and stamped all over with sacred emblems, was a part of life itself. And it still persisted. In some homes the host looked apologetic when the *kulitch* appeared; he was a member of the Party, but his wife, poor deluded creature, was a Christian; he excused the lapse on that ground. The household where we stayed could plead no such extenuating circumstances, and yet the *kulitch* appeared – but with a difference. A stream diverted will take strange courses, as our host's *kulitch* plainly showed. Instead of seeing the cross on this noble cake, we were confronted with the hammer and sickle, with pictures of Lenin and Stalin, and with slogans in place of texts around its base. It had all been regularised: no one could possibly object.

A few days after the Easter service came a distressing blow to us as temporary exiles – the General Strike broke out in Britain. Delighted Soviet officials showed us a cartoon in *Pravda* depicting King George V perched precariously on a mound of coal being hacked away by British miners. It seemed strange that only a short time before *Pravda* had announced the birth, in London, of Princess Elizabeth, the present Queen. The Litvinovs had said it was an 'astonishing' thing for *Pravda* to do, and everyone else was surprised that a royal birth had been mentioned.

Now, well-wishers said to us: 'Oh! The world revolution has broken out. It is on its way everywhere, and the Soviet Union is the only safe country because we've already had our revolution. Send for your children and come here and settle.' 'Well,' I said, 'I don't think I'll do that!' 'It's a great mistake to go back to England,' they warned. 'Revolution is beginning there. You might be in danger.'

Unmoved by this advice, and concerned about our children, we began to make plans to leave. Before doing so we dined with the members of the British Commercial Mission, the nearest thing to an embassy then existing in Moscow. Housed in the sugar merchant's mansion, it functioned under Sir Robert Hodgson, the chargé d'affaires, and consisted, besides officials, of about thirty British businessmen operating in the USSR. At dinner, we were painfully impressed by the doleful mien of the chief butler, who had served in that capacity to the Tsar, and still grieved for his master, murdered eight years before.

Sir Robert had little news to give us about the position in England, and we were thankful to get our exit papers in order and make for home by way of Finland. Sailing overnight from Helsinki, we awoke, at dawn, to find the boat keeling over violently to starboard; not through accident, but owing to dangerously unbalanced loading.

After enjoying a few days' rest in Bruges, we went home to face the family, understandably annoyed at having been left with the care of our two children for months on end. We discovered that at the outbreak of the General Strike, Ernest and Gwen, fearing violence that, fortunately, never materialised, had left London and had gone to their country house. We were so happy to see our beautiful children again. Anthony, curly-haired and thirteen months old, had, alas, forgotten all about us, but we were greatly touched by the loving welcome of little Michael, nearly five, who jumped with joy to see us.

Now that our journey was over, William, once again immersed in British politics, was faced with the decision of whether or not to leave the party he had served in Parliament for two decades.

CHAPTER 6

1926–1929

Liberal prospects were not favourable in the spring and summer of 1926; the different positions taken up by the leaders towards the General Strike – Asquith demanding unconditional surrender, while Lloyd George backed negotiations with the strikers – had led to the disruption of the fragile unity so recently achieved. A further blow occurred when Asquith had a stroke and was unable to participate in active politics for several months. William continued to organise the Radical Group and was one of the few effective Liberal MPs opposing the Conservative Government. Most Liberal MPs were very demoralised by the way the Party had split into different groups.

When Parliament broke up for the summer recess, William temporarily put his political anxieties behind him and we went to see Stansgate, the Benn family's old seaside house. The visit had been planned while we were travelling through Syria. The wide open spaces of the desert had made William nostalgic for the flat terrain of the Essex coast, and so we had decided to visit the place where he had enjoyed many happy holidays as a boy.

We had been warned that the owner of Stansgate, Captain Grey, was an unsociable man, but that did not put us off. When Mrs Grey opened the door, William said: 'I do hope you don't mind my calling. My father built this house in 1899 and I want to show it to my wife.' Mrs Grey was charmed and William went on to say: 'I very much want to bring my mother down next weekend. We'll stay in an hotel and call next Sunday.' There was a farmhouse in the grounds, and Lady Benn, not the type of woman to be intimidated by Captain Grey, even if his wife and children seemed in awe of him, said: 'Now, Captain Grey, I am going to ask you to let me have that house to rent for the summer for the use of my family.'

We used the farmhouse as our holiday home until Captain Grey died, whereupon his widow, wanting smaller accommodation and no longer able to bear the expense of keeping the sea wall in good repair, moved into the farmhouse and sold Stansgate to us. It became our weekend home and played a great part in our lives. William loved going there and enjoyed teaching the boys to sail. We went down as soon as Parliament rose at the end of the week, sometimes on a Thursday evening. When William was a minister he would take his papers with him in the ministerial 'red boxes' and work on them over the weekend.

The parliamentary session which began in the autumn of 1926 was the last that William spent in the Liberal Party. It was not a happy one; any MP who is contemplating a change in his political allegiance must, unless he is extremely insensitive, suffer a very great deal. One of the principal sources of unhappiness is the feeling that he is betraying, not only his colleagues but, even worse, his supporters in the constituency he represents. They have supported him through all the battles of past contests, stood by him without question, and now he has to let them down.

William finally made up his mind, after much agonising, when Asquith resigned from the leadership in October, and the Liberal Administrative Committee, in January 1927, accepted Lloyd George's offer to finance Liberal candidates from his private fund. William was not prepared to serve under Lloyd George's leadership.

After breaking the news to Asquith, William decided that we should visit Ramsay MacDonald so that he might personally make his 'submission' to the leader of the Labour Party. Accordingly, we went to his beautiful home in old Hampstead. It was in every way a gracious house, well set out and furnished, and, knowing Ramsay to have been for long a widower, and his elder daughter, Ishbel, to be only in her early twenties, I wondered if he had achieved this by himself. Since his main domestic help was a Dutch housekeeper, I came to the conclusion that Margaret Gladstone, his late wife, must have collected the furniture in her day.

All kinds of rumours were afloat about Ramsay. He was believed to be growing more and more out of sympathy with his Labour colleagues and was known to have been 'taken up' socially by Lord and Lady Londonderry and their wide circle of Tory associates. On one occasion he went to the door of the House of Lords and when Labour peers came out to greet him his only remark had been: 'Has anybody seen Lord Londonderry? I want him to take me home to lunch.' At this everybody's spirits had fallen.

Ramsay, a lonely man since his wife's death, received emotional support from his sentimental attachment to Lady Londonderry; a friendship which, later, was said to trouble King George V a good deal. He was believed to have said to the Marquis of Londonderry, in his blunt way: 'I hear that my Prime Minister is in love with your wife.' Londonderry, assuming that such a situation made the advent of socialism unlikely, replied enthusiastically: 'Oh yes, but don't you think it's a good thing?'

Ramsay welcomed us with warmth and affection. He had been a good friend of my father's, and had known William over the whole course of their political careers. Indeed, on my engagement, he had written me a most friendly letter saying: 'I am glad you are going to marry Wedgwood Benn. I'm fond of him too.'

Although his personal welcome was warm, however, his political one was strangely qualified. It seemed to say, in attitude, if not in plain language: 'Are you really sure you want to do this? Have you fully realised what it means to join the Labour Party today?' It was quite obvious that he was even more out of sympathy with it than rumour had hinted at. Warning us that 'the Party takes quite a bit of keeping straight', he spoke of 'tough-jawed men' whom William might find difficult to live with and hinted at his own hope that they would never take over the Party and party policy. William told Ramsay that his mind was firmly made up but assured him that he would not expect to be adopted by the Leith Labour Party, whose candidate had already fought the seat twice.

I was struck that everyone asked whether I was 'coming over' too. This would have been unlikely had William been joining any other party, but, for me as a Scot, it was never difficult to see the Radical wing of the Liberal Party as similar to the Labour Party. I was happy to give William my full support.

Having been to see in turn his old leader, Asquith, and his new leader, MacDonald, William's next, and most painful, duty of all was to go to Leith and hand back to the constituency the trust they had so generously placed in his keeping nine years before at the general election of 1918. I accompanied him on what was one of the saddest journeys of his life. Taking a day train to Edinburgh, we arrived just in time for the constituency meeting William had called.

Our assembled friends awaited us in stunned silence. They had only recently heard a rumour of this move and still hoped William had come to contradict it. He began by telling them the inside story of his increasing unhappiness at the state of the Liberal Party. Asquith had been his leader since the death of Campbell-Bannerman in 1908. Lloyd George under Asquith's principled leadership could no doubt be kept in check, but on his own he was totally unpredictable. 'He doesn't know right from wrong,' William told them. 'I cannot put my conscience in pawn to such a leader.'

William spoke quietly of all the difficulties that had surrounded a parliamentarian attempting to fight on as a Liberal in a party that had lost its way. As long as Asquith was leader it was just possible to ignore the things that had been done: Lloyd George had sold titles and had built up a large personal fund running into millions. But now Asquith was gone, Lloyd George was going to use the power this fund gave him to dictate to the Party and oblige it to take the course he wished.

William had never spoken this way before and the meeting sat stunned. But where to go? He told them, truthfully, that there was for him only one possible place – the Labour Party. One question faced him from the chairman of the constituency party: 'You told us, Captain Benn, that Liberal principles were totally indestructible. How then do you account for your desertion of them?' In much pain, he told them that he was no longer sincerely able to act as a Radical Liberal in the Liberal Party. It was more and more falling into the hands of what were rightly called 'old fashioned Liberals', adherents of free enterprise capitalism who did not believe in the ideals of a just society. His father, John Benn, for many years a Liberal MP, had always stood with the support of the labour movement and that was where both William's head and heart lay. Now the crisis had arrived, he must make the decisive step once and for all. In silence we left the meeting and caught the night train back to London.

William did not believe it to be right for an MP elected for one party to change to another without facing the electorate and so, a short time later, in February 1927, I watched William enter the Chamber for the last time as a Liberal member of the front bench; sit on the Labour back benches for a few moments; shake hands with his new colleagues and the Speaker; and, because MPs cannot resign, go home to apply to be Crown Steward Bailiff of the Chiltern Hundreds – an 'office of profit' under the Crown. William used to say that the Chiltern Hundreds, which, ironically, does not actually provide a 'profit' or salary, was the only job for which he had ever asked!

It was a traumatic experience. He was leaving the House of Commons utterly behind and going into the wilderness without having any sort of hope as to when, if ever, he would re-enter it again as a Labour MP. Never before had any door shut so decisively upon him and a much-loved career.

In the spring of 1927 William and I were spending a short time with my parents in Florence when William decided that this would give us a good opportunity to cross the Adriatic and visit Albania – a small country shrouded in mystery. It was known to be mixed in religion and economically backward. The only famous man it had produced in recent times was Mustafa Kemal Pasha, the President of Turkey. The ruler of Albania was a Muslim, Ahmed Zogu, later to be called King Zog, but the country was under the influence of the Italians, whose embassy was the leading one.

Arriving at nightfall by boat, we were somewhat daunted to find that the landing stage was lighted only by fireflies. This picturesque form of natural illumination did little to help us find our way. We asked to be shown to a hotel suitable for foreigners; William for once agreed that this might be wise, and, indeed, it would have been impossible to imagine what a native one would have been like. There was no running water, hot or cold, and the toilet was a hole in the stone floor. There was nothing hot to drink except coffee with goat's milk, and the solid food offered was impossible to identify. We asked for eggs and survived on them with black coffee and black bread.

Next day we walked by a secluded bay and were tempted, in the hope of getting clean, to have a bathe. Unfortunately, it was still early in the spring and I must have been attacked by something approaching hypothermia for, on our return to the hotel, and for the first and only time in my life, I fell down in a dead faint. William, thinking me desperately ill, asked the hotel to send a doctor at once. None being available, the local vet was asked to do his best. The medicine he administered was of a type and strength that any self-respecting horse would have blown back at him and I grew worse before I grew better. On my recovery we lunched with the Italian Ambassador, who was horrified to hear of the bathe: 'You had a bathe? You English – you will kill yourselves!'

William met Ahmed Zogu, from whom he was able to learn a good deal of the state of the country and the Italian domination. At the close of the audience, William was presented with a signed photograph of Zogu in full military attire and wearing very conspicuous white boots. To William's surprise, a day or so later, emissaries from Zogu appeared and exchanged the photograph for one in which he was wearing ordinary brown boots. No explanation was offered, but we heard that the white boots had been the object of many jokes in diplomatic circles and Zogu had been warned not to let this get abroad!

Throughout the spring and summer of 1927 no possible constituency made any sign of appearing and we had to exercise our souls in patience. Sometimes it seemed as if William would never be back in the House of Commons again. We had no alternative but to stay in London and be prepared, if the opportunity offered, to move into any constituency where William was chosen as prospective candidate for the next election, still two years ahead.

The Parliamentary Labour Party gave us a very warm welcome. Many of them had hoped for a long time that William might join their ranks and they were well prepared. The first thing we did in the autumn was to attend the Labour Party's annual conference. My fellow Scot, that lovable humorist James Maxton, did most to make us feel at home. His style was inimitable; indeed, it was said that in any ballot of parliamentarians he would have come out as the favourite MP. Addressing the Conference, he made everyone laugh by saying: 'Now I want you all to give a great welcome to Wedgwood Benn – a Stepney lad who has never had a chance!'

We were thrilled when, in November 1927, William was chosen to be the Labour candidate for the West Renfrew constituency. It was a hopeful, if not safe, seat and William had the prospect of nursing it till the next general election, whenever that might be. West Renfrew, then a safe Liberal seat, having been the local constituency of my girlhood, I was delighted to be associated with the district once more. This turn of events promised to bring together the two now widely separated parts of my life; and I even hoped to win William some votes.

Although we stayed friends with many of our old Liberal colleagues, especially Archie and Marigold Sinclair, inevitably we drew closer to some interesting members of the Labour Party. We had known Sir Oswald and

Lady Cynthia Mosley – always known as 'Tom' and 'Cimmie' – since the early twenties but got to know them better after William joined the Labour Party and Tom sent him a letter of welcome. They lived round the corner from us in Smith Square. Cimmie had been brought up in an enormous house at Kedleston but preferred a more intimate scale. 'I don't like great big houses. I like teensy little houses,' she would say.

Her regular features, deep-blue expressive eyes and perfect complexion came, undoubtedly, from her beautiful American mother, Mary Leiter, the daughter of a rich Chicago businessman. This marriage gave Cimmie's father, Marquess Curzon of Kedleston, substantial means with which to support any form of political life he wished. Already heir to a barony, he was elevated to the peerage in 1898 on his appointment as Viceroy of India. His mother-in-law who, with other Chicago relatives, attended the great Durbar to celebrate the succession of King Edward VII, said: 'I never knew what it was to be Lady Curzon, Vicereine of India, till I saw Mary on that elephant!'

It was a very happy marriage of mutual devotion, and three daughters were born before Lady Curzon's early death. The girls were fortunate in having kind aunts on their mother's side and a wonderful old nanny to bring them up. Eventually the nanny looked after Cimmie's children and was the mainstay of the family. On one occasion, when I mentioned to Cimmie that I had seen her children at Canon Woodward's children's service in St John's, Smith Square, she replied: 'I'd no idea that their nanny took them. She runs everything.'

I once had a talk to her about her father, Lord Curzon. She regretfully painted the picture of a remote and severe father: 'I think it is a great reproach to him that he never made any effort to become friends with us. He used, as we got older, to have lunch with us and I remember he seemed chiefly concerned to keep the conversation on serious lines. He would describe a series of scenes and in each case we had to name the occasion. When confronted with a verbal picture of armies crossing rivers, or deserts, or what not, we had to be prepared to name the event. It would be Caesar crossing the Alps or the Rubicon, or Xenophon describing approaching the sea, or Alexander the Great conquering the world. Woe betide us if we got it wrong! Above all my father hated the pursuit of any trivial object of conversation. Only epoch-making events were worth thinking about.'

Lord Curzon, it appeared, had a tremendous belief in his ability to do anything at all better than anybody else. He would frequently demonstrate this by being found on his knees laying a stair carpet. Never losing his great sense of dignity, he would invariably answer the phone with the words: 'This is Lord Curzon, himself, speaking . . .'

Cimmie, determined to make her own choice of husband, married Oswald Mosley in 1920. 'I didn't want to marry someone everyone thought I should marry,' she told me, 'I wanted to make my own choice, and nobody had ever heard of Tom when I married him.' It was assumed that the young couple would reflect the Curzon views, Tom being the Conservative MP for Harrow, but shortly after the wedding they began to attack Lloyd George's Coalition Government, especially its repressive Irish policy. Both Tom and Cimmie were reacting against their early upbringing and longed for a more liberal – even socialist – way of political life.

Criticism came along hard and fast from Lord Curzon, from Tom Mosley's father, the baronet Sir Oswald Mosley, and from Conservative MPs. Socially, the Mosleys were dropped by traditional Conservatives. The media joined in this persecution with enthusiasm. Stories of their great wealth were circulated as evidence of their hypocrisy. I recall a well-known journalist saying: 'If things are getting dull politically there's nothing to beat a good Mosley "rag".' This merciless pursuit of the young couple persisted for many years until, later on, it acquired a more serious basis with Mosley's nascent Fascism.

William and the other Independent Liberals – the 'Wee Frees' – being the most active opponents of Lloyd George's Government, it had been expected that, on resigning the Conservative whip, Tom Mosley should work with them. The Asquiths, having courted the Mosleys most as-siduously in the hope that they would become Independent Liberals, were consequently very disappointed when, in 1924, Tom joined the Labour Party, becoming MP for Smethwick.

We saw quite a lot of the Mosleys. Their two eldest children, Vivien and Nicholas, and ours played together in the Westminster parks, and attended each others' parties. Indeed, it is a family joke that the first speech my son Anthony ever made, after careful coaching by his nanny, was to say 'thank you' at a Mosley birthday tea!

Tom wanted a revitalised Labour Party that would, he hoped, elim-inate unemployment by pursuing expansionist economic policies rather than the traditional ones of a strong pound and a balanced budget. Needing as many MPs as possible to support him, he persuaded Cimmie, against her own inclination, to stand for Parliament in 1929.

We had a few talks about this and she told me of her terror at the situation in which she had been placed. However much Tom might help her, she was the candidate and would have to answer for herself. With characteristic honesty she said: 'Well, I really don't know what I'm going to do. If somebody asks me about the gold standard during the election I shall just have to say I don't know anything about it.' She would have preferred to stay at home with her family and have more children, but Tom was not happy with that idea.

Fortunately, she proved to be very popular both in her Stoke-on-Trent constituency and in the House of Commons, where she made a refreshing and elegant figure in her impeccably tailored haute couture black suit, worn with a white satin blouse, and a camellia that was delivered to her house daily. The House of Commons can be a generous assembly and it understood very well how the situation had been forced on her and treated this unusual member with friendship tempered with amusement.

It was a tremendous effort for Cimmie to make her maiden speech. William, who was an awful tease, told her that one MP, when it came to it, just could not make the speech. He got up and said: 'Mr Speaker, sir, I don't feel well,' and sat down!

She had a basic honesty that kept her from presenting herself as anything other than what she was. When she set out to make her maiden speech she took up the Tory challenge that socialism was the offer of 'something for nothing', which, if accepted as natural policy, would ruin both individuals and the country itself. She cited her own case as an illustration to the contrary. All her life, she pointed out, she had had not 'something', but 'everything', for nothing and this had not wrecked her character. The Labour Party cheered; the Tories remained politely sceptical.

She really was so completely ignorant of politics and what it was all about. Lord Curzon had not believed in educating daughters and Cimmie was a perfect illustration of a remark once made to William: 'The aristocracy bring up their daughters to look wistful.'

Although Cimmie and I became good friends, I always found Tom Mosley somewhat cold and distant; he reminded me of an electric fire with artificial coal – the coals glow with light but there is no warmth from them. He was unfaithful and not at all worthy of her. In the language of the period, he was 'an awful cad'. Whereas Cimmie dearly and devotedly loved her 'Tomkin' and had no one else in her life, his feelings were quite different. Needing many relationships, he took a room in London and entertained his women friends there. We all thought this was a very raw deal for Cimmie, who had an extremely difficult time with him.

A very ambitious politician, Tom was extremely disappointed that Ramsay MacDonald did not give him a seat in the Cabinet when the second Labour Government was formed in 1929. He had to be satisfied with the minor office of Chancellor of the Duchy of Lancaster, where his task was to assist J. R. Thomas, the Lord Privy Seal, to deal with the persistent, and growing, problem of unemployment. This he found very unrewarding. Full of new ideas, he discovered that Jimmy Thomas did not think them worth attending to.

Thomas was a rather sad figure. A former railwayman, he was mocked as a social climber who increasingly preferred the company of Conservatives. When a budget leak in 1936 led to his dismissal from the overwhelmingly Conservative National Government, a cruel cartoon, with the caption 'Parting is such sweet sorrow', depicted a disconsolate Thomas watching his evening clothes disappear down the drive of his expensive house. 'Alas!' William remarked. 'There comes the inevitable end to the value of blasphemy from the footplate on behalf of the upper classes.' Thomas's language was as unrestrained as his incipient Toryism. Even

(*Below*) Daniel Turner Holmes, the author's father
(*Foot*) Margaret Stansgate at the time of her engagement

(*Top*) Margaret Eadie Holmes, the author's mother

(*Above*) Margaret Stansgate with her mother

(*Above*) Margaret Stansgate with her husband Captain William Wedgwood Benn, later Viscount Stansgate, at their wedding reception

(*Left*) Margaret Stansgate with her sons (left to right) Michael, David and Anthony

(*Below*) Margaret Stansgate's parents with her sister, Hermione, and her children

Oswald 'Tom' Mosley and
Lady Cynthia Mosley at the
Smethwick by-election, 1926

Waldorf and Nancy Astor at
Epsom, 1925

Margaret Stansgate with her
brother-in-law, Sir Ernest
Benn, and a group of boys
from the John Benn hostel
(named after her father-in-
law), 1930

The Earl and
Countess of
Oxford and
Asquith, 1924

Sidney and Beatrice
Webb (Lord and
Lady Passfield) at
Passfield Corner

1929 Labour Cabinet. Ramsay MacDonald is in the centre and the author's husband, retary of State for India, is on the extreme right of the front row. Margaret Bondfield was the woman Cabinet minister

Margaret Stansgate's eldest son, and husband: Flight Lt Michael Wedgwood Benn and Air Commodore, Viscount Stansgate, during the Second World War

Margaret Stansgate
and her husband
enjoy a luncheon
party with members
of the Knesset –
Israeli Parliament –
in Jerusalem

Margaret Stansgate
with her husband
and President Nasser
of Egypt

Margaret Stansgate watches her husband lay a wreath on Mahatma Gandhi's samadhi (memorial). Viscount Stansgate had been responsible for Gandhi's visit to Britain in 1931

Margaret Stansgate and her husband relax in front of Taj Mahal during their visit to India

(*Right*) A family group at Stansgate in 1988

(*Below*) David and June Benn in 1985

(*Top left*) Margaret Stansgate with her daughter-in-law, Caroline Benn, grandson Stephen, and son Anthony after he had been refused entry to the chamber of the House of Commons in 1960 on the grounds that he had succeeded to his father's viscountcy and could not renounce it

(*Top right*) Margaret Stansgate holds up the Charter of the Congregational Federation. She was the first President and, subsequently, Emeritus President

when reporting other people's remarks he made no attempt to moderate his vocabulary. 'A very intelligent woman, Queen Mary,' he once told me. 'She said to me: "Mr Thomas, you're bloody well right!" '

Tom Mosley's frustration with Thomas and other members of the Labour Government, particularly the Chancellor of the Exchequer, Philip Snowden, led to his becoming increasingly interested in Mussolini and Italian Fascism. His future career became a sad one to watch and we ceased to associate with him. There is little doubt that Tom had an ardent desire to end our country's deep economic depression, but he undoubtedly had a power-loving streak in his nature which more and more took over his life and dictated his way. Resigning from the Labour Government, he set up the 'New Party', which was Fascist in all but name.

Cimmie left Parliament and returned, thankfully, to family life, giving birth to a much-desired third child. The next stage in Tom's rejection of democratic methods was when he founded the British Union of Fascists – the 'Blackshirts'. Puzzled, doubtful, but loyal, Cimmie reluctantly supported him.

Then a most sad event occurred. In 1933, she suddenly developed acute appendicitis and, in the days before antibiotics, developed peritonitis and died at the tragically early age of thirty-four. I saw the old nanny, once again looking after motherless children, out pushing the new baby, just a year old, and she said: 'Poor Lady Cynthia. She wanted this baby so much and here he is and she's gone.' Cimmie's life with Tom had been a full cup but not always a sweet one, and it is doubtful if he would have chosen to remain with her despite her great love for him.

He was undoubtedly distressed by her death and this, together, perhaps, with feelings of remorse, led him to build a tomb for her in the grounds of their country home at Denham. During the year it took to build, Cimmie's body lay in the chapel at Cliveden. It was not long, however, before he married the beautiful woman to whom he had, for some time, been attached – Diana Guinness, one of the famous Mitford sisters.

Cimmie always appeared to her friends as a woman of great sincerity who cared deeply for the principles of a just society. A woman of astonishing beauty and goodness of heart, she was lovely to look at and lovely to be with. In supporting Tom when he became a Fascist, she followed her heart rather than her head. Her premature death was a blow to us all.

Another couple with whom we became better acquainted when William left the Liberal Party were our next-door neighbours at Grosvenor Road, Sidney and Beatrice Webb, whose reputation as social investigators was unrivalled. Founders of the London School of Economics, there was nothing they did not know about social issues; and all the necessary information was at their fingertips. As soon as William joined the Labour Party, they kindly invited us to spend a weekend at their country retreat, Passfield Corner.

Our first sight of their sitting room brought a shock. It had several windows, looking on to different parts of the garden, every one of which was curtained in an entirely different kind of figured material. I felt instantly that here was a spontaneous reaction to the Webbs' lifelong habit of precise classification. At the tail-end of their lives they were indulging in a glorious break-away from system and all the limits it imposed on personal inclination.

Beatrice Webb, on noting my astonished gaze, laughed and said with satisfaction: 'We had the greatest difficulty in having those put up. At first, Harvey Nichols refused outright to do it, thinking we should immediately repent and have them pulled down, but, as you see, they were wrong. I like them more and more.'

The sitting room at Passfield was provided with the same arrangement of furniture as at Grosvenor Road. Beatrice sat comfortably in a large armchair, suitable to her length and breadth; Sidney, much shorter, his head supported by cushions, stretched himself out, full length, on a medium-sized couch. From these adjacent stances, they chipped into each other's conversation, adding spicy bits to what the other was saying. Sidney, for example, might be quoting from something Bernard Shaw had told him and Beatrice would make a long digression to give us details of how difficult it was for Shaw to get on with his wife and why.

They were very entertaining and amusing conversationalists but so unlike in temperament that I wondered why they had ever decided to marry. Beatrice, still, in her late sixties, a beautiful woman, had in her youth been deeply in love with the Liberal Unionist statesman Joseph Chamberlain, and might have become his third wife; but, on asking him if he expected his views to prevail in his household, and receiving the reply 'That is so,' she knew that she would never be happy with him and wisely turned elsewhere. She settled for Sidney Webb, whose political ideas were compatible with her own. Nothing else mattered.

Beatrice talked freely about their life together. When she decided to marry Sidney Webb, she told us, they had agreed that he would settle the important things and she would settle the unimportant things; but she would settle which was which. There were many differences, physical and mental, between them: 'Sidney and I are poles apart. He's never ill: he's solid through and through. I'm not. And he's absolutely self-contained and self-sufficient. He doesn't need to think there's a Presence behind him. Now, I have to pray. I can't get by without a Presence. I have to be guided by It and acknowledge my accountability.' Whether she felt that 'It' was the Christian God, I do not know; but, obviously, whatever she believed was sufficiently satisfying to carry her through life. It was clearly a happy and stable marriage.

They were much travelled and Sidney told us an amusing story of their stay in a Japanese Buddhist monastery. The abbot was a very agreeable, cultured man with an excellent knowledge of English, Western civilisation, and the Christian religion. During the course of their stay, he invited Sidney to give the monks a lecture comparing Christianity and Buddhism. Sidney, explaining that he had no knowledge of either, regretfully refused; offering, instead, to speak on the development of the Poor Law in England during the nineteenth century, a subject on which the Webbs were the leading authorities. The abbot assured him that this would be most welcome. Sidney gave the lecture, stopping after every paragraph to enable the abbot to give his translations. As these proceeded, Sidney became aware, from the occurrence of the names of Christ and Buddha, that the abbot was himself giving the lecture he had asked for!

The only trying occasion for me came when, despite bad weather, the Webbs decided that we must all go for a long walk. I am at best a bad walker and, not having brought wet-weather clothing, was obliged to don Beatrice's mackintosh, which was long and trailed on the ground, and Sidney's goloshes, which were too big and flapped; my misery was complete!

From their conversation, we were confirmed, after this weekend, in our belief that neither of the Webbs really had much use for Parliament or, indeed, parliamentary institutions. Great admirers of the Soviet Union, they were thrilled when they eventually visited that country to find what they were convinced, with a few reservations, was Webbism come true.

Sidney's authoritarian style of speaking was not acceptable to the House of Commons. This he never understood. I remember two incidents in 1924, when he was President of the Board of Trade in the first Labour Government, in which he came off much the worst. On the first occasion, when he was asked to explain some policy or other, his reply, 'You must read my books,' was greeted with laughter and jeers. On the other, when he adopted the attitude of a lecturer, not a minister in debate, an impudent young member of the opposition shouted: 'Oh, lie down, Nanny!' This was too much for a loyal old Scottish MP, who rose and drew the Speaker's attention to this outrageous remark. 'Mr Speaker, sir, did you hear what yon member said to our revered leader, Mr Webb?' At this point the whole front bench, including the victim himself, were vigorously trying to silence the loyal friend before he actually repeated the fatal words, but to no effect. On he went, getting nearer and nearer to disaster: 'He said: "Lie down, Nanny!" ' at which the House roared with delight.

When Sidney became Colonial Secretary in the 1929 Government, he took a peerage and found the House of Lords much more congenial to his particular gifts and style. Beatrice, however – after, not before the event – let it be known that she would not be known as Lady Passfield. Ramsay MacDonald complained that he had received no warning of this awkwardness. Beatrice explained it to me in her forthright way: 'I am a middle-class socialist and, as such, I shall neither be called Comrade, nor

Lady Passfield; just Mrs Webb.' So the distinguished couple were addressed formally as Lord Passfield and Mrs Sidney Webb. One evening at a dinner at Buckingham Palace, however, I noticed that she had to endure the indignity of taking her seat at a place marked 'The Lady Passfield' – her official name.

We were next-door neighbours of the Webbs from 1925 until 1929, when their house was taken over by the Labour MP and junior minister Susan Lawrence, who had been a tenant of the Webbs. She had a great sense of humour. On one occasion, when William, thinking that our boys were making too much noise, took them in to apologise, she said: 'Well, if you tell me what you have done I am prepared to be perfectly furious!'

From Susan, we rented the ground-floor room in which Sidney and Beatrice had written all their books. It stretched the length of the house, with long windows looking out on to the river. We got planning permission to make a door through the party wall and for many years it was our library and favourite sitting room. William, who had gained an expert knowledge of interior decoration from his father, had it panelled and painted a beautiful Georgian green. Both the appearance and the atmosphere were very pleasant.

While the Webbs were still our neighbours, our comfortable life in Grosvenor Road was rudely shaken when, at about one o'clock in the morning of 8 January 1928, our cook, rushing into my top-floor room, threw herself across the bed with the words: 'The Thames is in the house!' Hearing the sound of many waters, I leapt up, went to the window, and saw a sight like the Niagara Falls. At a point exactly opposite our house, the Thames had burst through the wall that normally held it back, and the road had disappeared. Where it had been was a mighty flood. Leaving my bedroom, I heard the waves lashing against the front door, and the river pouring loudly into the basement, filling it in a few minutes.

We had turned our sunny basement, which was not overlooked, back or front, into a pleasant flat for our domestic helpers and it had proved popular in giving them their own self-contained home. Now, to my horror, I saw them struggling out of the basement with as many of their personal possessions as they could save, up to their waists in the steadily rising water.

Rushing to the nearest telephone, I rang the exchange. The operator only had time to say: 'The police know all about it. Get up as high in your house as you can and take a ladder – you may have to get on the roof . . . ' before the phone was cut off by the tide. Our only ladder was in the basement, so there was no chance of taking it with me.

In great concern, I woke the children's nurse and we got Michael, then seven, and Anthony, nearly four, up and dressed. They were entranced by the exciting view from the window and I remember hearing Nanny saying to Anthony: 'No, you can't have ginger beer at one in the morning, even if the Thames has overflowed!'

For a ghastly hour no one could tell us what was going to happen, and I actually felt more frightened than during the Blitz, twelve years later. It took me about a month to recover from the shock. Certainly the house was solidly built – as good a Victorian structure as one could hope for – but even so it trembled and shook under the impact of two tides. The previous one had been kept from taking its usual course because of violent winds and, on its way back, had met with newly melting floodwater from the upper reaches. We later learned that fourteen people had been drowned by the flood, some in the basements of Grosvenor Road.

Mercifully the tide turned and, little by little, the waters subsided and the police came along in boats. In an hour or so everyone along Grosvenor Road came out to see how much damage had been done. It was a truly memorable occasion. Most of the residents had never even met their long-standing neighbours face to face, far less spoken to each other. Now the river Thames had introduced us, and we went on talking far into the night.

The roadway had thrown up its macadamised surface and it was plain that no wheeled traffic would be able to come to rescue us. On the footpath, paving stones had also been dislodged and it would not be easy to carry any luggage with us when we left. The great gash in the wall loomed threateningly before us. As we were in danger from every tide until it was mended, the first priority became that of finding some safe place to take the children.

William was in Scotland, engaged in a round of political meetings in his West Renfrew constituency, and I was not expecting him home until the evening. Fortunately, my brother-in-law, Ernest Benn, came straight up from Oxted when he heard the news. His solution was a good one and he arranged for all of us to go to a flat, fortunately vacant, in a Victoria Street block. I considered leaving a message in a bottle to let William know where we were, but, in the end, adopted the less romantic solution of pinning a note to the front door! We must, indeed, have looked a strange party as we left, the grown-ups carrying their most immediately necessary possessions in the sheets off their beds. No other container was usable; all our leather suitcases and trunks, stored in the basement, were the consistency of wet paper.

Inspection showed the house to be in a thoroughly insanitary state. Mud, potato peelings, and other, less identifiable pieces of rubbish dripped from the ceilings and walls of the basement: it was a truly miserable form of Neptune's cave. Our linen was filthy, and William's papers were badly damaged.

A number of strange and hitherto unknown objects lay about. One was a trunk which, when opened, was found to contain Sidney Webb's summer underwear! Another was a beautiful oriental rug. At first I thought it belonged to my mother-in-law, who stored some possessions in our basement. I had it cleaned, and later, after the house had been repaired, put it in the hall. I noticed that Susan Lawrence kept looking anxiously through the window in our front door so, catching her at it one day, I enquired: 'Is there something that interests you here?' 'Yes, that's my rug!' It was duly returned.

We experienced various reactions, good and not so good, to our unfortunate situation. Our laundry rang up and offered to wash all our badly drenched linen free of charge. This kindness we most gratefully accepted. When approaching our insurance company for compensation we encountered for the first time that ambiguous phrase 'Act of God'. I believe the insurance company was prevailed upon to moderate its early certainty about what was or was not the will of God and we got something. My mother wrote to say that she had 'seen' the flood in a dream at the exact time it happened. Clearly, she assured us, it was a case of second sight, which she had always claimed to possess!

As the house had sustained so much damage, we decided to leave Grosvenor Road for a while, make our way up to West Renfrewshire, and set our minds to winning the next election. We moved into Clyde-bank House on the beautiful esplanade that overlooks the bay at Green-ock, with a view towards Helensburgh and the nearby hills on the other side of the water. It was a delightful house from which we could conveniently visit the widely spread constituency and in which we would be able to hold meetings and garden parties.

I was expecting our third child at Christmas, and with the election a year or more away the whole prospect seemed pleasantly unhurried. Alas! We had no sooner established ourselves in West Renfrewshire and begun to meet new friends, than North Aberdeen, on the other side of Scot-land, fell vacant in the summer of 1928, and the constituency association began to ask urgently for William's immediate transference to them as candidate to fight the by-election. The Labour Whips in London intim-ated urgently that they would like William to contest this and return to the House of Commons, if successful, forthwith.

With West Renfrew's approval, there was nothing for it but to drive up to Aberdeen and set to work at once. We travelled in our first car, a dark maroon Morris Oxford of the new variety, which had cost £200; a gift from my mother. Our lack of experience in driving presented the only difficulty. In those days driving tests had not been thought of. When you bought a car from a shop or garage you took as little instruction as you thought you could get away with, or as much as you thought you needed, before driving it on the highway – nobody asking how well. Neither William nor I had had more than a lesson or so, but we bravely set off on the unknown journey, which involved negotiating such daunt-ing obstacles as the Spital of Glenshee. In the middle of this small mountain the car stopped and refused to move until I got out and walked.

Fortunately it was beautiful, late summer weather and the views were breathtaking: Dinnet Moor covered with purple heather from horizon to horizon; Loch Lomond lying still and sunlit at the foot of the Ben; and a profusion of wild strawberries to refresh us on the way.

Once arrived in Aberdeen it was useless to say: 'I am sorry I cannot climb on to rickety chairs at street corners and address open-air meetings just now.' There was the street corner, and the wobbly chair, and the meeting gathered firmly round it. People had helped me up before I knew what I was doing. This made me fear for the new baby, expected three months later. Nothing could have been less agreeable than campaigning in such circumstances; on one occasion, I lost my voice completely. The evening meetings were less alarming, though I had to go through all of them unsupported by the candidate, as we divided the meetings between us and addressed them separately.

The speeches became routine. It is surprising how a few ideas will begin to take shape into different speeches as a campaign begins. My great inspiration has always come from the prophets of Israel and their teaching on justice and mercy, and I have always tried to communicate this to others. I have never failed to find at least some warm support in a meeting for a speech along those lines.

Finally the seat was won, on 16 August 1928, and to celebrate we decided to take a few days' holiday, returning in leisurely fashion to Greenock – still my home for a few months more. Our London house had been let, after the flood repairs, till the next summer and it was obvious that I must remain in Scotland until our third child was born.

When the parliamentary session resumed in October William stayed during the week at Whitehall Court with Ernest and Gwen, returning to Scotland at weekends. It was characteristic of their generosity that they should have invited him while disliking his politics as intensely as they did. Sadly, however, the two brothers were never as close as when they were both Liberals. By this time, Ernest had become internationally known for his energetic advocacy of monetarism. He arranged regular meetings at which well-known opponents of socialism addressed his Society of Individualists.

Ernest's attitude towards me was rather amusing. He believed that women should not have minds of their own but should, in every circumstance, echo and support their husbands. Before William joined the Labour Party, Ernest had looked on me with considerable disapproval. He believed, quite wrongly, that I was trying to push William into it. Then, when William had made an irreversible decision, Ernest changed his tune completely. Looking at me with just as much severity, he announced, in a warning voice: 'Of course, you'll join the Labour Party too.'

Living in Scotland meant that I had to miss an important few months of William's life – the period in which he made the readjustment to the House of Commons, necessary on first sitting there as a Labour MP after spending twenty-three years as a left-of-centre Liberal in the Campbell-

Bannerman tradition. Ethel Snowden had often said: 'The distance is very short,' but in fact it is in some ways much bigger than might be expected. The existence of the mixed economy was taken for granted in the Liberal Party. In the Labour Party this was often true, but always with a respectful look at Clause IV of the Labour Party Constitution with its basic affirmation of the nationalisation of the means of production, distribution and exchange.

There was much more freedom in the Liberal Party, in my father's and William's day, for MPs to act on their own initiative than there was in the Labour Party. As a guerrilla fighter with the 'Wee Frees' and the Radical Group, William constantly acted according to his own judgement in conducting the fight. When he tried to produce a daily bulletin for Labour MPs, as he had done for the Liberals, he soon found his way blocked. I well remember his genuine astonishment when he was told, with good humour but with a pointed finality that allowed of no discussion, that acting on his own was 'sharp practice'. Leadership was collective. Individualism had no place in socialist politics. Everything came from below.

Whatever 'draught' he may have felt, he accepted this limitation on his liberty without complaining or looking backwards. He himself, in the generation of life that still remained to him of public service, moved steadily to the left in doctrine. In his eighties he used to speak of the 'winter sunshine' that suffused his life at home and in Parliament; and he called the Labour Party that 'warm-hearted fellowship' he had never regretted joining.

To my great delight, our third son, David, was born on 28 December 1928. Unlike my first two pregnancies, this had not been an easy one, for I had been in poor health for the whole of the time he was expected. Fortunately, during our stay in Greenock I had met and made friends with Mrs Baine, a local woman of much character whose outlook and way of life helped me by degrees to become stronger. She was a Christian Scientist of long experience who had overcome adverse circumstances in her own life and was anxious to be of help to me, among many others.

To her great disappointment I never became a Christian Scientist myself, but this in no way prevented me from experiencing a warm appreciation of all she did. I have always been grateful in particular for the acute analysis she made of my home circumstances, at a critical time, that enabled me to set right dangerously adverse circumstances within it.

I suffered so severely for months on end from weakness, lethargy and breathlessness that she asked me, one day, if there was, by any chance, some excessively dominant personality at work anywhere in my life. I could assure her that the family – and especially, my husband on whom I thought her suspicions were possibly falling – were supportive to the last degree.

Then I added that I was exceptionally fortunate in having a nanny much devoted to the children, so that whatever happened they would be cared for. In fact, I said, 'she would be wonderful with motherless children'. This remark was enough. My friend sat up straight! 'That is not your thought,' she said. 'If you don't get rid of her, she *will* be looking after motherless children.'

A little discussion of the situation called to mind the fact that this nurse was constantly leaving letters on my breakfast table demanding changes in the family routine and saying she could not stay if they were not conceded. On Mrs Baine's advice I quietly accepted the next letter of notice written to me. 'Where will you be going when you leave here?' I asked, in a matter-of-fact way. The nurse was plainly dumbfounded and could reply only: 'I don't know . . .'

I had always been interested in the scheme by which the Norland Institute trained educated girls to be children's nurses. Indeed, an aunt of mine had employed one of the earliest of these nurses to go on duty, with great success. I contacted the Institute, in London, and they wrote back to say they had only one nurse interested in a post in Scotland, a young woman called Olive Winch. Well, no mother ever had so splendid a colleague in the work of bringing up a family. From the moment she entered our home in September 1928 there was an atmosphere of peace and understanding based on willing discipline.

Many years later, a child gave me the clue to it all. I asked a little granddaughter of eight why she so much enjoyed being with Nurse Olive, whether at her home, my home or Nurse Olive's home. It was always enjoyed and looked forward to. What was the secret? The child paused thoughtfully before replying, then answered: 'Because she makes it fun to be good.' When children were with her they wanted to do what they ought to do and enjoyed doing it.

A few days after David's birth, William suggested a drive up on the hills behind our house. Rather cautiously, I agreed. We had been driving for about an hour over the moors when the car stuck and William could not move it. At first I was depressed about the situation, but, remembering Mrs Baine's advice about altering your thoughts according to your wishes, I suggested that we should get out and have an enjoyable walk across the moorland. After about an hour we came to a cottage and William knocked at the door. 'May we come in?' he said. 'My wife's just had a baby.' Not surprisingly, the couple started looking about for the baby! When the situation was explained to them they took us in, gave us a lovely tea, and then William set off, on foot, for Greenock to get help. We eventually got home at eleven at night. I had not suffered at all from my unexpected walk, and soon, with the help of Mrs Baine and Olive Winch, my general health was fully restored.

CHAPTER 7
1929–1931

We had let our house in Grosvenor Road, soon to be renamed Millbank, for a year, and now that the end of the let was approaching we were preparing to move back to our Thamesside home in the early summer of 1929. Until we could move in, we stayed at a guesthouse in Chislehurst near William's two sisters.

A general election was called for 30 May 1929. I could not go and help, as all three children were ill with whooping cough, but I was, of course, thrilled when the news came through that William had successfully defended his North Aberdeen seat. The Labour Party, with 288 seats in the House of Commons, was able to form a minority government with the support of the Liberals. Knowing that Ramsay MacDonald was in the process of forming his Cabinet, I ventured to point out that the Prime Minister would not know that William was in Chislehurst. He brushed this aside, saying: 'If he wants me he'll find me.'

Soon a telegram, forwarded from London, arrived from the Prime Minister's personal aide, Rose Rosenberg: 'Please attend Transport House immediately.' On arriving at the Labour Party headquarters, William was asked to wait in a corridor outside the Prime Minister's room. Shortly afterwards, a most unusually flushed and dishevelled Ramsay MacDonald put his head round the door and asked: 'Have you ever made a speech on India?' William replied: 'Never. I am sympathetic to Indian aims, but it's not a subject I have ever taken up in public.' Ramsay replied: 'Good. You shall take the India Office. You must have a silk hat on Saturday and we're going to Windsor,' and he disappeared without another word.

The names of the members of the new Cabinet were announced on the nine o'clock news on 7 June, my thirty-second birthday, and I realised I was the youngest of any of the Cabinet ministers' wives. Knowing that the other people in the guesthouse were not sympathetic to the Labour Party, I listened to the bulletin on the stairs outside the main sitting room. My fellow residents did not mention the subject when they saw me later.

The King was still convalescing from a severe illness, hence the need for the Cabinet to go to Windsor to kiss hands. William never forgot the journey itself. The royal train awaited them at Paddington, and both there and all along the route rows of delighted railwaymen waved their greetings. It was indeed a joyful occasion. On his way home, William took the Underground and, lapsing into a most unusual absent-mindedness, left the newly bestowed seals of office – 'those performing seals', he called them – on the train when he left it at Westminster. Their recovery took some time and trouble.

I soon found that to be the wife of the Secretary of State for India brought more duties than fell upon most Cabinet wives. Within a day or two I received an urgent communication from Colonel Patterson, William's social secretary, who announced that I should attend the royal courts, held at Buckingham Palace for a large range of people from diplomats to debutantes, and present to their Majesties all the Indian ladies who had applied and received permission to attend. The next court would take place in a week or two's time and twenty-seven ladies would require my services.

My mother's dislike of public occasions, combined with her poor health, meant that she had not been presented at court and consequently had not been able to present me. I had never taken the time or made the effort myself; now I had to do so. I immediately set about learning all the drill.

The first necessity was very pleasant: I must order a beautiful new dress with the regulation three-foot train. My dressmaker and I decided on a gold lamé, severely plain in cut, with a train to match. This was hung from the shoulders and, at the court, must be carried over the left arm except for the actual presentation, when an official would spread it out with a stick on the floor behind me. I feared that a new dress and train would be required on each occasion but was soon reassured by the fact that Queen Mary, as often as not, wore the same outfit at two successive courts.

Then there were the three 'Prince of Wales' white ostrich feathers, clustered above a flowing white tulle veil that must be attached firmly at the back of my head and slightly to the left. All this was a matter of professional arrangement with my hairdresser, who knew all the ropes. What I had to learn to do was to curtsy in the approved manner. To do it gracefully and keep one's balance, while managing a handbag and a bouquet of flowers, took quite a lot of time and effort. William also wore court dress and looked very splendid in his Privy Councillor's uniform of gold coat, knee-breeches and cocked hat.

I was under the strict direction of several court officials, one of whom told me exactly what to do and the right moment at which to do it. The courts were opened by the wives and daughters of foreign diplomats, who passed in front of the throne in order of seniority. Normally they were followed by the wife of the Secretary of State for India with the ladies she presented, and then it was the turn of the young debutantes. On this first occasion, although I was told that I would open the court, it so happened that the young Duke of Norfolk had just come of age and was making his first appearance as hereditary Earl Marshal. An official whispered in my ear: 'We're going to let his mother go before you this time,' as if I should have some objection! As soon as the Duchess of Norfolk had made her curtsy, my train was taken off my arm by a gentleman in attendance and carefully spread out behind me with a stick. I was duly launched.

On my left was the throne, elevated on a platform that held many other royalties. I advanced, made my curtsy to the King, then walked on a few steps and repeated it before the Queen, who was sitting on her throne. Both bowed graciously. Then one at a time the twenty-seven Indian ladies went forward and curtsied. I had asked Queen Mary what she wanted them to wear and she had replied, most agreeably: 'Oh, they can wear what they like. I don't mind.' They decided to wear saris with trains and feathers.

Another official deftly picked up my train and put it back over my arm, and I was then free to enjoy myself among friends and, in particular, the ladies whom I had presented and their husbands, for the rest of the evening. Flowers were in abundance, but we had been requested not to make our bouquets from heavily scented flowers as the Queen was apt to find the general effect overwhelming. After the presentations the King and Queen walked about and people would be brought up to speak to them. King George was never very talkative, but Queen Mary asked about my children and told me she believed very strongly in competitive education – 'that desirable emulation'.

All went well at my first court, but I have seen some strange sights, particularly one hilariously funny event that called for quick and unexpected action on the part of the officials in charge. A dowager peeress, clothed from head to foot, train and all, in black, with a gown embroidered with glittering sequins, was presenting a young debutante, presumably her granddaughter, swathed in white tulle. The dowager paused in front of their Majesties with impeccable and leisured dignity, making her two curtsies before moving on. Unfortunately, the girl, frightened and nervous, moved on too quickly and collided with her grandmother. Inevitably, as she turned to go, the white tulle stuck to the sequins and the whole front of the girl's dress was glued to the back of her grandmother's. In distress they tried to separate by moving first in one direction and then another, but became more and more hopelessly involved in a joint wobble, backwards and forwards, before the throne. Nothing could break them apart.

After much whispering between two senior regimental officers in full uniform, one of them drew his sword and, advancing on the hapless pair from behind, with a skilful stroke of the blade cut them apart, thus spoiling two beautiful court dresses, to say nothing of the evening for the two concerned.

Everyone present, with the exception of King George and Queen Mary, who gazed into space with admirably blank expressions, was in agonising fits of suppressed laughter. It must have been the first time that a naked sword had been brandished before a sovereign for a very long time. 'Poor pet,' murmured one compassionate woman, thinking, no doubt, of the storm awaiting the debutante on the way home.

These courts with all their rules, regulations and protocol were swept away with the outbreak of the Second World War, never to return. That was a good thing, but, for the privileged young, the courts were a delight. The surroundings were magnificent. People wore the best clothes they could afford, and such jewels as they possessed or could borrow. They met friends, also looking their best, and enjoyed it immensely.

During William's period of office it fell on us to carry out a certain amount of entertaining and this I enjoyed very much. Our dinner table at home, when extended, only held twelve, and as there were large numbers to entertain, our parties were usually held in one of the private dining rooms at the House of Commons. Once we had a very large gathering at the Banqueting Hall in Whitehall. Meeting our guest of honour, Margot Asquith, at the door, I presented her to the company. Margot, who liked to entertain in her own characteristic way with little parties and who always spoke her mind, took one look at the assembled guests and remarked, only too audibly: 'This is my idea of hell!' Unfortunately, the small intimate party we all favour is not always possible when one is officially bound to deal with large numbers in a limited time.

It was a very difficult period for William to be taking over the India Office, as the growing demand for self-government was accompanied by unrest. While sympathetic to the national aspirations of the Indian people, he realised that the great distrust that existed between the Hindu majority and the Muslim minority, who feared that an independent India would mean domination by the Hindus, would make the achievement of self-rule very difficult.

William, and Ramsay MacDonald, believed that it was necessary to proceed slowly. This meant that William found himself attacked, on one side, by members of the Independent Labour Party, such as Fenner Brockway, who wanted independence immediately, and, on the other, by the Conservative and Liberal Imperialists, such as Winston Churchill and the Marquess of Reading, a former Viceroy, who wanted Britain to continue ruling India and feared for the break-up of the Empire. William had to do almost daily battle with Winston Churchill, whose opposition was severe and unremitting.

It may seem surprising, but William had most support from the leader of the Conservatives and former Prime Minister, Stanley Baldwin; and from Lord Irwin, later Lord Halifax, whom Baldwin had appointed

Viceroy of India. When news of Cabinet appointments came out, William received a personal letter from Lord Irwin, whom he had long known in the House of Commons as the Conservative MP Edward Wood, heir of Lord Halifax. The letter expressed a warm personal welcome, saying as well: 'I believe a Labour Government was elected on the prayers of India.' Over the next two years William and Lord Irwin worked together very hard indeed.

As soon as we met Indian statesmen, we began to realise the very special relationship in which Lord Irwin stood towards India. This had begun at the moment of his arrival in Bombay on the morning of Good Friday. As soon as his ship docked, he went straight to the Cathedral without taking part in any ceremony of welcome until the service of worship was over. I can think of few, if any, British diplomats who would have taken this course. Whatever their own personal feelings might have been, they would have feared to slight the people of India by such an action.

Lord Irwin was a man of deep religious sincerity who, without any hesitation, put what to his mind were first things first. As it happened, he could not have done anything that would so quickly and completely have made the Indian people take him to their hearts. Here was a man whose integrity they immediately saw and understood and, indeed, revered.

While the Viceroy was on leave in England in the summer of 1929, he had discussions with William which led, in October, to the issuing of the so-called Irwin Declaration, making it clear that the British Government wanted eventual Dominion status for India. This meant that, after a period of time, India would be on the same footing as Canada, Australia, New Zealand and South Africa. William, Lord Irwin and Ramsay MacDonald had also decided to hold a Round Table Conference in London to discuss the way ahead. All points of view would be represented by the delegates from Britain, British India and the Indian princely states. This policy was supported by Baldwin, but opposed by Churchill and Lloyd George in the Commons, and by Reading, and Birkenhead, William's predecessor as Secretary of State, in the Lords.

During the India Bill debate on the proposals, on 7 November 1929, Lloyd George referred to William, who was short in stature, as 'this pocket edition of Moses'. Quick as a flash, William replied: 'But I never worshipped the Golden Calf.' This reference to Lloyd George's private fund was picked up at once and the joke went down very well. I have never heard such a laugh as rang out in the House of Commons; at least three times there was laughter. Lloyd George got up and said: 'Well, the calf that was sacrificed for you when you joined the Labour Party had its golden side,' referring to William's Cabinet office. Margot Asquith, who was sitting beside me in the gallery, said: 'Saying you're another is no good.'

The promise of eventual Dominion status was not enough for the main political organisation in India, the Indian National Congress, which soon demanded complete independence. In March 1930, the great Indian nationalist leader Mahatma Gandhi began a campaign of civil disobedience. British cloth was boycotted and, deciding to break the Government's salt monopoly, Gandhi marched with a group of followers to the coast and made salt, illegally, from sea water.

India was never out of our thoughts and daily lives. There was a fresh problem every morning, a fresh setback every afternoon and a fresh hope every evening. William spent hours on the telephone making state-of-the-nation calls to Lord Irwin. I used to stand by the desk supplying him with coffee and sandwiches during these nightly vigils, sometimes into the early hours of the morning. William would then wake up, after a few hours' sleep, to hear, for example, that 30,000 people were lying across the tram lines, disrupting life totally in the great cities.

Although William respected Gandhi, who advocated non-violent opposition, some of his followers were violent, and this put William, who sympathised with the Indian nationalists, in a very difficult position. He said to me: 'You must govern a country if you are in charge of it. We can't let lawlessness prevail in India.' In May 1930, the decision was taken to arrest Gandhi and his supporters. There were waves of civil unrest throughout the subcontinent, and the President of Congress, Motilal Nehru, and his son Jawaharlal, the future Prime Minister, were also arrested.

The left-wing Labour MPs found this intolerable and attacked the Government. Fenner Brockway was suspended from Parliament for not obeying the Speaker and, in the course of the commotion, Fenner Brockway's friend John Beckett seized the mace and tried to walk out with it. He was subsequently suspended too.

All through those troubled times, the statesman who gave William most help was Stanley Baldwin. When William wanted support and encouragement, as was the case during the India Bill controversy, he would often go to see Baldwin, rather than Ramsay. William and the ex-premier were personally very friendly and they used to exchange reminiscences of their youth. William told Baldwin: 'I was always being accused of getting too excited and so my parents never told me if I was going to a party in the afternoon, and when I set off they always said: "Now don't get excited at the party." ' Many years later, just before Baldwin's death, William saw him for the last time, at the Athenaeum. Sitting in an armchair, Baldwin opened his eyes when William touched his hand, and said: 'Don't get excited at the party, Willie!'

The closing months of 1930 were crowded with incident. In October an Imperial Conference was held in London for representatives from the

Dominions and India, and one occasion in particular stands out in my mind. We dined at Buckingham Palace and I wore the loveliest dress I have ever had. Made of pale turquoise chiffon, the dress and train were hand embroidered with paillettes in many shades of the same colour. The whole effect was enchanting and it attracted the attention of Winston Churchill, who was sitting opposite.

At the end of the party my friend Lesley Jowitt, the wife of the Attorney-General, Sir William Jowitt, came up to me and said: 'I've been sitting next to Winston and he pointed at you and said: "Who's that?" and I said: "Oh, that's Wedgie's wife, Peggy Benn," and he said: "Did you ever see anything more charming?" ' I have always cherished that unexpected compliment from Winston Churchill, especially as he went on to acknowledge William's war record. Looking down the table towards William, who at that time was his greatest parliamentary opponent, he said to Lesley: 'Quite right. None but the brave deserves the fair.'

Just a few days after this glittering dinner party a terrible tragedy occurred. Everyone's imagination had been excited at the prospects that seemed to lie ahead for the development of a fleet of airships, so when the experimental R101 set off for her maiden flight to India there was great enthusiasm and interest. Sadly, the airship had only got as far as France when it hit the ground near Beauvais and was destroyed by fire. There were only a few survivors out of about fifty passengers and crew. The Secretary of State for Air, Lord Thomson, who had been the driving force behind the Government-backed R101, was among those killed. Ramsay MacDonald was devastated at the loss of a man who had not only been an energetic Cabinet minister but also a close friend.

It was in sombre mood that William, representing the Government, and I made the journey to France in order to accompany the bodies back to Britain. The coffins lay in state in a large room in the Town Hall at Beauvais. We were told that the local people had been very moved by the accident and had stripped the surrounding area of flowers; they were certainly everywhere in abundance. The bodies were brought to Dover and then taken by a special train to Victoria. Arriving in the early hours of the morning, the train was met by Ramsay and his daughter, Ishbel. Thousands of people were waiting in the streets to pay tribute as the bodies were taken to lie in state. The airship programme was never resumed.

Despite the disturbances in India, and the refusal of the Congress Party to send representatives, it was decided to go ahead with the Round Table Conference. The opening ceremony was held on 12 November 1930 in the magnificent setting of the Royal Gallery of the House of Lords. Flanked by Ramsay MacDonald on his right and William on his left, King George, who was also Emperor of India, made a short speech to the assembled delegates that was broadcast by radio throughout the world.

William was at the heart of the Conference at all times. Unfortunately, neither Lord Sankey the Chairman nor Ramsay MacDonald was wholly at ease with the situation. They were constantly subjected to pressure from Lord Reading, the Liberal Leader in the Lords, who, as a former Viceroy, regarded himself as specially qualified to pronounce on Indian affairs. Without ceasing he told Sankey and Ramsay that India understood nothing but power. Let the red carpet be well kept in evidence and all would be well. Any show of weakness and all would be lost. Behind this advice there was always the unspoken 'Do this or else . . .' which kept in evidence the fact that Labour was in office, not in power, and could be removed at any moment by the Liberals.

The great problem for the delegates was to try and get an agreement between the Muslims and the Hindus. A small amount of progress appeared to have been made, despite the absence of the Congress Party, when the rulers of princely India, who were linked to British India by treaties, agreed to participate in an all-India federation as long as there were safeguards for Muslims. It was hoped that this would enable more and more power to be given to the Indian people. The conference was adjourned for further consultations on 19 January 1931 and, shortly afterwards, Gandhi and his associates were released from prison. After talks with Lord Irwin, which were supported by Baldwin but savagely attacked by Churchill, Gandhi called off the policy of civil disobedience.

We did not visit India during these years, as it was not considered proper for the Secretary of State to overshadow the Viceroy, the King's representative, but William's period of office gave me the opportunity to meet many interesting Indians who came to London. One of these was the famous Aga Khan. Best known for his racing stables, he was an astute politician and played an important role at the Round Table Conferences. I think of him, above all the people I have known, as a citizen of the world. There was no country in which he was not perfectly at home, and many in which he possessed a unique standing of his own as leader of the Ismaili sect of the Shia Muslims. It was even said that his servants sold his bathwater to believers.

Shortly before one of his visits he had married a beautiful young Frenchwoman, Andrée Carron, and I was informed that he would be asking me to present his wife at a forthcoming court. Rumour had it that she had been a seller of chocolates at the Paris Opera and, unlike the other young women to whom the Aga Khan was attracted, had had a very determined father! They called at our house and presented a lovely bunch of flowers.

As the wife of so important a subject of the King, the Begum Aga Khan would 'open' the court, that is, be presented immediately after the foreign ambassadors' wives. Faultlessly garbed in a most elegant example of Parisian haute couture, she enjoyed the occasion immensely and showed herself to be amused rather than impressed by the traditional attire of the Aga Khan, who was standing on the royal dais. 'Look at the Prince,' she whispered to me in French. 'Doesn't he look just like a sorcerer?' And she laughed heartily. When next I met her, the following year, she had become the mother of a son, Sadruddin. 'It has certainly changed my life,' she said. Many years later when I asked the Aga Khan how his wife was he replied: 'Oh, we have separated. She was too busy playing golf to look after me.'

The convening of the first Round Table Conference in 1930 brought meetings with a large number of Indian statesmen and princes, and their wives. Dinner parties abounded, varying in size from a dozen or so guests gathered at the hotel where the host was staying, to immense parties for some hundreds of people.

As I am not first and foremost a politician, what I particularly enjoyed was meeting so many people of different religious beliefs and encouraging them to talk to me about them. I always found much interest in listening to the guests between whom I was placed. On one side might be sat a maharajah who followed the Buddhist faith; on the other a Hindu or a Muslim statesman. Among these I specially remember Sir Akbar Hydari, Finance Minister of His Exalted Highness the Nizam of Hyderabad, and friend of the novelist E. M. Forster. He was a delightful man, witty, learned, kindly, humorous, and a devout Muslim. When I found myself beside him at dinner I knew that our conversation would go far beyond the bounds of current politics. He was delighted to find a British woman happy and eager to share in his long search for truth and to hear what he had discovered.

Sir Akbar told me how, for a very long time, it had been difficult for him to accept the beliefs and discipline of his faith. Laughing, he said: 'I fear that I was for many years, intellectually, a very bad man!' Then, by degrees, he began to understand what the Prophet was saying and to enter into the essential meaning and message of Islam. This had brought him complete contentment and a certainty that he was pursuing the path intended. Peace abounded in his presence.

Sir Akbar and his wife were opposed to the system whereby Muslim women led secluded lives, and Lady Hydari had caused a sensation by coming out of purdah. Sir Akbar jokingly said that on that day the shopping his wife did cost him hundreds of pounds! They were a most delightful couple, and when they came to see us at our house brought lovely traditional costumes for our children which they very much enjoyed wearing.

I was given two beautiful saris as presents, one of which, in gold and yellow, I still have; the other, in a lovely, most beautifully contrasted sky blue and pink, I eventually gave to the Victoria and Albert Museum.

When I wore the saris at parties I was pleased that people liked and admired them.

Among the other Muslim delegates, I remember Sir Mohammed Shafi and his daughter, the Begum Shah Nawaz, one of the two female delegates at the Round Table Conference. The presence of these two women gave great satisfaction as it showed the rate at which progress by Indian women in public life was being achieved. The Begum Shah Nawaz wrote a book *Father and Daughter at the Round Table Conference*, about her experiences.

There were, however, some Indian statesmen, like the Muslim Mohammed Ali Jinnah, with whom it was impossible to make any warm contact at all. He gave the appearance of being wrapped in impenetrable bitterness. Muslims such as Jinnah made it difficult to see how people of the two faiths could ever become one nation and live together. So it ultimately proved, and when India became independent the predominantly Muslim areas became Pakistan, with Jinnah as President.

Among the princes whom we saw frequently was Sir Hari Singh, the Maharajah of Kashmir. On a previous visit he had become a blackmail victim, and although, in the ensuing court case, he was named only as 'Mr A', his identity inevitably leaked out and caused some embarrassment. He now hoped to put it all behind him and appeared with a new young wife, who was introduced as the fourth Maharanee. As a third marriage was considered unlucky, it was rumoured that after divorcing his second wife he had been married to a tree. This left him free to marry for a fourth time with some hope of success.

The Maharanee of Kashmir was plainly not overawed by her new status and was up to many pranks. Sir Hari appeared to be somewhat concerned when his wife was placed next to William at dinner. Anxiously he whispered in William's ear: 'Please look out. She'll probably shower your soup with pepper!' After dinner the Maharajah entertained us to the theatre where, by an unfortunate piece of misjudgement on the part of his advisers, the play chosen was all about blackmail!

The princes varied greatly in nature and outlook. I particularly recall one sad case of a maharajah who belonged to an exclusive Brahmin sect. On his first appearance in London he gave a dinner party for us at which he sat neither eating nor drinking as his faith demanded. But the next year, when he came a second time, the desire to move nearer to the West had completely overruled this exclusiveness. The result was that he had quite obviously become an alcoholic, and one dinner party at which he entertained William and me had to break up early because he was no longer able to preside.

I was much attracted by the quiet, poised charm of the Nawab of Bhopal and his wife. His charm was due to his great integrity. After dinner a servant brought in the complicated apparatus of a 'hubble-bubble' hookah pipe and he sat in perfect contentment smoking it.

The Maharajah of Bikaner was completely at home in both East and West. He gave wonderful dinner parties, always with some purely Indian courses prepared by his own chef and assistants. He showed a considerate interest in the welfare of his guests. Once, when a plate of oysters was put before me, he said: 'If you get a bitter one, spit it out – never mind who's there!' The Maharajah also gave us information on some of his brother princes. About one in particular there was endless gossip. The Maharajah of Bikaner and his party had been given a sunny suite of hotel rooms which the other Maharajah coveted. He sent a message to Bikaner asking for an exchange, as his wife was expecting a baby. 'Of course I agreed at once,' said Bikaner, 'knowing perfectly well the reason was bogus.' 'Why bogus?' I asked. 'Oh,' said the Maharajah, 'no senior maharanee from that state would come to London, particularly if she was pregnant!'

The India Office did their best to get my husband to ignore this notorious maharajah. They said he was probably the most evil human being alive – very nearly a savage – and should not be entertained by the Secretary of State. He taxed his peasants to the limit and was rumoured to be a sadist. He would capture lions, tie them to the ground and run over them in his motor car. Knowing that the princes would be asked to give up a great deal in the coming reforms and wanting to keep them well in the picture, William took no notice of the warning. This prince, the Maharajah of Alwar, happened to give a dinner party for us at the Hyde Park Hotel and during the course of it declared that he had a great wish to visit us in our own home and meet our children, Michael then aged nine, Anthony aged five and two-year-old David.

An afternoon was duly fixed and I set out to prepare the children for what to expect when he arrived. The Maharajah of Alwar dressed in a very exotic fashion: an ankle-length robe, often of gold brocade; ropes of pearls, and other jewellery, round his neck; diamonds in his nose and both ears; a magnificent coronet, set with glittering diamonds, on his head. Believing himself to be descended from the Sun Goddess, he wore white gloves at all times so that he would not be corrupted by touching the hand of a mere mortal. I knew the children would not have seen anything like this before and was afraid that the strangeness might frighten them.

At tea-time on the appointed day the Maharajah duly arrived with an aide who remained waiting in an adjoining room. To our surprise, when His Highness came into our library we saw that for the first time ever he was not wearing his gloves. We seated him in an armchair and immediately he called to the three children. Beckoning Michael and Anthony to sit down on adjoining chairs, he invited David to sit on his knee. Then I trembled indeed! Would the Round Table Conference be wrecked by the children's frightened reaction? But my anxiety was quite unnecessary. To my relief and astonishment, David immediately climbed on to our visitor's knee and, looking first at the Maharajah's feet and then at his own, remarked in the most friendly fashion: 'I've got red shoes, too!'

From then on for the next half-hour or so the Maharajah ignored us completely and devoted himself entirely to entertaining the children. He told them fascinating tales, one after the other, of the jungle in his native Alwar and of other places he had visited. 'The lion', he told them, 'is a bold beast. He does not mind who sees him and believes he is the master of any situation. But the tiger is quite different. He is a crafty creature. He keeps himself hidden and you will only know he is there by the gleaming of his eyes through the undergrowth.' The boys were enthralled.

After this delightful home interlude to the Round Table negotiations, I always found it difficult to believe that the Maharajah was as bad as he was painted. Not long afterwards I heard something of his state of mind that threw light on the situation. Among the members of the India Council, based at the India Office for purposes of consultation and advice to the Secretary of State, was a highly experienced man of great warmth and perception who had the gift of getting into personal touch with Indians of all sorts. When I told him of Alwar's visit to us, he said that only recently the Maharajah had come to him for a long talk, during the course of which he had confessed to a deep personal depression. 'My life', he said in despair, 'is a complete failure. Tell me how to put it right.' To which came the harsh but sincere and friendly reply: 'Reverse everything you do.'

Alwar, it appeared, had been totally under the influence of his guru, who died during the Maharajah's visit to London. 'The best news I've had,' said my friend on the India Council. How far the Maharajah changed his way of life I do not know, but I was very pleased that he sent me interesting books on Buddhism for some years. He certainly had few friends and many enemies and sadly, but probably inevitably, he was assassinated some years later in Paris when returning to his hotel after a round of tennis.

Before he returned to India at the end of the first Round Table Conference there was further fun in store for us with the Maharajah of Alwar. William and I had been invited by Ramsay MacDonald to see in the new year, 1931, with him and his family at Number 10 Downing Street. We were to go along after dinner and stay into the small hours. On that evening we dined with the Maharajah of Alwar, who said that he was going to the country directly after the meal.

I then told him that in my native Scotland the last day of the old year was an important occasion called Hogmanay. It was the custom for families to stay at home and await some special person who would call and pay them the first visit of the New Year. 'First footing' it was called and the visitor, who always arrived with a gift, brought particularly good luck if he happened to have dark hair.

I reminded him that the Prime Minister was a Scot like myself and would especially appreciate having this honour paid to him. Would not the Maharajah put off his visit to the country till next day and appear at the stroke of midnight bearing a small gift? He was much taken with the whole idea and immediately said he would carry it out to the letter.

William and I duly arrived at 10 Downing Street at about ten-thirty, where we found a family party of Ramsay, Ishbel, Sheila, and Ramsay's younger son, Malcolm, whom his father always called 'Molcolm'. Also present was the distinguished portrait painter Sir John Lavery. I was interested to meet him because he had painted a portrait of my mother the year before her marriage.

Unfortunately, John Lavery was at that time much enamoured of the artist Whistler, and was determined to paint my mother in Whistler's style. The result was a 'one-eyed picture' done in profile of my mother in a sombre black dress wearing a bonnet – the only one she ever had. The whole outfit quenched her buoyant personality completely and was regarded as a failure by the family. It was done at an early time in his career when he was poor and struggling and my mother said he took fifty sittings, each followed by a hot lunch! When he became better known he had asked to retouch the painting, and when it came back my mother discovered that he had removed his signature! By the time of our meeting, Sir John Lavery was rich and famous and accompanied by a lively wife.

While we waited for the New Year to come in we all exchanged memories of life in Scotland, and when it came to first footing Lady Lavery said: 'Well, if there should be a visitor tonight I guarantee to throw my arms round him and embrace him warmly.' And so the jokes went on. As the chimes of Big Ben rang out, the door opened and the parlourmaid announced: 'The Maharajah of Alwar.' In came our 'first footer' bearing a bottle of whisky! We all pressed forward to welcome him and receive his greetings for 1931 while Lady Lavery collapsed in shock on the sofa! It was noticed that the Maharajah had left his gloves in the hall and was shaking hands, unprotected, with us ordinary mortals. The rest of the evening went with a swing and the Maharajah joined in the fun with much relish.

Just before this incident there had been an unscheduled two-day conference at Chequers, the Prime Minister's country house, to try and resolve the differences between the Hindus and the Muslims. Chequers itself was full and the British delegates were asked to stay at an hotel. Wives were not invited to this conference, but William and I decided to make a short holiday of it together. On the last night Ramsay told his secretary, Rose Rosenberg, to ask me to dinner. She replied in surprise: 'But Mrs Benn's not here!' 'Are you so sure?' replied Ramsay. 'I have never known the Benns be far apart.' So I duly attended.

It was late when the party broke up, and we set off for London with some misgivings. Soon a heavy snowstorm came down and visibility was poor. London seemed an impossible target. We should probably be snowed up and freeze to death. I suggested that we sought the well-known Quaker guesthouse, Jordans, and beg for a night's lodging. It was midnight, or later, before we found it and only one upstairs window was still lit up. With much trepidation we knocked on the great front door. Presently a woman's cautious voice called down to ask what we wanted. William told her our difficulty and asked for shelter. Not surprisingly, the Quaker lady asked: 'Are you Friends?' A look of amazement crossed William's face. He threw up his hands in shocked denial of the supposed implication. 'Certainly not! We're man and wife,' he assured her. Gusts of laughter floated down and, in greater astonishment than before, William turned to me. 'Whatever have I said?' he asked.

Soon the great doors opened and we were taken in to enjoy one of the most pleasant weekends I can remember. There was that wonderful peace and quiet – refreshing and energising – that Quakers know how to create. I was told that this story went all round the Society of Friends, and we certainly met it over and over again.

The years 1929 to 1931 were years of economic depression and rising unemployment and the Labour Government was put under increasing pressure. After Tom Mosley resigned from the Government because his programme of economic expansion was not taken up, Ramsay MacDonald began to think tariffs on imports were the answer but was opposed by Snowden. William, a lifelong free-trader, was also against protectionism.

In May 1931 a financial collapse in Austria and Germany affected Britain and by August a quarter of the sterling reserves had gone. The Cabinet was told by the financial institutions that foreign confidence had to be restored by balancing the budget and cutting government spending. Eventually the Cabinet voted on whether unemployment benefits should be cut. A small majority, including William, voted for cuts, but MacDonald realised the Labour Government could not continue with such a divided cabinet.

On 24 August 1931 the Labour Government resigned and Ramsay MacDonald, on the urging of King George, formed a National Government. It was overwhelmingly Conservative, and Ramsay, flattered to be told that he was needed to keep the country together, was really a prime minister without a party. Most of the Liberals joined the Coalition, but only a tiny number of Labour MPs. We knew, from much conversation with him ever since joining the Labour Party, that Ramsay was deeply estranged from it, and so the eventual break-up was no surprise. William detested coalitions. He considered that it was impossible for members of them to be themselves. Everyone had to accept a lot of what they thought wrong in order to get a little of what they believed to be right.

On the morning the National Government was formed, I was in the room when Ramsay phoned William to say goodbye. He was in an unexpectedly doleful mood and thoroughly downhearted about his own position: 'You see what is happening? I've been asked to lead this coalition because it's felt that it's what the country needs – I think it is the end of my career. I don't think I shall last very long, but they've said I'm needed. It will take time but a few of you will bring the Party round to sanity again. You will be able to save the soul of the Party. I am doing the only thing I can do at the moment.' He indicated that the way he himself was taking was not the path of sanity. This of course differed widely from the substance of all his speeches made to the nation at the time. He was suffering from many conflicting thoughts, fears and emotions and it is quite possible that his words expressed one genuine aspect of these.

Finally, he said: 'I'm not going to ask you to join the National Government, because I don't think it's your job. It's the job of you and a few people like you to pull the Party straight again and keep it as straight as you possibly can. That will be a very big job to do.' William and Ramsay parted with words of friendship and good will. I really do not think Ramsay expected to stay in the National Government as long as he did.

The Maharajah of Alwar sent him a telegram from India saying, 'See what success my visit brought you!' Ishbel MacDonald, who did not like her father being Prime Minister of the National Government, had her own views about that! She always believed that if her mother had been alive, Ramsay would not have taken the way that he did.

A general election was held on 27 October 1931 and the result was disastrous for the Labour opposition, which won only fifty-two seats. William was decisively defeated in North Aberdeen. The campaign was unlike any other in which I have taken part. Our meetings were huge and completely silent. There were no cheers and no boos. People were exceedingly puzzled and had clearly come for information and meant to get it. Rumours flew around like wildfire. One of the most persistent was the malicious one that, if returned, Labour would confiscate Post Office savings accounts to meet the crisis. Lord Grey, the former Foreign Secretary, normally a much-respected statesman, gave it as his considered opinion that it would be a good thing if the Parliament now to be elected did not contain a single Labour member.

The election had taken place during the second Round Table Conference, which had opened in September 1931. William was fully involved in this although ceasing to be Secretary of State in August. He had been largely responsible for organising the conference and had arranged for Gandhi to come to London to represent the Congress Party, much against the advice of the India Office. Gandhi stayed in the East End of London and lived a genuinely simple life, but the right-wing press was very snide and, assuming that his lifestyle was just a pretence, suggested that he ordered all his meals from Fortnum and Mason.

William had an extremely difficult time getting King George to consent to Gandhi's coming to an afternoon party at Buckingham Palace. Finally agreeing, the King said: 'Well, I hope he puts in his false teeth!' Gandhi only used false teeth for eating and after a meal put them in his pocket. William said to me: 'Well really! Doesn't the King know what a rare character he's got in Mr Gandhi? How strange he doesn't realise.' Gandhi arrived at the party wearing his loincloth and an old shawl. He came in, put in his false teeth and gave the King a double handshake. A few words were exchanged and Gandhi turned, took out his teeth and walked out!

One day while the conference was in progress, the Liberal Indian politician V. S. Srinavasa Sastri told me that he had met Ramsay Mac-Donald and Gandhi that morning and each, without prompting, had told him that they found the other intolerably vain!

Unfortunately, the Second Round Table Conference did not resolve the problems of India, and although a Government of India Act was passed in 1935, the princes changed their minds about a federal system. When independence finally came in 1947, India was divided into two states, one predominantly Hindu, the other predominantly Muslim. This was accompanied by terrible bloodshed.

When we visited India in the 1950s William and Mr Mavalankar, the Speaker of the Indian Parliament, discussed, with the benefit of hindsight, the early years of the civil disobedience campaign. William spoke of the distaste and reluctance with which the Labour Government had imprisoned Gandhi and thousands of his supporters in the necessary interests of public order while they themselves unswervingly supported the ultimate aims of Congress for self-government. When William said that this attitude had been widely shared in Britain, Mr Mavalankar declared it had been at the heart of the whole matter: 'Gandhi was inseparable from the British. A dictator would have crushed him from the outset!'

CHAPTER 8

Germany, USA, Japan, 1931–1934

Now that William was again out of Parliament, his first thought was to use this unusual spare time to learn something new. Beginning by quoting vigorously from the posters we had seen in the Soviet Union – 'Workers of the World – Improve your Qualifications!' – he decided that becoming more proficient in foreign languages would be the most useful means of pursuing his overarching aim of world peace. French and Italian he spoke fluently; his German, on the other hand, was still halting. So to Germany we went, in the summer of 1932.

William's decision was part of the fundamental change in his aims and outlook brought about by the war. From 1906 to 1914 he had concentrated on the Liberal agenda of social reform; but of what use was a perfectly ordered society in Great Britain if the world outside showed the constant likelihood of disrupting it by constant threats of war?

The situation in Germany was increasingly, and alarmingly, unstable. At the end of the First World War the Weimar Republic had been set up with a government based in the city of that name; but by 1932 the economic conditions were so bad that the Republic was coming under increasing pressure from Adolf Hitler's National Socialist Party – the Nazis – and it was to be only a matter of months before it fell.

Enquiries at the Foreign Office as to where their intending diplomats were trained in the German language, gave us the name of Marburg, the university city on the river Lahn, fifty miles north of Frankfurt; and the address of Frau von Pritzelwitz, the lady who received students in her large and hospitable home.

We set out for our two-month visit with a good supply of books. William's were in German; mine in English and classical Hebrew. When our baggage was searched at the frontier, I found that the security guards, already under the influence of Hitler, did not take kindly to my theological pursuits. In a country where anti-Semitism was growing, my interest in Hebrew made me an object of great suspicion. I recall vividly the lengthy and puzzled examination to which we were subjected. 'All these books? Why?' demanded the inquisitor. Fortunately, William was able to explain that we were students. Our combined ages at the time being ninety, this took some swallowing, but we eventually crossed the frontier without anything being confiscated.

To stay with a group of young people of several nationalities busy obtaining qualifications was a new and delightful experience. Among them we found some whose parents we knew and who, later, made a name for themselves, such as Anthony Greenwood, a future Labour Cabinet minister.

In one respect we really were happy and carefree students. We talked and laughed in Frau von Pritzelwitz's home, and every day, after lunch, I enjoyed sitting in the nearby Café Schloss. But, at the same time, a sinister atmosphere pervaded everything, and, as I drank my coffee, bands of brown-shirted Hitler Youth marched past. They sang a song with a haunting lilt with which I was unfamiliar. Alas! we were all to know it too well later on in Britain: it was the 'Horst Wessel Song', the Nazi anthem. William and I bought a recording of it, which I still have.

We became particularly friendly with an elderly teacher, Fräulein Ditzen. The aunt of Hans Fallada, the novelist, she was much travelled, very knowledgeable about European affairs, and contemptuous of Mussolini and Hitler. She knew many of the leading academics in Marburg and gave us introductions to such internationally renowned biblical scholars as the Old Testament specialist Professor Karl Budde and, above all, the very eminent Professor Rudolf Otto, famous for his book *Das Heilige – The Idea of The Holy.*

Dr Budde received William and me most cordially, fearing only that his English would not be equal to answering my questions. This was more than a little daunting, but fortunately I had some examples of his work with me and could ask him to elaborate on such matters as the controversial passage in the Old Testament which had been translated as 'Behold, a virgin shall conceive, and bear a son, and shall call his name Immanuel', and which had been taken as the prophecy believed to be fulfilled in the virgin birth of Jesus of Nazareth. Budde believed that this translation of Isaiah 7:14 was questionable and that the word 'virgin' was more likely to mean 'young woman'. He answered my questions most courteously, adding disarmingly that at his age he really did not remember much beyond what he was studying at the time. When he spoke he displayed a complete set of gold teeth that gave him a strangely affluent appearance.

He was known as not only a distinguished scholar but a deeply committed and most devout Christian worshipper, always in his place Sunday by Sunday in church. This, said Fräulein Ditzen, could not be said of Rudolf Otto: 'You will not see him in church: the air doesn't agree with him.'

Unlike Karl Budde, Dr Otto did not give the impression of being a happy man. It seemed as if his great learning had set him apart in a world where the penalty was to suffer a perpetual and unbridgeable loneliness.

His vivid blue eyes had a great sadness in them. It was, however, reassuring, and even cheering, to note a touch of human vanity in the bright blue tie and socks that were clearly chosen to match them.

William and I had many walks with him round Marburg. The conversation at these meetings was mainly about contemporary politics, about which Dr Otto was most unhappy, as were all the 'good' Germans we met. He could see no future for his country if the Weimar Government was overturned.

Unfortunately, I gained the impression that he did not care for women in general. He surveyed me with some disfavour and thought my interest in the Old Testament 'a strange one for a woman'. I know from what I have read and heard of his conversations with the great scholar Dr Martin Buber, whom I met in Jerusalem many years later, that Rudolf Otto was himself deeply interested in the Old Testament, and I wondered if it was his dislike of women that made him want them to keep out of it. I much regretted that I could make no headway with him in conversation.

Our meeting had one good effect, however, for it led me to study Dr Otto's famous book, where he writes with such profound learning and understanding of the 'numinous'. He believed that it is only when a sense of this spiritual dimension of life has been brought to the knowledge of a human being that religious experience can begin, and not before. When I thought this over there came before me a scene from my very early life when at the age of four at the French hospice I followed the gracious nuns round the chapel and dropped to my knees when they dropped to theirs in silent worship. This was my first encounter with the numinous, and from that time there came into my life a sense of presence that has been its most precious possession ever since.

For six years we kept in touch with our German friends, receiving from Fräulein Ditzen a number of ironical postcards whose *doubles entendres* had been entirely missed, as she knew they would be, by the Nazi authorities who had come to power the year after our visit. 'What do you think', she would write of some crazy new policy, 'about our Government's latest move to make all Aryans embrace?' At Christmas a postcard would wish us well and relate that 'our German he-men celebrate the festival round a mulberry bush'. This was a reference to the rejection of Christianity by the Nazis in favour of pagan celebrations.

The relationship between Britain and Germany deteriorated during these years, bringing us to the brink of war by the autumn of 1938. But as a result of the fateful Munich agreement by which the British Prime Minister, Neville Chamberlain, appeased Hitler and allowed him to annex a part of Czechoslovakia, the threat receded. Putting aside our recently issued gas-masks, we set off post haste to see what had been happening to our friends in Marburg during those dark and ominous days. We arrived in time to watch the German troops returning from Czechoslovakia.

Happy crowds pelted them with flowers and they themselves carried thankful banners reading: 'The War is Over. Home to Mother.'

Frau von Pritzelwitz ridiculed Hitler in a most outspoken manner. Knowing that her niece was a supporter of the Nazis, I cautioned: 'Is it wise to say these things in front of your niece?' Our hostess replied: 'She won't denounce me, she gets a free meal here every day.' There was at that time great poverty in Germany.

'We are in the hands of amateurs,' was the distressed cry of Fräulein Ditzen – a view echoed by other responsible German citizens. Their relief at the passing of the crisis was tremendous. Alas! It was to be short-lived. Soon they all vanished from our ken in the chaos of war. Fräulein Ditzen remained longest in sight and, while communications were open, her postcards came triumphantly through. No doubt the Nazi postal authorities, with no sense of humour, took them all at their face value. But, finally, there was silence.

In January 1933 we decided to visit the United States for the first time. William planned to pay for the two-month trip by a lecture tour – a crowd-pulling activity in the days before television. Seeking advice from the doyen of lecturers, the journalist S. K. Ratcliffe, who had spent every spring in the States for many years and knew exactly what audiences wanted, we invited him and his wife to dinner.

After discussing the American lecture scene very fully over the meal, we adjourned to our library. Looking back on that evening, I realise it was the only occasion when the actual seating of a visitor in my home changed the course of my subsequent life. I gave Mrs Ratcliffe my own easy chair, specially sited next to my bookshelves. From there she turned her eyes on their contents and asked me, presently: 'Are you a daughter of the manse?' 'No,' I replied, 'why?' 'I wondered if you had inherited these theological books.' 'They were either bought by me or were gifts,' I was able to tell her.

She thereupon wrote down and gave me a name and address in New York. 'As soon as you arrive,' she said, 'you must get in touch with a great friend of mine and our daughter's, Ursula Keppel-Compton, who graduated from Oxford with first-class honours in Theology, was sent on a scholarship to Union Theological Seminary and has just married the rising star of Union, Dr Reinhold Niebuhr, Professor of Christian Ethics.'

Arriving in New York, we made contact with the Niebuhrs. Ursula told me a great deal about her year of research at Union and how Reinhold, a confirmed bachelor sixteen years older than herself, had become a devoted suitor. Eventually, his proposal, like William's, had taken the form of a statement, not a question: 'Well, Ursula, I suppose it's inevitable!'

They were married at Winchester Cathedral and someone told me that it was the only marriage he had ever attended at which there had been a spirit of worship. But it was not easy for Reinhold's mother to adjust to the new situation. Widowed at an early age, she had got used to running Reinhold's home for him and wanted to remain the most important woman in his life. She said to him: 'If you're going to marry you must live at home. Ursula can go on being an intellectual and I'll take care of the house.' Well, Ursula would not accept that arrangement and insisted on having her own home. They had only been married a year when we arrived, and were having a very difficult time trying to make Reinhold's mother understand the new situation. Ursula was pleased to see another British woman and I was able to sympathise with her predicament, having experienced something similar myself with William's mother. I was pleased to be able to give Ursula and Reinhold some helpful advice and support at a crucial stage of their marriage.

It is not easy to describe such a great man as Reinhold Niebuhr in a few words. The son of German immigrants, he followed his father into the ministry and eventually became pastor of a church in Detroit. Having observed the struggle between the car workers and their employers, he devoted his whole life to trying to bring into being a society that was just, compassionate and free, for he believed that Christianity should be applied to political issues. He cared greatly for people, telling me on one occasion that the appropriate gesture for a preacher, a pastor and a parent was not 'push' but 'pull'. People should be charmed into righteousness. His favourite figure of speech was the paradox and, for me, his most seminal phrase was: 'Man's capacity for justice makes democracy possible; but man's inclination to injustice makes democracy necessary.' By the late 1930s he was one of the most respected theologians in the United States and had established an international reputation which continued to grow throughout the next decade. When war broke out, at a time when many Americans were isolationist, he urged the American Government to aid the Allied cause and to take in more Jewish immigrants. In 1948 he achieved the distinction of being on the front cover of *Time* magazine's twenty-fifth anniversary edition.

I was intrigued by the differences between Ursula and Reinhold. Ursula, for example, loved flowers and always had them in the house. Reinhold, looking at a vase of them, was likely to remark: 'Look at that doggone thing!' On one occasion when he was lecturing in Glasgow, his friends, quite desperate about his addiction to politics, took him to Loch Lomond for the day. On being asked for his reaction, Reinhold remarked: 'Oh, well – in the ultimate analysis . . .'

Ursula told me that Reinhold had sometimes felt the difference in their ages to be unfair to her, but that after seeing how happy William and I were with an even greater gap of twenty years, he was reassured. In many ways they complemented each other perfectly. Both were academics but of a different variety. Reinhold used to say that Ursula was more the theologian while he concerned himself with the issues of the day and their political implications for the Christian churches and society.

After our first meeting, whenever we went to the United States or they came to Britain we would call on each other. I was overjoyed that my political family should meet Ursula and Reinhold and should be enabled to hear them ask: 'Is religion necessary?' and answer it in the affirmative. This was the great question I wanted them to consider seriously. The meeting with Ursula and Reinhold was the beginning of a lifelong friendship. However scattered the family might be, they all made for home when the Niebuhrs were coming.

While in New York I decided to track down Uncle James, my father's brother. After much detective work a clue arrived in a letter from the postmaster of Greenwich Village, just before we had to leave for London: 'About sixteen years ago a James Holmes lived here – a genial, steady man and he came from Scotland.' Following it up, I was delighted to discover that the man in question was indeed my Uncle James. On my next visit I wrote to my uncle and invited him to lunch at my hotel in New York. I sat by the door and I knew him the minute he came in as the upper part of his face was just like my father's. I had a charming letter from him afterwards.

We enjoyed our first visit to a country where everyone was so hospitable – 'a nation "pleased to meet you"' was William's description – but were very distressed by evidence of the economic hardship caused by the Great Depression. While William was lecturing, I travelled on my own by Greyhound buses from New York to Florida and from the Gulf of Mexico to New England. Usually I slept in the bus but sometimes in a hotel. A notice in one hotel warned me: 'Soliciting is strictly forbidden!'

On the journey to Florida, I sat over the wheel and the bus was so primitive that it gave me a permanent throb in my ears. People were boarding the bus and offering the driver bits of jewellery because all the banks had defaulted and they could not get their money out. The financial system was in chaos and there was mass unemployment and great poverty.

But the turning point was only a few days away. Listening to the radio on 4 March 1933, from the comfort of a swimming pool in Florida, I heard President Roosevelt's first inaugural address. With the famous words 'the only thing we have to fear is fear itself', he launched the New Deal and promised to put the unemployed back to work.

Not only his politics, but also his character and personal courage, inspired the American people. One woman said to me: 'If anybody can save us, he can; because he is a Christian man and has suffered himself.' She was referring to Roosevelt's fight against polio. With great determination, he had defied the doctors' advice to retire and, by adopting a strict exercise regime, had managed to continue his political career. He certainly was a very remarkable man, and his battle against disability set an example for the nation.

William's lectures had been so well received that we returned to the United States the following year for a nationwide tour. As before, we left our children and the house in the capable hands of our trusted colleague, Nurse Olive Winch. She answered our mail with a supply of postcards which informed the recipients of our absence and promised a reply on our return.

On this occasion William and I had the fascinating experience of a meeting with Henry Ford at his enormous Dearborn car works in Detroit. His lean body, agile manner and rippling grey hair parted near the middle made him appear younger than his seventy years. The severity of his face was modified by keen blue-grey eyes with a kindly twinkle. In dress, he seemed something of a dandy because his shirt and tie were made to match a suit of brown and white with a largish check.

Something he said during the conversation made me ask: 'Mr Ford, do you believe in reincarnation?' Dropping his former reserved manner, he became very animated: 'Yes, ma'am, I most certainly do. I've been here millions of times before and I'll come back millions of times in the future.' 'On the same sort of job?' I enquired. 'Oh no, I've done all sorts of jobs.' Leaning forward he said with great deliberation: 'I feel quite certain that I brought nothing into this world but my past experience and I shall take nothing out but what I am now adding to that store.' He justified privilege because it was the reward for a virtuous previous life. As we left he pressed my hand and said: 'You and I could converse for a week without exchanging a word.' I thought: 'Goodness me, am I a soul mate of Henry Ford?' I asked his aide: 'Does Mr Ford find time to study Oriental philosophy?' 'No, ma'am, I've never known Mr Ford to be a student of anything other than his own ideas.'

Touring the works, we saw the famous production line where each man did his own special operation every few seconds. It seemed a most deadening and soulless experience for the worker as the whole emphasis was on increasing the speed of the process, while the only point of contact between the employee and the employer was the wage packet. No unions were allowed in the plant and Henry Ford did not concern himself with the provision of old age pensions or welfare work. At the Ford works individual effort was everything. Later, in the Soviet Union, we observed the reverse: there the team was supposed to be everything, the individual nothing. Neither of the two extremes was to our liking.

After journeying throughout the States and staying for a while on the West Coast of America, William thought it would be sensible to travel home through Japan, China and the Soviet Union. We sailed for Yokohama after enjoying a short stay in Hawaii, where Pearl Harbor was then hardly known. Arriving in Japan nine days after leaving Honolulu we were met, as we came down the gangway of the *President Hoover,* by an icy wind which numbed our hands and feet. It was woefully far from being the rare enchanted moment that we hoped our first arrival in Japan would be, especially at a time when daily radio bulletins, picked up by the ship, had been informing the world that, within a few days, the 'Cherry Blossom viewing' would be at its height. I bought a recording of the 'Cherry Blossom Song', which I still possess.

All the way from Yokohama to Tokyo we saw the decorations going up. Even the meanest street had produced its quota of trees, set in tubs and realistically hung with clouds of pinky-white paper blossoms. When we arrived, in brilliant sunshine, the perfect snow-capped cone of Mount Fuji had just risen majestically out of the mists below and stood, eerily isolated, on the horizon. Throughout our stay we noticed that on those 'lucky days' when Fujiyama was visible everyone in the hotel smiled more than ever and seemed even happier than usual.

Even during the course of our short stay we could see that the scenery of Japan had deeply affected its people. Every home contained not one but many representations of nature. The world of nature had been brought indoors to inspire, to rest and to refresh the people during those hours that they had to spend away from it. Each Japanese room contained a little raised platform set in an open recess and known as the 'Most Honourable Place', where there hung, invariably, one seasonable scroll: in the heat of the summer perhaps a waterfall, in winter something that suggested the returning life of spring; and underneath the picture there was always one exquisite piece of floral decoration.

In Tokyo alone, we were told, there were two thousand teachers of flower arranging. Fixed principles and rigid rules underlay unlimited possibilities of variation. Of these we grasped only two. First, flowers must be arranged in three degrees, or lengths, representing, respectively, the tallest, Heaven; the lowest, Earth; and the middle group, Man. Secondly, they must look as though they were growing. The fewest possible flowers, leaves and branches were used, and the result was always restrained, exquisite and satisfying.

But this was not the only form of decoration; there were also the nature scenes that young girls were taught how to make for the adornment of the home. The material consisted of a black lacquer tray, without rim, and an endless quantity and variety of real silver-white sand, pebbles, infinitesimal boulders, little mother-of-pearl sailing ships, sampans, sea-gulls and moons, and of course the snowy cone of Fujiyama. William and I watched as, under skilful fingers and the touch of many finely graded quill brushes, a picture arose in a few moments that was an ethereal idealisation and yet full of realistic truth.

We observed that Japanese gardens never suggested man's triumphant toil but always nature made perfect. A Japanese garden carries you a step beyond nature itself and suddenly shows you some abstract idea, such as peace and solitude. This world in miniature with its tiny lake in which are mirrored the clouds, bridges, lanterns, flowers and trees suggests not an empty stillness but the brooding tranquillity of a reflecting mind.

All the time we were in Japan we were conscious of some idea being conveyed: always, whether in a garden or in a theatre or in a picture, art was holding up the mirror to nature and to society. And everywhere we were conscious of that harmonious order, that disciplined subordination to some central thought, that we found in the gardens and in the flower arranging. Not only the individual home but all society was instinct with it.

It was characteristic of the land and of the people that the Emperor's two garden parties – one in the spring and one in the autumn – should be for the purpose of viewing respectively the cherry blossom and the chrysanthemum. We were present at the Cherry Blossom party, held at the Imperial Palace. All the guests assembled to await the arrival of Emperor Hirohito and the Imperial family. The women guests wore kimonos but the men wore formal European attire. It was amusing to see these men squatting, in the characteristic Japanese manner, all over the garden while dressed in frock coats and black silk top hats.

After not too long the Emperor Hirohito appeared and we were seated eight to a table. In front of every seat there was a very pretty crinkled cardboard box sprinkled with gold. Opening mine, I discovered with delight that it was filled with meringues in the shape of cherry blossom. I had only eaten a few mouthfuls when I noticed a look of horror appear on everybody's face. 'Oh, have I done something wrong?' I exclaimed. 'No, not at all,' came the polite reply. They would not enlighten me, but I could see that I had made a terrible social gaffe. It was only later that I realised that the meringues had been blessed by the Emperor, a divine figure to the Japanese, and what everybody did, and what I had been expected to do, was to take them home and summon all the relatives to a sacred feast. I took the remains home with me and still have them!

I only really understood the meaning of democracy after this visit to feudal Japan, where human beings were rigidly ordered, classed and graded. Everyone was subordinated to somebody else all the way through, in society and in the home. At the topmost pinnacle stood the Emperor. Next to him came the privileged and idolised military caste, followed by the middle classes, workers and peasants. Minorities were entirely subordinated to majorities. In the home children were subordinated to parents, parents to grandparents and, ceaselessly and all the time, women were subject to men. Japanese women walked behind their husbands, carried all the parcels, watched over all the children and had babies strapped to their backs. In the house they sat on cushions just outside the inner circle. We met several well-educated women who clearly resented their inferior status.

William and I felt that Japanese gentlemen, while intent on meeting the Western world on its own ground and beating it at its own game, were quite determined not to change their homes. This depended upon keeping women exactly as they had always been. We discovered that Japanese businessmen came home, took off their European clothes, soaked in hot baths up to their necks and then put on their comfortable kimonos and slippers while their wives fluttered round them anticipating every want.

But we were aware during our visit that the soldier was much more significant than the businessman. In Japan in the 1930s war was still a splendid and glorious thing, conceived of as a way of patriotism, self-sacrifice and chivalry. Militarism and nationalism were of overriding importance in a country which had recently invaded Manchuria, a part of China, and had left the League of Nations. A Japanese boy's training in warlike affairs began from his earliest years. The national symbol of boyhood was the carp, the fish that fights hardest and longest. We learnt that a Japanese must fight fearlessly and die fearlessly for his Emperor. We asked one uniformed youth, who spoke a little English, how long his military service would continue, but he, misunderstanding, alarmed us by striking his chest and declaring: 'I fight – till my death.'

We visited General Araki, who had been War Minister during the conquest of Manchuria. Although he lived in a modest villa in a Tokyo suburb, the suit of ancient armour and the big statue of hobgoblin type – typifying martial valour – were reminders that this was the house of a warrior whom the interpreter seemed quite naturally to address as Araki Shogun. He talked of martial virtue and of the simple life and, above all, of devotion to the Emperor. We were told that, in conversation with George Bernard Shaw, General Araki had enlarged on the moral value of earthquakes in keeping before the mind of the people the vanity of material possessions. Thereupon Shaw is said to have lamented the seismic deficiency of England and proposed himself to make it good by increasing the supply of volcanic thought!

Araki saw Japan as the eastern barrier against Communism, which was not only the ideology of the Soviet Union but was becoming increasingly influential in China. Communism was checked with the utmost severity by the police, and a well-informed Japanese, when asked about left-wing movements, replied curtly: 'The best brains in Japan are in gaol.'

'Politics does not explain everything,' I said to William. 'We must get an insight into the religion of Japan.' We visited the popular Asakusa Temple in Tokyo on the Sunday in April devoted to viewing the cherry blossoms. Ueno Park, which we passed on the way, suggested Hampstead on a bank holiday. Thousands of families thronged its shrines and lanterned lanes. They purchased toys, let loose paper parachutes, or set off

fireworks in the intervals of consuming their lunch and almost obscuring
the ground with discarded newspaper wrappings.

We approached the Temple of Kwannon at Asakusa through a lane of
booths, on this day thickly beset by a seething mob. The largest crowd
in the temple was pressing round a priest who constantly shook a box
of rods and according to the one which protruded selected printed paper
slips which foretold the future. But to speak of the priest 'telling fortunes'
brought forth a reproof: these were oracles of the Goddess of Mercy.

I went up with the crowd, paid a sen, saw the operation of the rods,
watched the priest open one of many drawers and was duly handed my
'fortune'. Our Japanese host, Baron Harada, picked this up to translate
it. As he read, his face grew increasingly gloomy; finally, crumpling it
up in his hand, he returned it with the brief words: 'It is not good.' In
that moment I sensed a little of the terrific force of suggestion that is
put forth by minds intent on their own self-created beliefs. I am not
superstitious, but next year everything went wrong and I realised how
coincidences like that reinforce people's belief in fortune-telling.

We also visited the beautiful shrines at Nikko. Deciding to travel from
Tokyo by tram, we managed to find the right platform and secured cheap
excursion tickets. The journey took three hours and gave a wonderful
impression of the people and the country. The car was full nearly all the
way and contained every sort and kind of traveller. We were the only
strangers. Although the car had the usual benches, whenever the chance
presented itself the people slipped off their pattens and squatted on the
seats in comfortable Japanese fashion. The conductor removed his hat
and bowed to the passengers, recited some information apparently about
the stations or tickets, after which, with a further bow, he replaced his
hat and again became one of us.

We observed the intensity of cultivation in Japan. Every square foot
of soil was carefully tilled and looked exceedingly fertile and tidy. Two
hours of travelling over the flat were succeeded by a view of the
mountains just before sunset, and at half past seven we were in Nikko.
The spirit of the enterprise of course forbade us to be whisked off to
the extremely comfortable and famous international hotel. Its uniformed
officials at the station showed some surprise when we declined their
pressing invitations. We told them that it was our intention to stay at
the Japanese inn, and we started out on foot to climb the brightly lit
street of bazaars.

We had made no more than a few hundred yards when a boy appeared
and politely enquired of us if we were the strangers who were seeking
the Konoshi Inn. Lighting the candle in his brightly decorated yellow
paper lantern, he led us onwards. The host and the many hostesses of
the inn were waiting in the ample porch.

Our pilgrim's pack was taken from us and our shoes removed and
replaced by slippers. With the aid of a few pages torn from a book

entitled *Easy English for Hotel Employees*, and a great deal of pantomime, the room and rate were fixed. We were shown up a staircase – broad, carpetless, highly polished and spotlessly clean. Sliding doors with paper panels were drawn back and we found ourselves ushered into a completely empty apartment. Some soft rush matting covered the floor and a small mirror with a Japanese scroll hung on the wall above a little raised platform. In this place was also set a great bowl of cherry blossom. Some of the girls produced cushions, padded kimonos and charcoal braziers and we sat down to the traditional threshold hospitality of green tea and sweetmeats.

We enjoyed a bath as it should be. We washed first and, when clean, entered the tub. Returning to our room for a meal, we discovered that cushions had been spread and by each was set an elbow-rest on one side, and on the other a little lacquer table. Lacquer dishes contained all manner of food. Eating with chopsticks, we made a good meal on eggs, rice, toast and innumerable bowls of soup containing various kinds of fish and fungus, two sorts of boiled and fried seafood and more green tea. With this appeared bamboo shoots, seaweed and other, more ordinary vegetables.

One older Japanese woman and three young girls sat on the floor before us, handing out everything as we required it, laughing, twittering, and repeating every English word they had managed to pick up. Sometimes they would stroke our clothes and say: 'Very nice.' We, in turn, read phrases from the guidebook, at which they were highly delighted. Their way of expressing approval was inimitable: it sounded like a very effective gargle. The entire hotel staff appeared, carrying mattresses and quilts. Two beds were soon made up, consisting each of three mattresses and about six quilts, the innermost of which one was supposed to wear, for it had sleeves like a kimono. The pillows were small, round and hard.

The next morning, no sooner was it known that we were awake than the same numerous staff, some of whom we suspected of coming more from curiosity than from official duty, gathered to give us our breakfast. In a gallery with six wash-basins was a gentleman in vest and trousers busy washing. 'Now isn't this all the fun in the world,' he exclaimed as we retreated, 'just one big family!' He himself was a Canadian professor fresh from Central Asian research and he had for companion a tall Tibetan, whose long white coat, lined with scarlet, and round Chinese hat with a scarlet button, set off the real distinction of his appearance and carriage.

Before long we were ready with maps and guidebooks to visit the shrines, and we maintained the spirit of the affair by the purchase in the bazaar of oranges and biscuits for the day's food. It is not easy to convey the brilliance of the temples of Nikko with their gold and red lacquer, their exquisite hand-carvings, and their many colours glittering in the forest settings. A fitting prelude was found in a walk through the seldom

visited garden of the Prince Abbot. We joined the crowds of Japanese
pilgrims who had come on this, the birthday of Buddha himself, to pay
their devotions at his temple. Above the steps of the first and largest
building hung a long rope and, by swinging it, the worshipper could
sound a deep-toned gong near the roof, for the double purpose of
attracting the attention of the deity and carrying off his own prayers on
its receding echoes.

The gigantic gold images of Buddha at this shrine were perhaps the
most impressive single spectacle at Nikko, but the Sacred Horse had a
quaint charm of its own, and the richness of 'the Gate before which one
lingers all day' cannot be overpraised. Finally there was the climb, passing
gate after gate – known as *toris* – and mounting ever steeper steps, to
the Temple of Iyemitsu, the Emperor who had shut off Japan from the
West in the seventeenth century. The sound of a gong took us down to
the Futara-San shrine. This was the oldest of all and had stood for over
a thousand years. Here was to be seen real Japanese worship, the pure
Shinto. Against a dark green background of cryptomeria trees rising from
a hillside, stood the crimson temple. Its altar lay hidden behind a stage
that faced a wide open courtyard. At one side squatted several priests
fingering musical instruments and, on the other, two young girls conversed with each other in low tones. Their clothing was that of temple
dancers: bright scarlet skirts surmounted by white silk bodices, over
which their long black hair hung in a tight roll of white rice-paper. At
a given signal the gong vibrated as the maidens rose slowly to perform
their daily intercession for the favour of the Sun Goddess.

Their movements had the angular precision of figures in a marionette
show. To the clash of cymbals and the thin piping of flutes the slow
posturing began. First, the air must be cleared from evil spirits by the
rhythmic movement of blades, held tightly at each end by a delicate
hand. Then flowers must be strewn and tempting music played to entice
the reluctant deity from the Cave of Night. Here, indeed, was the world
we had been seeking. This was the true Japan, the home of the Children
of the Sun.

Shinto means 'The Way of the Gods'. Found in no other country, it
was the soul of Japan, externalised, idealised and worshipped. Beginning
at the family shrine, Shinto is based on a firm regard for the loved and
honoured dead. Centring upon the doctrine of direct physical descent
from the gods, it made for a deep-seated pride and confidence. It did
not surprise me that people who believed they were descended from the
Sun Goddess and that she in turn sprang from the right eye of a Higher
Power, should have made such difficult neighbours at the League of
Nations.

It was later, at Ise, the supreme shrine of the people, that we saw
Shinto in its sheer grandeur as the deification of Japan. First the peerless
setting: the mountains and cryptomeria trees; the clear stream, with its

sacred fish. Then the noble planning and tireless care expended on the graceful bridges and stately avenues which, winding from *tori* to *tori* and growing ever darker, led pilgrims upward to the limit of their permitted advance, to the outward gate of the shrine, a simple and perfect specimen of massive joinery. The two temples, dedicated respectively to the Sun Goddess and the Goddess of Food, were not in themselves old, although the actual site of the shrines had been the same for nearly two thousand years. They were of the simplest kind and built of plain, unvarnished wood heavily studded with brass nails, in exact imitation of the archaic tents that the people used in the earliest days of their history. Every twenty years they were both pulled down, the wood cut up and sent out in the form of charms to every family in Japan and the goddesses had new homes provided on alternative sites to which they were moved with great ceremonial.

We learnt that what Jerusalem is to the Jew, and Mecca to the Muslim, Ise is to the Japanese. It was the dream of every loyal citizen to offer his dutiful respects to his divine patron in her immemorial home at least once in a lifetime. With deep satisfaction the devotee kneels before a pure white veil at the outermost court of the deity, in an atmosphere of profound adoration. In the gatehouse squats a priest in a white robe, holding a scroll in his motionless hand.

I realised that this was no formal cult, capable of ethical sublimation into a similarity with Western beliefs. It was the soul of the land. Captured Russian guns, hideously smeared with red paint, seemed to desecrate the place, but in reality they were of a piece with it. Here Admiral Togo brought his victorious fleet after defeating the Russians in 1905; here the Emperor gave thanks after the First World War; it was here that Hirohito donned his sacerdotal robes and, as High Priest, made intercession for the nation. And it was to this sacred spot that he sent messengers to announce to the goddess the birth of an heir to the ancient throne of her people. Here, I sensed, was a race that felt itself to be 'chosen' by its goddess to work, not for the brotherhood of man, but for the greatness of Japan.

This ecstatic nationalism, underpinned by Shinto, explained what seemed inexplicable in the 1930s – how it came about that the Japanese people, in territory and resources incomparably poorer than their competitors, proudly chose the lamentable path of isolation which led, within a few years, to war with China, and the attacks on Pearl Harbor and Singapore.

Interestingly, though, one religious innovation had been brought about in pre-war Japan by some of the women. Observing that the girls belonging to Christian families were married in church, the Shinto girls were more and more insisting on a similar ceremony. We witnessed the preparations for a marriage at a Shinto shrine where the bride wore a European wedding dress and the groom a morning coat.

William and I visited a number of mission churches of all Christian denominations. The ones of which I have the happiest memories were those built in Japanese design outside and in, with a porch in which one took off one's outdoor shoes in proper native fashion before going forward to worship. I met an English missionary in Japan whose church was more like a Shinto temple than a Christian place of worship. He explained it on the grounds that if you want to entice someone to a certain way of thinking you must proceed from the known to the unknown in order to give them something to work on.

We were determined to visit the theatre as often as we could. In Kyoto we saw the uniquely lovely *Miyako-Odori*, the seasonal cherry-dance play, with its many exquisite scenes and tableaux, but most of the plays we saw were in Tokyo. When we arrived for the first time, at about six-thirty one evening, at the famous Kabuki-Za Theatre in Tokyo, we found that the play had been in progress since early that afternoon. At eleven o'clock, when we reluctantly followed our solicitous hosts – fearful of exhausting us – out of the theatre, the performance was still unconcluded.

A series of scenes was being represented, dealing with the history and glory of Japan. The most effective of these gave the story of the capture of Osaka castle by Iyeyasu. The stage was immensely wide – eighty feet at least. One curtain was pulled across from side to side and another huge curtain was worked on a roller. There was a great deal of real gunpowder used and the castle was attacked by bands of soldiers who ran on, firing and shouting, along a raised platform from the back of the auditorium. This trick of bringing the players right through the body of the theatre on to the stage, so much favoured in the Soviet Union as well as Japan, had the effect of creating a bond between players and people and was no doubt employed for that reason. The fights were magnificent examples of choreography, the actors posturing according to recognised classic rules.

The performance was entirely conventional, both in the choice of topic, the rendering of the dialogue – including long passages of monologue delivered by a female impersonator in a shrill voice – and the movements of the actors. The programme provided a précis of the plot in English and we realised afterwards with surprise that, throughout an evening of superb acting, we had never missed the spoken word. To our great regret the Noh plays were not given in Tokyo during our visit there, but to the Kabuki-Za we went as often as we could.

In Tokyo, perhaps the most significant of all performances was that given by the Shimbashi geisha girls to celebrate 'the birth of the Crown Prince, and the exaltation of Japanese prestige'. The series of beautiful tableaux was named 'One Joy after Another'. Beginning with a reference to the divine storm which in 1281 beat off the Mongolian invaders, the performance ended with a dance by many children –

Japanese and Chinese – who celebrated, in the waving of a five-coloured flag, the foundation of the new Empire of Manchukuo, the former Manchuria.

We could well understand, after seeing these plays, how the martial and patriotic ardour of the country and the chivalrous idealism of the people, involving the readiness to give any service and to court death in war or even by suicide, was fostered by the repetition of the national stories on the stage and by strolling players. In pre-war Japan the theatre not only kept alive the romantic spirit of the past, but inspired public enthusiasm at a time when government policy was meeting with the disapproval of the world.

We were constantly aware of the Japanese perfection of detail. For an example of finished skill, plus a little joking something, it would have been hard to beat Mr Hamacho's fish shop in Tokyo, where we enjoyed a delicious meal. After removing our shoes we entered a reception room and were given green and black tea, salted beans, raw fish and seaweed, with a sauce served in small round cups. Through the open window we glimpsed a beautiful garden, with its pond, its lantern and its Japanese trees.

Our hands were wiped with steaming hot towels and we entered the dining room. Facing us was a large screen shaped like a *tori* and bearing the inscription 'I cook good fish for many clients.' Bent in a semicircle in front of the screen was a table about twenty inches wide and four inches high, of burnished ebony, round which on the floor were placed five brilliantly coloured cushions. Immediately inside the ebony arc was a steel table and within it, and in the centre, were a large bowl of raw fish of many kinds and over some sort of charcoal brazier a seething pot of butter and flour.

In the midst of all, resembling in posture, appearance and gravity a Buddha on an altar, sat Mr Hamacho himself, said to have been a stockbroker before becoming a restaurateur. He squatted in perfect ease and comfort on his seat behind the stove and bowed while the attendants tied round our necks large bibs and served us with tea, rice, pickles and horse-radish. Our host picked up the raw fish from the receptacle, fried it in the pot, and put it on a paper plate in front of each guest. As soon as it was empty the plate was replenished. A sense of repletion rapidly began to cause anxiety, but there seemed no way to defeat the indefatigable cook. At last, however, a general united and grateful protest from the party convinced Mr Hamacho that hospitality had been done.

He then pressed a button and the cook and his food disappeared on a revolving platform to be replaced with pots of blossoming flowers. As we rose, our ears caught the sounds of a welcome to other guests, who had assembled on the further side to take their fill at the complementary semicircle. We then moved to a third room, reserved for our party, where tea was served in deep cups, oranges were sliced and handed round, and scented, hot, steaming napkins removed all traces of the meal.

We passed downstairs to the porch, our shoes were replaced, the rickshaws were called into the little courtyard and, as we cast a backward glance, we saw the rows of attendants forming a bright foreground to the figure, still squatting and bowing and smiling, of the stockbroker turned cook.

Our three weeks in Tokyo had been packed tight with events. Every day and almost every hour we had been overwhelmed with generous hospitality. Our protests that we were critics of Japanese policy and took a strong League of Nations view made no difference. On the day of our departure from Tokyo we were sitting in the room at our hotel when we both noticed a slow swinging of the window-curtains, followed by a slight rattling among the furniture – it was an earthquake. Leaving Tokyo, we travelled across Japan to Moji, where we embarked for Shanghai.

CHAPTER 9
CHINA AND USSR, 1934

The ship taking us to China rocked and rolled for twenty-four hours and then was held up for another twelve in thick fog. Much to William's amusement, I tried on my lifebelt before going to bed. The next morning I was thrilled to see the thick yellow waves of the aptly named Yellow Sea and realised that we were getting close to the muddy Yangtze River and would be at Shanghai very shortly. I found it as exciting as first seeing the Euphrates, which was much the same colour.

As we drew up the river Whangpoo it got hotter and hotter. The river was humming with junks, sampans on which people lived all their lives and brought up their children, liners, battleships belonging to every country except China, and river craft of every kind. I had never seen such crowded streets, such bright lights, such large numbers of people; and the noise was deafening. Shanghai had been an international port until the Nationalists had taken it over in 1927. We found that the long-established merchants were not happy with the new government and preferred the old system.

After a brief stay we left for Hangchow, the ancient capital of China, in order to meet the Panchen Lama, the spiritual teacher of the ruler of Tibet, the Dalai Lama. These two leading Tibetan Buddhists had quarrelled and for the previous ten years the Panchen Lama had been living in China. Shortly after we met him, he returned to Tibet when the Dalai Lama, on his deathbed, begged him to return so that he could give guidance to the next Dalai Lama.

At the time of our visit the Panchen Lama was attending a large prayer-meeting at the monastery of Ling Ying, near Hangchow. After spending the night at an hotel overlooking the lake, we were met by our guide at eight o'clock the following morning and driven through hot, steaming rain to the monastery. Reaching the gate, we found crowds of pilgrims and vehicles, including many of the sedan chairs that abounded in the neighbourhood. On the far side of the main gate the road wound on, lined on both sides with curio shops and teahouses. Policemen with pistols and bayonets were on duty here and there, and photographers solicited custom, offering as a special inducement the chance of having one's picture taken against the rocks and cuddling the carved stone figure of a 'laughing' Buddha. William had his photograph taken with his trilby hat perched on the statue's head.

In the centre of the temple, railed off by a cordon and protected from the group of worshippers in the courtyard by two sentries with bayonets, sat a chapter of lamas – Tibetan Buddhist monks – facing each other in two rows at right angles to the high altar. We were told by our guide that they were 'very high indeed' to merit this position, for in their midst, with his back to three colossal statues and enjoying the full comfort of an electric fan which was cooling the air, sat the Panchen Lama himself. They had all been at prayer since three o'clock that morning and were still performing their chant.

Before them on a sort of low bench were many musical instruments. From time to time, interrupting their chanting, the monks would play in unison on the trumpets, bells and drums and the temple echoed with a wild primeval harmony. In front of each lama was laid a plate filled with rice, which at intervals he appeared to scatter. Before the altar similar offerings of rice, nuts, raisins and dates were to be seen. The air was thick with incense, which clouded the light of many simple wicks burning in oil. Above, in the roof, birds were flying about and singing so loudly as almost to take first place in the festival. The rain still poured down.

At last the celebration was over and the time had come for the Panchen Lama to retire to his quarters, where he was to receive us. He rose and moved off, and after a short interval we followed. A young man was very hastily unrolling a narrow width of yellow muslin which was to cover every inch of ground on which the holy man would step. While waiting to be summoned we sat on beautifully carved Chinese chairs in a courtyard which was partly roofed over. In the far corner of the open court were servants gossiping or preparing tea, the pigtails here and there of the Tibetans seeming very strange in Republican China, but stranger still the trilby hats by which so many of them were surmounted.

The Panchen Lama's secretary came out to bid us enter, and accordingly we went into the large room in which our interview was to be held. The Panchen Lama greeted us most charmingly with both hands and, motioning William to a yellow satin armchair, sat in its twin himself. I, as befitted my sex, was put in a high-backed chair a little further away. The two interpreters stood. The conversation went through French, Chinese and Tibetan and so it took rather a long time.

He was about fifty, dark-haired with very bright hazel eyes. His arms were bare and he wore embroidered shoes whose toes curled upwards. His clothing was various, the chief article being a maroon-coloured gown covering scarlet undergarments. But what I shall never forget was his outstandingly serene countenance, refined and made beautiful by much spiritual reflection and discipline. No ugly thought could have found expression in his presence.

As we left, the Panchen Lama presented each of us with a pale blue silk scarf. These, we discovered, were guaranteed to drive out all 'ghosts' from any room. He embraced William, who completely disappeared from view under the Lama's cape and emerged, looking as if he had had a struggle, with very dishevelled hair. Unused to being embraced by another man, William looked most uncomfortable!

From Hangchow we made our way to Nanking, which was then the capital of China, where we parted. I crossed the river and went by the Tientsin–Pukow railway to the north, while William went up the Yangtze to visit the Nationalist leader, General Chiang Kai-shek, at Nanchung.

William would not take me, because the last woman who had made the trip had been kidnapped. Although her ransom had been paid by the *Daily Mail*, William was certain the paper would not pay mine as it disapproved of his politics. 'I'm not involving the family in a lot of unnecessary expense,' he said firmly. I recall the moment of his departure on Whit Sunday 1934 as a grim one for me. I had to make my way across China alone and hope we should meet again in Peking about a fortnight or so later. But would we? I sat down and counted my blessings, remembered my friends and home; and above all thought of my three precious children half-way across the world, and Nurse Olive who had cared for them for so long and now did not even know my address.

That night I boarded the Shanghai Express. I was the only European on a train committed to carry me to Peking by an uneasy passage through the lively war raging between a number of warlords. 'Fighting usually breaks out at dusk,' I was told by railway officials. 'As soon as you hear firing get on the floor at once.' Fortunately, this only proved to be necessary for short periods, but there was evidence of the war everywhere. A large number of fully armed troops were travelling on the train; each station was surrounded by barbed wire and was swarming with soldiers; and I noticed that every field had at least one square-towered lookout place. It was quite a journey. I took my own food and drank endless cups of hot fragrant tea, green and black, supplied for twopence a day.

It was intensely hot, and I kept the curtains back just enough to look out all the way at the farms and the little mud- or stone-walled cottages. Towns and villages lay on the plains like the design on a willow-pattern plate. Always members of the population came and stared at the passengers, but no one asked for alms as in the Soviet Union.

Towards sunset on the second day we came into the mountains. I longed to stop and climb the sacred Mount Tai-shan, but I could not spare the five hours it took to make the ascent in a sedan chair carried by Muslim bearers. It had been a place of worship and pilgrimage for over four thousand years and was so close to the birthplace of Confucius as to be identified with it. I learnt that any Chinese whose home happened to be in an unlucky position – at the foot, for example, of a street, where all the evil influences congregated – could not rest until he had obtained a stone from Mount Tai-shan on which he brushed the words: 'The Most Holy Mountain takes responsibility.'

At ten o'clock the next morning the Shanghai Express came to a standstill by the walls of Peking. A week or so later, when I was reunited with William, I discovered that his train journey to Peking had been much less comfortable than mine: a shortage of seats meant that he had travelled in the luggage rack of a compartment. As he got down he tore his trousers, enabling a fellow passenger to display his knowledge of English by commenting: 'Broken bottom!'

By good fortune the First Lady's Apartment happened to be vacant on my arrival at the Chinese Guest House, run by an Englishwoman, where William and I had chosen to stay. The house, with its many shady courtyards and painted gates, was a source of new delight and rest after nearly five months spent in hotels and on steamers. In the middle of my courtyard was a little pond full of those strange Chinese goldfish that have faces like Pekinese dogs.

For a couple of hours at lunchtime the principal courtyard was filled with Chinese merchants who laid out their various wares temptingly before us. Ancestor pictures hung on the stone walls; silks, satins, rugs lay unrolled on the pavement. Mandarin coats of every colour, stiff with magnificent embroidery of incredibly fine stitching, rings, necklaces, bracelets of jade and many other semi-precious stones, awaited our inspection.

Making my selection from these delightful wares, I decided I wanted for ever after to live with two lovely camels, with rapt gaze, in shades of yellow. I also bought some reproduction Ming vases; a screen on which Chinese men and women, made of semi-precious stones, were in an almost living contact – obviously telling each other news of great importance; a set of Cantonese black wood furniture, including an ancestor table; and some lovely Khansu rugs. 'How will you get them home?' asked my practical husband. 'I shall do it,' I declared emphatically. Months later a packing case weighing three cubic tons arrived in London; everything was there. Miraculously, all my purchases survived the Second World War, with the exception of one of the camels, who lost half an ear in a bombing raid; but even that was eventually found and stuck on again. The Chinese camels are still marching across my mantelpiece.

William and I were provided with rickshaws, and at whatever hour we might happen to set out on the day's programme, Wang and Ting, our rickshaw boys, were always there waiting with smiles of welcome and helpful suggestions. They explained to us that they knew only 'outside English', which meant they could talk about things that happened in the street but not inside a house.

It took three mornings to cover the Forbidden City. For centuries it had been taboo to the ordinary person. Brides, when once they had entered, were not allowed to return to their homes, even for a visit, but had to be content to see their relatives from time to time in a small reception room near the inner side of the main gate.

Inside the Forbidden City's huge walls, moated outside and adorned by magnificent gates and watch-towers, lie the myriad palaces, temples, courtyards and gardens of the Imperial household. Yellow tiles predominate, for that was the Emperor's colour. Each palace is painted on gables and eves in every sort of colour, and the whole shimmers and glitters like a succession of jewelled caskets.

There had been a republic in China since 1911 and the Chinese did not appear to mourn the departed glory of the Empire. The Dragon Throne was empty, the brass bedstead of Pu-yi, the last Emperor, and his bicycle – both English – were left behind, but there was no note of regret evident in the voice of the guide who showed us these relics. 'Mr Pu-yi is now at Changchun,' was his only comment, smilingly made with the wave of a fan vaguely towards the north.

Next to the Forbidden City, or perhaps even before it, in august sanctity was the Altar of Heaven and the Temple of Fasting. Here, at the winter solstice, the Emperor, known as the Son of Heaven, came in former times to offer sacrifice to his only superior. This centre of national worship stood outside the city walls in a beautiful meadow, sweet with the scent of grass and the fragrance of a eucalyptus grove. On a rain-washed morning in May it was unforgettably beautiful: the temple with its austere white marble courtyards, staircases and round walls surmounted by a sapphire roof, blue as the night sky; and, even more impressive, the circular, open altar – 'the Centre of the Universe' – rising from its three tiers of steps. Here, as in the Forbidden City, bullocks of one colour and without blemish were slain on great occasions, an immemorial custom which the Emperor carried with him to his new capital at Hsinking, the former Changchun, where he reigned, under Japanese control, as Emperor of Manchukuo.

I walked through the temples and monasteries unable either to converse with the worshippers or to read their inscriptions, yet the expressions of the people, their petitioning faces and posturing bodies, all spoke to me in the universal language of the heart. I have never felt less need for words.

Buddhist temples, thronged as in Japan with devotees, musical with the deep vibration of gongs and hazy with incense, were always in every city the easiest places of worship to find; indeed, it was almost an exception to come upon any other. In order to visit a Taoist temple I made a short journey outside the walls of Peking to visit the Temple of the 'White Cloud'. In its shady courtyards, completely devoid of worshippers, the priests sat in groups conversing quietly. They were unshaven and their long hair was pinned up into a topknot. The sudden arrival of myself and a woman companion filled them with amused curiosity.

With an ever-increasing company of priests we were taken through many courtyards to the main temple, where we received our first introduction to the images of the Taoist Supreme God and His Immortals. The sense of ineffable inward peace that is expressed so unerringly in the quiet, rapt features of Buddhist gods and saints was here notably absent. The Immortals, on the contrary, all gave the appearance of contented Chinese people who had met with more than usual success in their daily undertakings. From the temple we were led into a succession of little shrines, each with its attendant priest. Sometimes the deity on the altar was benevolent; sometimes fearsome. In every case offerings of food lay before him and incense curled upwards from a carved metal brazier. Our hosts readily posed for photographs and displayed considerable interest in the camera.

The star of the educated classes was Confucius, the philosopher who believed that given the perfect government, the perfect people will appear. His temple, in the heart of Peking, was peacefully free from images, crowds or coin-throwing. A glorified professorial chair, from which Emperors once read aloud portions of the sage's wisdom to the people, stood in that central position usually reserved for some representations of the Divine.

But it was impossible to breathe the air of China for long without realising that here was a country where, despite an immemorial culture and two and a half millennia of philosophy, the great bulk of men and women still lived and moved in a spirit-peopled world. On the threshold of temples and rich homesteads stood always two giant gods, frowning hideously to turn aside the evil spirits that seemed always more numerous than the good. Farther on, a large dragon-screen invariably guarded the front entrance to the main courtyard. Evil spirits, happily, could proceed only in a straight line: this timely obstacle turned them back. The delightfully crooked lacquer bridges that spanned little streams and lakes were all planned for the same purpose. Prominent in funeral processions were the little boys carrying long white brushes to sweep away evil spirits.

In day-to-day family life myriad precautions were necessary. An eldest son required special protection until he had passed the 'dangerous' age. In an English household where we were entertained the house-boy brought his children to visit us and we saw what appeared to be a girl of eight and a boy of six. Actually, the beautiful little 'girl' was the precious elder son, who had been dressed in this way since birth to deceive the evil spirits.

There was always the additional possibility that some unwitting neglect might, at any moment, turn a benevolent demon into a malignant one.

This was guarded against with the aid of persons possessing the necessary knowledge and skill. The priesthood, particularly the Taoist branch of it, played a large part. Priests could be hired singly or in groups to keep the atmosphere 'safe' at weddings and funerals, as well as for purposes of exorcism and magic.

When driving by car we were often puzzled and uneasy at the spectacle of a Chinese darting suddenly across our path. Having barely escaped with his life, he would turn and laugh heartily in our direction. We soon learned the reason. By this nimble action he had freed himself of the evil spirit that followed him and as surely transformed its unwelcome attentions to ourselves.

We enjoyed our visit to the theatre, where there was a pleasant party atmosphere. The building appeared to be unfinished, but it was brightly lit and adorned with garish illustrated posters after the style of a second-rate picture-house. The balcony, divided into open boxes, was reached by a wooden stairway. Provision was made for our comfort in the shape of a pot of tea and some peanuts and melon-seeds arranged on a tray in front of our places. From time to time vendors came round offering sweets and steaming hot towels to wipe our fingers. This luxurious custom had only one drawback, for I suspected, and rightly, that these towels had passed through many hands before reaching ours. On the ground floor attendants were handing them along the rows of seats like sidesmen offering a collecting plate. Occasionally there was a sharp slapping sound when, to save time, these towels were thrown smartly over the heads of the audience and neatly caught.

The theatre was filled with a buzz of conversation and nobody appeared to be paying any attention to the stage, though the curtain was up – in fact we were told it had been up long before any of us had arrived. Everybody was coming and going, laughing, talking and nibbling. Some were even stretched out asleep on the seats. The stage was filled with people wearing ordinary clothes and with props obviously out of place and not related to any scene. On the right were a few men constituting a band, the most effective member of which beat a gong, creating a ceaseless din. But we soon realised, from the tones, gestures and postures of a group of the players, that they were carrying on some scene. This did not appear to be noticed by the attendants, who wandered on to sections of the stage not occupied by the actual players, conversed, and even drank tea.

As a setting for the rapid series of acts, chairs, screens and backgrounds were placed at that part of the proscenium where the speaking was taking place. The theme was the success of a sprightly concubine over a dull legitimate wife, and the animation of the plot continually grew. Gradually the scenery became more and more magnificent; the loiterers and loafers faded out; the audience began to pay attention to what was going on; conversation ceased; the gong became louder. It was strange how this noise, which had been a decided nuisance at first, really came to play a part in stirring emotions. It was rather like the roll of drums which in a circus heralds the most daring acts on the trapeze. Soon the whole stage was a mass of brilliant banners, screens, chairs and costumes, and what had started with the look of an unexciting dress rehearsal finished up with all the blazing thrill of a great spectacle. This crescendo was certainly the most striking feature of the whole evening.

On whatever fascinating excursion we might go – to the Great Wall, to palace or temple, to theatre, or to the teeming bazaars of the Chinese city – it was always Peking itself that held us in bondage by its own charm. By sunlight or moonlight we never tired of watching the life that flowed through it. Here were coolies staggering under incredible loads; blind men with gongs; scholars with faces as pale as their own parchments; men as fat as Dives drawn by rickshaw boys as thin as skeletons; endless babies rolling naked in the dust; trousered grandmothers smoking contentedly by the door of some wrecked dwelling of straw and matting that clung like a fungus to the wall behind. Occasionally a motor car drove by carrying Europeans with tennis rackets, or a 'four-wheeler' with aristocratic-looking Chinese ladies in flowered coats. Hardly an hour went by without the passage of a funeral or a wedding party. For these the traffic had to move to one side. The richer the family, the more gorgeous the display.

We left Peking for an audience with Emperor Pu-yi in his new state of Manchukuo. Removed from the throne of China in 1911, he had been allowed to remain in the Forbidden City, where he had been taught by an Englishman, Reginald Johnson, who, just before our visit to China, had written a fascinating book about his experiences, *Twilight in the Forbidden City*. Many decades later it was used as the basis of a film about the Emperor's life. The Japanese courted Pu-yi, and when they took over Manchuria in northern China made him the ruler of the puppet state of Manchukuo. In March 1934, a few months before our visit, he was proclaimed Emperor.

We travelled by train from Mukden to the capital, Hsinking. Japanese troops were everywhere, and soldiers were continually passing through the coach, each with his automatic rifle in a wooden case. Officers were inspecting papers with the assistance of cavalry swords. As we arrived we noticed that the Japanese were building large numbers of new houses, and that a palace for Emperor Pu-yi was in the process of construction. He was at the time of our visit lodged in an office which had been used in connection with the administration of the salt tax. There was no vast moat or turreted encircling wall, as in the Emperor's last dwelling in Peking. The drive was through ill-paved streets and slums, which might have been removed, but remained there, we were told, on account of the Emperor's consideration for his humble subjects.

The car drove into a courtyard past two sentries and, alighting, we walked a few steps into a largish, undistinguished building, the main apartment of which was a sort of hall or waiting room. Here we began at once to realise that we were in an Imperial atmosphere. It was a world of satellites, graded and bemedalled. There were the special folk wearing some emblem of the Emperor, there were generals, there was a Court Chamberlain, there were traces, perhaps from the old time, perhaps from the new regime, of the charming manners which are associated with an Imperial court. Conversation was pleasant, yet all minor politeness between ourselves seemed to be merged in, and a part of, a wider deference to the Unseen.

This impression was deepened when we were summoned across the courtyard to a small two-storey house which was the actual residence of the Emperor. The entrance hall was not large, but in it were crowded eight or nine young officers in uniform, who came to attention as our small party passed along. There were no further formalities and a door was thrown open, admitting us to the Presence. The room was of no great size and seemed mid-Victorian in type. There were settees almost resembling what our grandfathers would have called 'conversation seats'. There were chairs with antimacassars. There were a few clocks on a shelf. Under a glass cover was a cannon, modelled in silver. The carpet had a large, rather startling pattern. There was a purple rug with a blue border, and small tables with green plush covers. On the walls were some raised, embossed pictures, one photograph, and one picture of some divinity. There were also framed pictures, apparently of the Emperor's family, standing on tables and ledges. The end of the room was hidden by a brocade curtain.

The Emperor motioned us each to an armchair and himself took a seat on a couch between us. He was tall and slim; his hair had the appearance of being blue-black; his face was pale, thoughtful, intelligent and dignified. His lips were thick and protruding – concealing, or revealing, excellent teeth. Behind his glasses were pleasant brown eyes, which lit up often with a humorous smile. His hands were very expressive and artistic and he used them effectively in conversation. He wore a gold wedding ring and was dressed in a light fawn suit, with a soft collar.

The conversation was conducted through an interpreter – apparently for some formal reason, because it was obvious that the Emperor understood what we said, and we were under the impression that his English was quite equal to the task of making his own replies. As is usual on such occasions, the interchange began with questions put by the Emperor; but very soon his unaffected good nature, combined with our own eager interest, had inverted the roles, so that we were putting the questions and the Emperor was providing the answers.

He criticised the government of China and then said that it was love that ruled the world. To the heavens above, all races seemed alike: all men were born equal and the distinctions that existed were the making of men and not of Heaven. We ventured to suggest that His Majesty should make a journey to the West and preach these doctrines to the various dictators of Europe. 'Ah, you mean Mussolini and Hitler,' he said. He went on to say: 'These are not my sentiments: they are the old philosophy of my country. Goodwill is the secret. Just as you love your children and you extend your love to other children, so you must learn to extend it to the whole human race, and that is the key to the riddle.'

After our audience we were required to walk out backwards from the presence of the man who had been the last Emperor of China. His later life was not a happy one, as his association with the Japanese invaders led to his imprisonment when the Communists came to power in China. On his release he worked in the Botanical Gardens in Peking until his death in the 1960s.

Leaving Hsinking by train at ten o'clock one night, we arrived, shortly after dawn, at Harbin, which had been under the influence of the Japanese since their defeat of Russia in 1905. An amazing spectacle of racial medley met our eyes. There were Chinese men in long, loosely made gowns wearing felt slippers; some bare-headed, but others, who could afford it, with a topee or the popular boater. Jostling them were Russian officers who, until a nearer approach showed their clothes to be threadbare, seemed to have stepped straight out of the old regime. One, over six feet in height, with grey pointed beard and moustache, was wearing a white tunic, black breeches and top-boots, his lordly head crowned by a military cap of the smartest type.

Alongside were tiny Japanese officers, with brightly polished brown riding-boots which, despite their patrician cut, seemed to be of cheap manufacture. There were Chinese soldiers in green and yellow cotton uniforms, and Japanese with a similar inexpensive outfit, dignified by red facings. Through this maze of the trappings of officialdom slipped little Japanese, bare-legged and, with their awkward and inappropriate sandals, uncovered heads and exposed necks, looking pitiably underclothed.

The womenfolk included Chinese, with the usual long gown buttoned at the neck, and good-looking Korean peasants with high straw hats. The Japanese women, in their doll-like perfection, with their hair arranged in buns or sometimes in geisha fashion, and their necks carefully whitened, were smiling and bowing to their acquaintances. The Russian peasant women had heads bound in handkerchiefs. A sharp note from the West was struck by the sight of a cluster of German Jews, escaping Nazi persecution and putting all Asia between themselves and their memories.

In the waiting-hall of the station was a samovar of tea with which the new arrivals were fortifying themselves for the incalculable adventure of another day. This mingled stream of humanity surged round the central feature of the place: a tall and gaudy shrine, railed in and adorned with artificial flowers and the light of many little lamps, where a Christian peasant knelt to perform his devotions.

Our passports and papers were courteously and rapidly examined jointly by Russian and Japanese officials. We then left the railway station and saw the boulevards, built under Russian influence, which converged upon it. The East seemed to disappear and we were plunged into the West. Electric trams shrieked and an occasional carful of Japanese officials raced along, apparently above subservience to traffic regulations. A shabby droshky whisked us round to our hotel.

It surely must have been grander in former days. There was a look of neglect about the front hall; the ambitious pillars were grimy and chipped; the stairs were uncarpeted, and the corridor almost seemed as if it were being prepared for the housebreakers. Now and again there hurried past us some of the strange dwellers in this caravanserai – a woman, for instance, cheaply *soignée*, slipped into her small apartment, giving the odd impression of an exiled Grand Duchess in a shabby bed-sit. Our own bedroom was roomy, rather grand, heated, and connecting with a tiled bathroom, peopled by many large but unaggressive insects.

In the restaurant of our hotel, a glassed-in balcony overlooking the street, we became acquainted with the elderly White Russian men who sat for hours toying with an ice-cream or a cup of coffee. We were told that there were eighteen separate parties of White Russian exiles. All were pitifully dependent upon the Japanese, and they had a touching belief that the new power in the East, at the conclusion of a successful war with the Soviet Union, would restore at least an independent Siberian government and then gracefully retire, leaving the White State to enjoy its freedom. These dreamers cherished every custom of the old times. The Christian churches which dotted the city were their centres and stood for earthly triumph as well as heavenly salvation. They showed Old Russia in stained glass.

Harbin was a dangerous place with many bandits preying on the Russian exiles and the Chinese. When we spent one Sunday afternoon on the banks of the Sungari River, our kind hosts had to provide themselves with cartridges as well as sandwiches; and we picknicked with a pistol.

In order to demoralise the Chinese, the Japanese had encouraged opium dens to flourish. With the assistance of a Chinese business agent we visited some of these establishments. Entering by the back door of the first shop, we reached the first-class department by a wooden outside staircase, which gave upon a long room divided into cubicles, each shut off from the public gaze by a curtain hanging to the level of the knees. Inside these cubicles were beds, or shelves, covered with rush matting and bearing stumpy, hard-looking cylindrical pillows. On each bed was a flame-lamp for heating the opium, and here and there a pot of tea.

There were only one or two patrons in the first class, but downstairs things were busier. Here the customers had not the privacy of a cubicle, for they all shared one shelf. One woman, who was sharing a lamp with a man, looked up in a dazed way, with puffy eyes. The opium she was rolling in her fingers over the flame was, we were told, being used for the second time; it having already done service in prime condition for the first-class customers. In the second opium den we visited, a man with glittering eyes approached and offered to sell us heroin, supposing that only a search for some such drug could have brought foreigners to so filthy and revolting a lair.

We found in a public street a much better type of opium shop. It was ostensibly a restaurant, but the customer, having entered and passed through a back door, found a flight of stairs leading to rooms arranged after the common model. The whole shop was enlivened by some music of a shrill monotonous kind in a minor key, played on a one-stringed fiddle by a wizened old man. As he scraped out the melody – if such a word could be used – the tune was taken up by the occupants of some of the adjacent cubicles, and so the air was filled with weird sound. As we entered, a little boy of about seven hurriedly sought shelter behind the prostrate form of his father, who turned his stupefied and indifferent eyes from us to his frightened child.

We hurried off to the car, and as it turned out of the street it pulled up sharp, with harsh braking. A strange figure lay across our path. A mangy oilskin cap crowned his head, blue cotton trousers hung loosely on his limbs: otherwise he was naked and every rib and bone showed in sharp relief. This opium addict was quite young, tall, and had been handsome: his neck and chest were covered with loathsome, leprous-looking sores. He made no move in response to the approach of the hooting car, but at last, aroused by some passer-by, he rose up, looking at us out of his hollow eyes with a foggy and incomprehending smile. He asked for nothing, but moved away very slowly, dragging one foot after the other. He might have been twenty-five years of age. Someone in the car said: 'He will be dead with the first frost.' Another man, more experienced, answered: 'Long before that!' And he added: 'One hundred and ninety-four dead were picked up in these streets last winter.'

After leaving Harbin we crossed Northern Manchuria to Hailar on the fringes of Mongolia. There were many 'soldier-bandits' in the area, opposed to the Japanese presence, and many precautions were taken on our train, including an armoured truck, next to the engine, that contained machine guns. Fortunately, our journey was without incident, and at 3 am the train pulled into Hailar station, where we were met on the platform by the Japanese Consul. A day's rain had reduced the unpaved streets to a deep, soft mud, through which the Consul's elegant American car rolled uneasily.

The people appeared to be mostly Russians, but Chinese were also much in evidence. Most novel and absorbing of all, however, were the Mongols who came in from the surrounding country. Every few minutes we were delighted by the sight of some picturesque group. Sometimes it was a long row of carts drawn by oxen, led by a party of young men, that came riding by; sometimes it was one woman alone on a splendid pony. In every case there was the same sense of poise and freedom in their movements; the same dignity and calm on their unfamiliar broad brown faces. Their clothing was a strange jumble of oddments. Both sexes wore top-boots curling upwards at the toe, and skirted garments gathered in at the waist by a belt, into which the men thrust their long pigtails. For men the usual headgear was the familiar round hat surmounted by a button; for women, a more closely fitting cap.

Once outside the town, where roads soon vanished, the magnificent horsemanship of the Mongols was immediately evident. One man cantered for miles beside our car, sitting easily and gracefully on his peaked saddle, one hand on the reins and the other holding a long whip. His loosened pigtail streamed behind him in the wind. Every few miles he turned on us a friendly but slightly satirical smile. Something about that smile made William and me a trifle nervous and our apprehensions were in no wise allayed when the Consul remarked: 'That Mongolian knows me well!' This news depressed us considerably. For the rest of the journey each of us gave way to silent fears that the other might at any moment stop a bullet intended for our host. But it was all a needless and groundless foreboding.

We crossed Siberia by train. Gradually the prairie-land turned into hills and forests as we skirted the north of Outer Mongolia. Everywhere there were billboards bearing maxims, welcomes, encouragements. I noticed a greeting, from Stalin, to the Conference of Cooperative Farmers: 'Advance to New Conquests!' Figures of the favourites, stuck on wood and cut out, adorned the roofs of many stations. Lenin and, less frequently, Stalin were there, but their images were companioned in each district by that of some local official.

Our train constantly passed men and materials being moved east. This was to protect the Soviet Union from a possible attack from Japan. By the railway there were brand-new wooden villages in course of erection, compounds, and, in places, large aeroplane hangars. Then, every hour or so, there was a long goods train, carrying scores of motor trucks, many of them decked with garlands. A train of wagons, linked in pairs, was carrying the huge wings of bombers. It was undesirable to go near these trains, as armed men picketed them at every few yards. In addition to all this unmistakable military material were the ordinary troop trains carrying uniformed and equipped soldiers.

We decided to leave the international Lux Express at Novosibirsk in Western Siberia in order to visit a collective farm. We travelled along a road that was terribly bad in parts but was in the process of reconstruction. We passed the collective sawmill and blacksmith's shop and were surprised to see a few countrywomen displaying for sale, on small tables before them, their eggs and butter. They constituted that rarity, the individual trader.

We paid a visit to the Children's Holiday Home, which was the pride of the village. The behaviour of these children was the subject of proud comment by our guides but, alas, it was a pride that went before a fall, for as the car moved away, some little boys in the street threw stones at us. The Mayor explained the behaviour by saying that these children were 'rude little individualists'.

We were told that the collective farm had been made by the union of 167 individual owners, and 450 persons depended upon it for their living. Those participating received a preliminary advance on account of the year's yield, and at the end of the financial period were paid according to the number of 'man-hours' worked by them or their families.

The chairman, the director and the local controller were clearly fired with zeal about the whole collective enterprise, but we were conscious all the time that the medium-size farmers, known as *kulaks*, who had employed a few labourers and who had objected to collectivisation, had been 'liquidated' and that villages throughout the Soviet Union had lost much skill and experience because of Stalin's uncompromising collectivist programme.

On our return from the collective farm we had planned to rest for an hour or two in preparation for the night journey which was to take us forwards to Sverdlovsk. Almost at the moment of our departure, when we were busy strapping up our bags, there descended upon us, literally from the Siberian skies, George Andreychin, who was to be our guide and companion for nearly the whole remaining time of our visit to the Soviet Union, and who became a real friend.

When the news of our arrival in Siberia had been telegraphed to Moscow, he had been dispatched by air to meet us as we left the so-called Lux train. Unfortunately, his machine had come to grief and he had had to travel for some days by train. Now he had arrived, bubbling over with enthusiastic plans and warm assurances of a welcome everywhere. From then on everything was easy. Places suddenly appeared on trains when we wished to board them. On expressing our uneasiness at what must have happened to travellers already booked for the same journey, George waved a casual hand. They had to step aside for us. But what, we asked, of the equal rights for all in a classless Soviet society? Of course, said George, all are workers in the Soviet Union. The only difference lay between more responsible workers and less responsible ones. The second had to give way to the first. So we learned that we belonged to the category of more responsible workers. Clearly this was a great honour.

For our journey to Sverdlovsk the weather was superb. Our quarters were our own and in them we fed ourselves meal after meal from the inexhaustible basket which we had brought from Harbin and replenished at the Torgsin – foreign currency – shop. Tea we made constantly. At the stations William or I would race with our kettle to the boiling tap, taking a place in the waiting queue and joining in the general indignation against any such comrades as brought large pots to fill and so made the rest of us risk getting no water at all. I was pleased to hear from George that Tolstoy also carried a kettle on his journeys and ran out, as we did, for hot water.

The countryside was richly clad in wild flowers, and in praise of these George was justly lyrical: 'Our people want life, the riches of fulfilment, air, sunshine, the chance to work and to achieve. See! Those wild flowers. When the train stops I will cull them for you. Armfuls you shall have. See that workers' dwelling. Look at the long high windows! Light! Light! Our people need sunshine. They have been in the dark so long. A carpet of wild flowers seven thousand miles long – that is Siberia! Ah! Look again at those flowers! Pink, blue, saffron, lavender. God himself could not have made anything so beautiful.' Difficulties, political and personal, he brushed out of the way with superb contempt.

Wherever we might be, I suffered much from the humbler creation. When I wailed about this George would call through the door of our sleeping compartment: 'What! A grown-up woman afraid of teeny-weeny insects. Come out of your bunk and I shall assassinate them all!' This incident reminded me of a family joke: 'What's the difference between travelling with Ernest Benn and travelling with William Benn?' 'With Ernest it's all creature comforts. With William it's all creatures and no comforts!'

One evening, shortly after our arrival in Sverdlovsk, George burst in with the news that a well-known Moscow drama producer was on tour in the town with his company and that one of his newest plays would be presented in ten minutes at the theatre opposite our hotel. These sudden and irresistible attractions were a constant feature of George's programme. We hurriedly made ourselves presentable and raced into the theatre, to find that the producer had most courteously kept some hundreds waiting so that we might see the beginning of the show.

The building was of the most modern type, the acoustics excellent, and the vision uninterrupted from every seat; at the same time it lacked the soft luxurious finish that would have been added as a matter of course in Europe, and even more so in America. The scenery was not elaborate, but it comprised a revolving stage, which was freely used, and a raised alleyway, as in the Chinese and Japanese theatre, so that the players could come on to the stage from the back of the auditorium.

The play dealt with the triumph of the Bolsheviks in and around Bokhara. The universal success of the Soviet forces in the face of opposition was perhaps a warning to any who contemplated counter-revolution. The caricaturing of the anti-Bolsheviks, who were shown as talkative, dirty, drunken and cowardly, was a regrettable blot on an artistic performance. It was not so flagrant, however, as similar 'guying' of Communists in a Nazi film we had seen in Germany. One of the most impressive scenes represented Muslims at prayer and we noted that Islam was treated with a respect denied to the Orthodox Church. The leading character was a woman general whose courage and steadfastness saved the situation.

To make the stage a mere instrument of propaganda is surely to degrade it, yet despite this, or perhaps because of it, the Russian stage seemed very near the audience. The revolutionary plays we saw in 1934, to a considerable though diminishing extent, dealt with events in which the onlookers themselves had participated. They made the same sort of appeal that Noël Coward's play *Cavalcade* – which follows the fortunes of an English family through the first decades of this century – made to a middle-aged English audience at the same period.

To dress the players in workaday clothes created a further link with the audience and so too did the absence of ordinary stage scenery. That living sympathy flowed across the footlights was unquestionable, for from time to time members of the audience, not satisfied with mere applause, handed up little notes to the players giving them hints as to how they should meet the developments of the plot.

For me, as probably for all foreign travellers, the chief interest of Sverdlovsk was its association, under its historic name of Ekaterinburg, with the fate of Nicholas II, the last Tsar of Russia, and his family. We visited the modest dwelling concerned, which by a strange coincidence was called 'The House of Ipatiev' – similar to the 'Monastery of Ipatiev' from which the first Romanov Tsar, Mikhail, came to the throne. The house, demolished in the 1970s, was set out as a museum and was open to the public. Guides placed straw slippers over our own shoes. The atmosphere was chilly but respectful. Smoking was forbidden and silence requested. The objects shown naturally concerned the last days of the Tsar and his family, and at the same time presented it all as the commemoration of a historic event.

Prominent on the walls were life-sized portraits of the Imperial family being received by the local soviet, the Tsarina Alexandra with a quiet bearing, apprehension in the eye of the Tsar. On the desk lay the photo of an intercepted letter from Nicholas to an unnamed person in which he intimated hopes of rescue and gave a plan of the house. Menus with the Imperial crest showed the simple food provided. The Grand Duchesses were shown in the uniforms of nurses. A note expressed the heartfelt joy of a father that 'Marie has had a happy nineteenth birthday'. It was all very moving. Moreover, from our discussions with the local soviet, I became convinced, and remained so for a long time, that nobody had planned murder, nor wished for it, but that the local soviet panicked when they thought the Tsar was about to be rescued by counter-revolutionaries. But it would now seem, from evidence released over the last year or so, that Moscow may have given some general orders to execute the Imperial family if the need arose. We were not shown the basement where the murders took place.

William and I made no comment as we walked round, but perhaps our faces expressed a sense of the heavy atmosphere of grief and terror that lay in those rooms. Outside in the car George scolded us fiercely. 'You have sympathy with Nikolai?' he cried. 'Don't you know . . .' – and he reeled off a long list of political and personal crimes which he laid at the door of the last Tsar. But we had no intention of discussing the matter with him.

The modern town was very different from the one that Nicholas and Alexandra had known in their final days. Sverdlovsk had grown enormously, and everywhere there were new factories, houses and offices. There were also the inevitable queues outside all the shops. We put several questions about this phenomenon and received many answers, perhaps the most unconvincing being 'Russian women are unpractical and leave their shopping to the last minute.'

After visiting Kazan, the capital of the Tartar Republic, we proceeded by boat to Gorky, previously named Nijni Novgorod. For two days of perfect sunshine we made our way through the broad reaches of the Volga, receiving many impressions of the Russian countryside at harvest time. Now and again we stopped at a pier where we could go ashore and buy raspberries and strawberries, appetisingly displayed on large green leaves.

As we were contemplating the lovely scenes, George ran along to us with the excited information that a new sawmill was coming into view on the other side of the river. Obligingly we went with him and were transported by the sight of a cluster of gilt and painted towers and cupolas. Opposite rose a mean building surmounted by an insignificant factory chimney. 'What is the name and history of that superb monastery?' we asked eagerly. 'Oh,' he replied, 'that must be a resthouse for the sawmill workers.'

At twilight, the coloured twinkling buoys shone out one by one. In the last glow of the sunset a whole village appeared, floating slowly past us on the face of the water: cottages, a larger house with a dinghy at its door, and a flag-pole bearing a lamp. A closer glance showed that this little settlement was in the centre of what seemed to be acres of treetrunks chained together and steered by immense rudders fixed at their extremity, many yards from the occupied dwellings. Here indeed was a migrant population: they had come from who knows where and their occupation was to guard and guide this mass of timber through half a dozen states down to the distant Caspian Sea.

The next day, at sundown, we approached the town of Gorky, set on a hill and hidden round the corner on the river Oka. George pointed proudly to the new bridge connecting the town with the fairground.

This bridge, he said, had for decades been urgently required but always left unbuilt, until the drive of a revolutionary government had constructed it in record time. As usual he had far more interest in these triumphs than in the beauties of the Kremlin or the fifty churches which the city boasted.

On the subject of Communism he was endlessly lyrical: everything in the Soviet Union, from the weather to the latest decree of Stalin, was superlatively perfect. His big arms opened and shut as though to catch and hold the entire world within the beneficent embrace of Bolshevism. Of course we had to see the Molotov motor factory, the glory of Gorky. George told us that it had been built by engineers from Ford's Dearborn works at Detroit but was run on Communist lines.

The working conditions in the factory, which was surrounded by large blocks of flats and a training school, were good. The workers were urged to produce more by slogans and incentives. I saw an enormous crane, crashing along with its load from one end to the other of the vast building, that carried a large cut-out figure of Stalin and a slogan urging a greater output. Individual workers who produced considerably more than the average – the 'shock' workers – received more money and had a separate canteen and a higher status. I was impressed by the interest in education shown by the workers who, during the dinner hour, thronged a bookstall that was full of advanced works on mathematics and engineering.

We continued our journey, and on arriving in Moscow visited the Anti-Religious Museum, which with intentional irony was housed in one of the city's former churches. There were many exhibits contrasting the discoveries of science, especially the theory of evolution, with the supposedly superstitious, exploitative nature of religion. All the time there was a small but continuous flow of Soviet visitors, looking round with interest at both the scientific and the sensational exhibits.

An English eyewitness told me that a short while before our visit she had seen a group of ardent young Communists bring in, for her education, an elderly relative. The old lady looked patiently at the skulls and fishes, but, catching sight of the religious icons, immediately felt at home. To the embarrassment of her friends, she began to bow and cross herself repeatedly before each in turn. Their urgent whispers of 'You mustn't do that! You can't do that here! This is an *anti*-religious museum!' echoed desperately round the aisles. They were totally unavailing. The old lady went her own way.

I was struck on this visit by the fact that Communism in the Soviet Union seemed itself to have become a form of 'religion'. One of the most noticeable features of Russian life in the 1930s was the worship lavished on Lenin. Busts and pictures, photographs and paintings adorned the walls of home, office, factory and ship, all over the Soviet Union. The chapel-like appearance of the 'Lenin Corners' with their raised 'altar' tables, supporting some representation of the hero, the devotional slogans of praise on the placards and banners that hung around it, all gave a religious atmosphere to the memory of the founder of the Bolshevik state.

Soviet Communism was also a very authoritarian 'religion'. The works of Marx and Lenin were 'scripture', and anything but authorised literature was strictly forbidden to all but 'Communists of good standing'. Many Communists we met had no desire to hear all sides of a question, or decide anything whatsoever upon evidence. One man told us: 'Marxian philosophy, when it is correctly known and used, solves all problems and unifies all diversities.'

It seemed to me that since our last visit in 1926 more people had been swept along the Communist road. Moscow was still a city of churches, but I was told that only about forty-five were still 'working'. St Basil's Cathedral, with its unique pineapple cupolas of every shape and colour, was a museum, and St Saviour's Cathedral, where William and I had had our frightening experience on Easter morning eight years before, had vanished altogether. Other churches had been converted into cinemas and offices.

When at length I found one of these remaining places of worship, I discovered that it was possible to wander into it on any day of the month – days of the week had been abolished – and find a service in progress. On one occasion we attended a service where the congregation consisted of about a dozen old people gathered together after their work. The church seemed in a sad state of disrepair. The carpet was in holes, the walls and pillars dingy. Outside, here and there, bricks from the building had fallen among the few forlorn blades of grass below. Outside, amidst bustle and laughter, surged the Communist world with its slogans and its singing. Inside, in an almost eerie quiet, stood the little remnant band, mournful, isolated and suffering.

We found Moscow changed in other respects. The streets and squares were better paved and cleaner than eight years before. We missed the British Leyland buses that had been a noticeable feature. The underground railway was being finished and above the works stood a great statue, made up of many square pieces of wood cunningly arranged in a futuristic fashion, not to represent any individual but to glorify a type – the workman who was digging below.

The beggars who used to lie across the pavement or huddle in corners seemed to have disappeared and there were no mobs of homeless children, though there were individual juvenile vagrants. Everyone seemed intent on some sort of job. There was none of the delightful chatter found in the cafés in Paris, and, before the rise of Fascism, in Berlin, Rome and Vienna. In a way reminiscent of the United States, the air was laden with a sense of the worship of the machine.

After travelling through Central and Western Europe we at last reached the end of our most memorable round-the-world journey, thankful to be reunited with our children. Michael and Anthony had been teasing our youngest, David, saying: 'You won't remember Mummy and Daddy.' When he saw us he jumped up and down and said: 'Of course I remember you, Mummy and Daddy – do you remember me?'

CHAPTER 10
1934–1938

With such extraordinary memories fresh in our minds, William and I decided to write a book about our experiences. I was delighted when we found a publisher but somewhat daunted by the extremely tight deadline. After a few months of intensive but enjoyable writing, we delivered the typescript of our book, *Beckoning Horizon*, which was published a few months later. The response was generally favourable, but some reviewers were puzzled by the dual approach of the book, described by one as a detailed analysis of the world political situation shot through with a strong belief in a personal God.

During the next year, 1935, everything seemed to go wrong and a superstitious person might well have felt that the Japanese bad luck prophecy was coming true. Michael had scarlet fever in the spring and shortly afterwards Anthony had his appendix removed.

On a happier note, William was selected to contest the Dudley constituency at the next election, but this was soon overshadowed by an event of great personal sorrow. I was expecting our fourth child in August and was looking forward with happy anticipation to the birth, which was to be at Stansgate. But, sadly, our fourth son, Jeremy, was stillborn.

That very evening, six-year-old David became ill and was eventually diagnosed as having tuberculosis caught from a cow. For a long while I feared for his life as he struggled against the disease, but after spending much of the next four years in bed he eventually recovered. The one benefit of the illness was that he learnt Russian from his émigré doctor. David's interest in Eastern European languages continued and he put his knowledge to good use in later life, becoming head of the Yugoslav Department of the BBC World Service. His Russian accent is so good that on visits to the Soviet Union people refuse to believe he is English.

Although the Labour Party increased its number of MPs at the general election of November 1935 – the last one for ten years – William was defeated at Dudley by 2,449 votes and the National Government, overwhelmingly Conservative, still had an enormous majority. Never daunted, William took up the offer to lecture for the British Council and undertook a number of tours. At the end of November 1936 I accompanied him on a visit to Central Europe and the Balkans.

The most interesting part of the trip was our stay in Vienna, where we were the guests of the British envoy, Sir Walford Selby, and Lady Selby. We attended a dinner given by Sir Walford's German counterpart, Franz von Papen. He was angry that the Austrians had refused to give him ambassadorial status, which would have elevated him above the rest of the diplomatic corps. The dinner was a specially planned occasion to demonstrate how natural it would be for Austria and Germany to become one state – eventually achieved by the Anschluss in 1938. After we had eaten, the guests, mainly German and Viennese notables with their wives, were entertained by a concert of old German songs, all traditional and part of the Austrian heritage as well as the German. As each was played von Papen would glance at his German and Viennese guests, looking for smiles of understanding in response to the unspoken question behind his caressing manner, 'Tradition, language, literature and life all combine to show us as already one. Is it not time to declare this to be so?' All the musicians and servants were in eighteenth-century dress and it seemed to be an attempt to reconcile aristocratic Austrian opinion to the Nazi idea.

Apart from the relationship between Germany and Austria, the one topic of conversation that everyone was interested in was the abdication of Edward VIII, which had occurred during our visit. Lady Selby always warmly defended his actions as being behaviour in accordance with the undeniable dictates of nature. I was not surprised when six months later she was one of the small number of guests at the wedding of Edward, now Duke of Windsor, and the recently divorced Wallis Simpson. It was just as well that he abdicated. I do not think that a man for whom personal happiness meant more than anything else would have made a good king during the war that was soon to engulf us.

The abdication meant that the Duke of York became King George VI, and in May 1937 William and I attended his Coronation. The Palace sent out a pronouncement that those people who could not afford to come in Coronation clothes could wear ordinary afternoon dress. Although William was not in that category, he decided that, as a gesture of support to the people of the Labour Party who could not afford special clothes, he would not wear his Privy Councillor's uniform. This decision infuriated some of the guests in the Abbey, who hissed at us as we walked to our places. A man near me said: 'Why don't you dress properly?' I said: 'Well, we are supporting friends who want to come and can't afford clothing we can afford, and so we're supporting them and we think that's right.'

At the time of the Coronation William was once again an MP, having won a by-election in February 1937 in the Manchester constituency of Gorton. Campaigning had been very exhausting, as William had been struck down by one of his recurring attacks of malaria just as election-eering had got under way. I nursed him throughout the campaign and made his speeches for him. I was particularly concerned about the need for better care for mothers and children and emphasised that the Labour Party wanted maternity and infant welfare centres, and nursery schools in all districts.

William was delighted to be back in the House of Commons after a gap of almost six years. He was popular with his fellow MPs, who elected him on to the Shadow Cabinet of the Parliamentary Labour Party. Coming second in the 1939 ballot, he achieved a higher place than MPs such as Herbert Morrison and Hugh Dalton. During these last years of peace William denounced the Government's policy of appeasing Hitler and stressed the need to support the League of Nations.

William's views were not considered, by some members of the Party, to be sufficiently left-wing. Sir Stafford Cripps, the future Chancellor of the Exchequer, thought that the best way to counter Hitler was for the Labour Party to form a union with Communists, and he invited William to several lunches in the hope of interesting him in this scheme. After one lunch, realising he was not going to get William's support, Stafford took a pink tulip from a vase and, presenting it to William, said: 'That's your colour, my dear – pale pink!'

William continued to lecture for the British Council and during December 1937 and January 1938 we travelled to the Near East. I vividly recall a most memorable meeting with Dr Chaim Weizmann, the future President of Israel, in what was then still the British mandated territory of Palestine. The political situation was very troubled. Resenting the influx of Jews escaping Nazi persecution, the Arabs had launched a revolt against the British authorities. Although Dr Weizmann, the leader of the Zionist movement, agreed to the British Government's suggestion of partitioning the land to form separate Arab and Jewish states, remarking that Jews would be foolish to refuse any offer of a state, 'even if it were the size of a tablecloth', the Arabs would not accept. When we arrived guerrilla activity was continuing.

Dr Weizmann had invited us to spend the night at his recently built mansion in Rehovot where he and Mrs Weizmann were now permanently settled, having lived in England for many years. Nearby was the Science Institute where Dr Weizmann worked. A research chemist by profession, he had made a crucial contribution to the Allied victory in the First World War by inventing an ingredient for high explosives. The high price that the Arab guerrillas had placed on the head of this foremost Zionist required the long journey to be undertaken in two heavily armed cars; Dr Weizmann and I in the first, William and Mrs Weizmann in the second. Travelling past the Garden of Gethsemane, my silent thoughts were accompanied by the low utterances of Dr Weizmann, who said – with deep emotion in his voice – 'There are trees there now that saw the destruction of the Temple . . .'

The long drive through the Judaean hills from Jerusalem to the coast

is a perfect situation for guerrillas to operate in and this part of the road
had been much fought over. Dr Weizmann was obviously uneasy as he
looked and listened for signs of trouble. At every turning our chauffeur
sounded the Gabriel Horn, a unique instrument that played a whole
melody. I doubt if there was another such in the Holy Land, and I felt
sure it must convey the news of Dr Weizmann's presence to any hidden
listener on the watch. The atmosphere was somewhat strained and the
conversation desultory during this part of the journey, but when we left
the surrounding hills and entered the lovely plain, Dr Weizmann sat up
and said with obvious relief: 'We're out of danger now.'

The evening that followed remains one of my most enchanted
memories. After tea and a rest we dined and settled down for an evening
of enlightenment. Dr Weizmann was an inspired interpreter of Jewish
history and Jewish hopes. In a low, intense voice he outlined the story
of his people down the ages from their first deliverance from slavery in
Egypt, the giving of the Law at Sinai, the long years wandering in the
wilderness up to their conquest and possession of the Promised Land. We
had no sense of the hours passing as, with him, we lived through these
years, and then on to the woeful time of loss when the people of Israel
were again wandering strangers dispersed among the nations but always
bringing the incorruptible treasures of their priceless heritage with them.

With the worst horrors then still in the future, Dr Weizmann spoke
passionately of the increasing persecution of the Jews by the Nazis. Now
was the time for Israel to be re-embodied as a sovereign state existing
again as a nation among the nations. 'That's what we desire: no more,
no less. We have no wish to re-establish any empire of old. We only
want to be ourselves again, living a secure and undisturbed life where
our roots lie here at home in Jerusalem. Our one wish is for a homeland,
however small; some land where we can be ourselves.' Continuing in a
quiet, hypnotic voice he said: 'These last two thousand years we have
carried our homeland with us,' reminding me of words spoken by Dr
Eliahu Elath, a future Israeli Ambassador: 'Somehow we've kept the
wine without the bottles.'

In the small hours of the morning we drove to the temporary house
a few miles away where guests were lodged until a new wing of the
main residence was completed. This was a fresh delight. Upstairs and
downstairs everything for a guest's comfort had been imaginatively
planned. A light meal was laid out. A variety of books were at hand,
armchairs and sofas abounded. The beds were inviting, although neither
of us as yet felt sleepy after so stimulating an evening. I felt like Goldi-
locks coming upon the home of the three bears. It was a glorious night,
and before we finally retired we looked out from the comfortable sitting
room on to a beautiful landscape and listened to the sound of jackals
calling to each other in the moonlight. Truly an experience to be
remembered.

Next morning we rose early and after breakfast went with Dr Weizmann to the Science Institute at Rehovot. Here we saw another side to this distinguished leader. The night before, he had been the historian statesman; this morning he was the practical mystic, the scientist showing how his hopes for a country were to be realised.

Donning his white laboratory coat, he explained to us the meaning of innumerable little bowls of earth that were placed methodically around, each one bearing a shoot of a green plant at some stage of growth. Jewish settlers from various parts of the land had written to him saying they did not know how to make a living in their hard struggle with the earth. To each he replied: 'Send me a sample of your soil. I will test it to discover all its possibilities, and if you then sow seed as I advise you will be able to make an ample living.' This plan he said was bearing excellent fruit.

Next day William left in the morning to give a lecture for the British Council in Egypt. Wishing to visit Galilee again, I decided to follow him to Cairo a few days later. When I arrived back in Jerusalem in the early afternoon I found to my dismay that the British mandatory government had ordered that I must be accompanied on my travels north by a British policeman. A car with a reliable, well-recommended driver had been booked to take me, but that was not regarded as providing enough security in a troubled situation.

The young policeman was very amenable, but it would have been difficult to find anyone who could offer less stimulating company. His mother was a member of some fundamentalist sect who believed that the end of the world was at hand, and under her urgent expectations he had recently come out to Palestine where he hoped for a ringside seat at the catastrophe. His knowledge of scripture was selective and somewhat confused and his conversation was sprinkled with such remarks as 'Do you think Noah's flood got as far as here?' Our helpful Arab driver was more concerned as to whether we should ever get as far as Galilee, where we hoped to stay for a night or two.

The whole atmosphere was one of great tension. Everywhere we could see that Jewish settlements had been strongly fortified in expectation of attack. Look-outs with telescopes kept watch from the roofs. Barbed wire was in evidence everywhere. We had been told that some settlements were established and fortified all within the hours of one day. By the amount of activity visible this seemed quite possible.

All went well for a time, and then suddenly at a turning we encountered a large tree lying across the road and were brought to a complete halt. Around it stood a band of Arab guerrillas who approached us from all sides. 'Who are you? What are you doing on the roads at such a time?' Turning crimson in the face, my policeman pulled out his revolver and pointed it here and there. He had only just been given it and I felt sure could not have hit a haystack had he tried. 'Please put that gun away,' I whispered urgently, and fortunately he did so.

A long argument ensued between our captors and the Arab driver. Apparently he declared that I was merely a harmless British tourist who had come out to see the Christian holy places and was no use to them. They took no notice of the policeman. He was wearing plain clothes and they probably mistook him for my son. Eventually the guerrillas announced that if we produced a sufficient number of cigarettes they would release us. I had not yet given up smoking and my policeman had several packs so we were able to satisfy them. The tree-trunk was removed and we were allowed to go our way. Fortunately, now denuded of cigarettes, we encountered no more guerrillas and arrived safely at a Christian guesthouse by the lake in Galilee.

Accommodation was warmly offered and after supper I betook myself to the shore with my Bible. I was much inspired by the thought that now for the first time I could read and enjoy it where its words had first been uttered.

Next morning a representative of the guesthouse announced that they were concerned about my policeman. For an hour he had defied all efforts to waken him and they feared something was wrong. Would I come? I succeeded in bringing him back to life, whereupon I learned that he was an unusually heavy sleeper. I was only at the beginning of several days' travel, during which I would be staying at a different hospice or kibbutz every night. I could not contemplate a repetition of this scene every morning.

I assured him that with the good car and reliable driver I was adequately provided for. Stressing that in no circumstances could I justifiably keep him from duties of real importance and urgency at HQ, I suggested that he should return that day to Jerusalem. But he was quite obstinate in his refusal; he had his orders, he assured me. When I asked for evidence he produced from his pocket a crumpled piece of paper bearing the instruction: 'Stick to Mrs Benn till she leaves.' So that was that!

While I was on this journey I heard of an ugly incident in Tel Aviv which, fortunately, had a rather amusing conclusion. A bomb was found in a café where a large group of British soldiers had gathered. On discovering it one of them unhesitatingly picked it up, took it to a safe distance, skilfully put it down and escaped just before it exploded. This act of selfless gallantry was widely praised and a senior officer came to decorate the soldier with an appropriate medal. Loudspeakers were laid on for the ceremony and he was asked if there was any wish that he might want to have granted. In a broad Scots voice that carried to the top of Mount Carmel he replied: 'Aye, there are just two things I want: oot o' Palestine and oot o' the Army . . .'

After a few days around the 'Sea' of Galilee, gaining an ever-deepening sense of its beauty and significance, I took the train that ran daily to Cairo. On arrival, I joined William at the residence of the British Ambassador, Sir Miles Lampson, the future Lord Killearn, and his wife,

Jaqueline. Often on our travels I received a particularly warm welcome from the wife of the British official, occasionally High Commissioner, but more often Ambassador, to be found in the places where we stayed. It might be that a long residence abroad had made her feel isolated from the society of other women of her own nationality. At other times – though not on this occasion – it might be that problems had arisen which she could not discuss with those around her.

Lady Lampson, like myself, was much younger than her husband. In her case the gap was wider and she had stepchildren of her own age group. This difference in age had never made any difference to the compatibility that so obviously existed between her husband and herself. 'Our ideas were so completely alike,' she told me, 'there was only one thing to do – marry!'

Relations between Egypt and Britain, although somewhat shaky, had improved since my last visit. The Egyptians, fearing that Mussolini, the recent invader of Abyssinia, might turn his attention to them, had signed an Anglo-Egyptian treaty. This was why Sir Miles had had his title changed from High Commissioner to Ambassador. A most imposing man, he was well over six feet in height and of a big build.

He asked me if there was anything special I should like to do and see and I said: 'Yes. I should like to have another look at the Great Pyramid.' Accompanied by two Nubian kavasses – Embassy servants – dressed in ceremonial gold and scarlet uniforms, I set off in great style in one of the Ambassador's cars. When I entered the Pyramid the chauffeur remained behind, but the other kavass came with me. As we walked up the eerie passage he suddenly spoke, and I have always thought that his remark was the most inappropriate I have ever heard. What he said was: 'Doesn't this remind you of Berwick-on-Tweed?' Unable to credit my ears I answered: 'I beg your pardon,' at which he repeated himself with some emphasis. I murmured something in reply and the subject lapsed. That night at dinner when I told the tale to Sir Miles he laughed heartily and remarked: 'That's easy to explain. The kavass came to me from a Scottish businessman who spent every summer at home in Berwick-on-Tweed. He just wanted you to know that he had travelled a bit and knew the world.'

CHAPTER 11
1939–1945

We arrived home from our visit to the Near East in January 1938, and William continued with his parliamentary work in an atmosphere of deepening gloom as Europe moved ever closer to catastrophe. Finally, after two days of agonising delay following the invasion of Poland, we were at war with Germany. The day war was declared, 3 September 1939, was a Sunday, and I was attending a service at Westminster Abbey when the declaration was made. Within minutes of the announcement the air raid sirens began to wail. I hurried over to the House of Commons and met William, who went with me to the Harcourt Room which had been converted into an air raid shelter. Leaving me there, he went upstairs to see what was going on. A terrific noise overhead made me think that bombs had fallen, but it was only furniture being moved. Fortunately, the air raid warning had been a false alarm and soon the all clear was given.

The outbreak of war inevitably meant the disruption of normal family life. Michael, just eighteen and waiting to go up to Cambridge, immediately applied to join the Royal Air Force Voluntary Reserve and did eye exercises to enable him to pass the test. Anthony was evacuated with the other boys of Westminster School to Lancing College in Sussex, where he joined the Air Cadet Corps.

William continued with his British Council work, visiting Central Europe in February and March 1940. He was offered the chairmanship in May of that year, but with the threat of invasion hanging over our heads he wanted a more active role. Knowing that I would be opposed to this, he did not consult me – for the only time in our married life of forty years – about a step in his career.

My suspicions were aroused when I surprised him as he was pressing a pair of trousers – something I had never seen him do before. When I asked him what he was up to, he replied: 'I'm just getting my clothes in order.' 'And why are you doing that all of a sudden?' I asked. He was very evasive and said: 'Will you meet me at St James's station at twelve o'clock tomorrow morning?' So, highly suspicious, I did and, to my amazement, was greeted with the sight of William wearing the uniform of a pilot officer – the most junior rank in the RAF – with three rows of decorations from the last war! I was horrified that, at sixty-three, he had volunteered for the Forces. 'Well, look at our housemaid's brothers,' he argued, 'they've all gone to the war.' 'But Jane's brothers are boys,' I replied. 'Oh well,' he said, 'I can't let these young men go and not go myself. I can't do it. I couldn't live with myself.' Referring to our great personal friend Sir Archibald Sinclair, who had just been appointed Secretary of State for Air in Churchill's new government, William continued: 'I'll ask Archie to send me where I can see action.' 'Well,' I said, 'I hope Archie doesn't send you anywhere.' And, fortunately, he did not!

Although thwarted in his ambition to be sent overseas, William was able to work at the Air Ministry. He slept in his office and, getting up in the early hours, collected all the newspapers in Fleet Street. From these he made a digest of the news that was distributed at the beginning of the day's work to the senior Air Force officers in the Ministry. Presently he became the Director of Public Relations with the rank of Air Commodore.

When William took up his duties at the Air Ministry, he asked me to deal with his constituency correspondence. I was somewhat daunted at first as I had never done this before, but I began to find a certain pastoral satisfaction in it. People wrote, often in great distress, about some problem that had arisen with which they had no idea how to deal. I remember the case of a boy who had lied about his age and had got into the army at fifteen. His distressed mother wanted him back and I set to work. My own sons warned me that if I were successful the boy would probably wreak a dire revenge on me. Happily, he was released, and nothing further happened!

After the fall of France in June 1940, there was a movement to send children to the United States and Canada out of harm's way. Although the Government offered assistance, Churchill was very worried about the effect on morale. At this time I received a letter from my youngest boy, David, then eleven: 'There's a rumour that our school is going to be taken to Canada and I beg you not to send me. It would only increase my homesickness and I should be sent to strangers and finish my happy childhood in a contrary fashion.' He was a very old-fashioned child! The letter continued: 'I implore you to see reason and not to send me. I would rather be bombed to fragments than to leave England now.'

I was very touched by this cry from the heart, and I believed that many children felt like this and did not want to go abroad. I sent it to *The Times* saying I thought that my son was speaking for his generation and that it was a mistake to send children out of the country. The letter was published on 4 July 1940. Churchill wrote to William, saying: 'A splendid letter from your boy. We must all try to live up to this standard.' We heard from Brendan Bracken, Churchill's secretary, that the letter had cheered the Prime Minister very much indeed.

David was thrilled to receive from Churchill a signed copy of *My Early Life*. He composed a thank-you letter which he and I delivered by hand to 10 Downing Street. The policeman on duty was very overbearing and told me that the letter should have been sent through the post; he took it nonetheless. Many years later David and I were surprised to be contacted by Churchill's biographer, Martin Gilbert, informing us that he had found David's letter in Churchill's files. It read as follows:

Dear Prime Minister,

I was greatly honoured to receive your book, on my return from school. I have read thirty-eight pages and find it very fascinating.

It will be interesting in my later life to remember your kindness and to keep your book as a relic for ever.

The Fortresses of London in which we shall fight for our lives 'street by street' will also be worthy of remembrance.

I am very glad that I am not to be ushered into safety.

The tragic sinking of a ship carrying evacuees across the Atlantic, together with the example of the King and Queen, who would not send the two Princesses abroad, led to the ending of the scheme.

Life became even more difficult when our house at Millbank was set on fire during an air raid in October 1940. During the day I worked in the house clearing everything out and sending what could be salvaged into storage. The smashed windows were boarded up and there was no electricity, so I worked with a miner's lamp strapped to my head! If the sirens went during the day I ran to the public shelter at Thames House, by Lambeth Bridge, where I also slept each night. It was a terrible time. I lived on crumbs of comfort, thankful if I knew the family were all right at any particular moment.

I could not go to Stansgate as it had been requisitioned, but I remembered that Blunt House in Oxted, Surrey, that had been owned by William's father and brother, was then a girls' school. Fortunately, there was space available and I was able to stay there for several years, giving some help by teaching the girls Religious Knowledge. Members of my family stayed there from time to time.

I worked with the Chaplains' Department in the WAAF, and I went round giving lectures. Sometimes the meetings were terrifyingly large – as many as seven hundred on one occasion. I lectured on the relationship between religion and politics and how important I believed it was that there should be an understanding of religion in the political sphere and the other way round. I travelled quite widely in the course of my lecture tours and I would often come back late at night in the thick of the bombing. Despite the blackout I never feared attack in the streets. There is certainly a wonderful spirit of companionship when everyone is committed to a common cause.

I also sat on the Committee for Work among Women in the Forces, where I found myself in disagreement with Rosamund Fisher, the wife of Geoffrey Fisher, the Bishop of London, later Archbishop of Canterbury. Being opposed to any innovation that appeared to be moving in the direction of the ordination of women, she was determined that women who were appointed chaplains' assistants should be in no way official, should not wear uniform, and should be no more than lay workers from the home base. I felt that this often stood in the way of their effectiveness when working within the discipline of the armed forces.

One day in 1941 William sought my advice on an important matter: 'Attlee says that Churchill wants to improve the representation of the Labour Party in the House of Lords and would like me to take a peerage; as I've been a Cabinet minister I'd become a viscount. What do you think?' We both loved the House of Commons, but by that time William was sixty-five, and elections were very energetic affairs. I replied: 'Well, I don't mind. It will lengthen your political life.'

At that time there were only hereditary peerages and so William asked our eldest son, Michael, whether he objected to inheriting a title. Hoping to become a clergyman at the end of the war, Michael said: 'I don't mind. I can make a disturbance in the Lords and Anthony can make a disturbance in the Commons!' So William decided to take the peerage. 'I love our house in the country and I'll enjoy signing myself Stansgate, but,' he added, 'I'm a fighter and the trouble with the House of Lords is the intolerable goodwill. It's very difficult to fight when people are so friendly.'

William's investiture took place in the Robing Room: the Commons' chamber had been bombed and the Lords' chamber was being used by the Commons. It had been made clear in the announcement to the press that William was not being given a traditional honour but was being made a peer for political reasons. Wearing his hired red robes, with his cocked hat slightly on one side, William walked in beside two peers. He winked at me as he passed and it was all I could do not to burst out laughing!

In 1943, more changes occurred to the family. Anthony joined the RAF when he reached the age of eighteen, and William, after leading an Empire parliamentary delegation to Ottawa and Washington, was appointed Vice President of the Allied Control Commission in Italy charged with reconstituting a free Italian government as the victorious Allied forces moved up to the north of the country.

I continued with my lecturing for the Chaplains' Department, working from a couple of offices in Caxton Street from the spring of 1944. I attended a conference of the Committee for Work among Women in the Forces in Cambridge. One of the speakers spoke slightingly of the Old Testament and I found myself impelled to launch a counter-attack of some violence. The Committee were divided in their views and I thought I was somewhat out of favour. To my surprise I received invitations from people present to speak at two other conferences, including a 'Life and Religion Week' in Cambridge.

In June 1944 a new hazard came from the skies. We had an alert that lasted all night, and every fifteen minutes or so one fearfully noisy nuisance raider – as we thought – came over. Towards dawn we had got used to its drill, which did not seem to vary, and we all felt there was something new about it. The plane did one of two things: it either went bumbling on and away, or at one point its engine would stop dead and after about ten seconds there would be an explosion. We later learnt that these were the unmanned flying bombs or V1s. In Oxted an old lady was heard saying she preferred the old Blitz bombs because these new ones 'lacked the personal touch'!

Our eldest son, Michael, had been sent to North Africa after his tours of duty in England, and we were extremely proud when he was decorated with the DFC after shooting down four German planes. At the end of 1943, aged twenty-two, he had been posted back to England to begin his last tour of duty, flying Mosquitoes. Based at Chichester, he was able, from time to time, to visit David and me in Oxted and had booked tickets to see a West End play on my birthday, 7 June 1944; but D-Day intervened and he was unable to be with us.

At lunchtime on 23 June, I received a telegram saying that Michael was dangerously ill with a fractured spine and was in St Richard's Hospital, Chichester. He was unconscious when I arrived, but I whispered to him, and I felt that he knew I was there. He died twenty minutes later. His navigator told me what had happened. Having flown four missions over occupied Europe, Michael took off from the airfield on what was to have been his very last operation, in the early hours of the morning of 23 June. Tragically, the mechanic who had serviced the plane had not checked the speed indicator. When Michael realised that the indicator was not working he returned immediately, but, unable to check his speed, he overshot the runway, the plane collided with the sea wall, and he broke his neck in the crash. The navigator held him up in the water for half an hour until help came.

I immediately sent cables to William in Italy and to Anthony, who was in Bulawayo, Southern Rhodesia – now Zimbabwe. The whole family was overwhelmed with grief. I had never experienced such heartache. William rushed home from Italy as soon as he heard the news, and was struck down by yet another bout of malaria. Determined to take Michael's place, he resigned from the Allied Control Commission and had himself transferred to a new job: lecturing at RAF stations on public affairs. He carefully arranged that his early lectures were all given at air gunnery schools, at each of which he persuaded the station commanders to allow him to undertake training, while he made sure his remaining lectures took place with active squadrons.

He was then sixty-seven and, before the authorities caught up with him and stopped it, had qualified and flown on a number of bombing operations. He had even been mentioned in dispatches. All the time he was on active service, express letters and telegrams were constantly arriving urging his attendance at critical Labour Party committees and House of Lords debates!

Michael had always hoped that a just and peaceful society would be established after the war and that, as a clergyman, he would be able to work towards those ends. Anthony was also passionately committed to the same aims and hoped to pursue them as an MP; indeed, his wartime experiences, especially when he compared the primitive conditions pro-vided for black patients in Rhodesian hospitals with the good-quality treatment provided for the whites, made him even more determined to achieve his goal. But Michael's death meant that Anthony became heir to the viscountcy, and William and I were as depressed as Anthony at the knowledge that this would damage his hoped-for parliamentary career. He was determined to do everything he could, with our full support, to renounce the peerage.

David bore the death of his much-loved brother very bravely and concentrated on preparing for his Oxford University entrance examin-ation. He was also taking a keen interest in politics, and I was delighted when he was elected to the committee of the Oxted and District Society for Anglo-Soviet Friendship.

Coping with my grief as best I could, I continued with my work, taking part in several conferences, including the 'Life and Religion Week' at Cambridge, where I spoke on the theme of 'Home'; and the conference of the British Council of Churches on 'Home and Family Life', being 'adopted' by the Congregationalists for the occasion.

I was somewhat surprised when, in 1945, I was asked to chair a Church of England committee to consider 'Recruiting and Training of Women for Service in the Church'. 'Service' does not mean 'ministry', and I wondered if they realised just how strong my views were on the ordina-tion of women. I felt rather like the wooden horse of Troy!

A few months later the longed-for surrender of Germany occurred, and on 8 May I celebrated VE Day in Oxted. William and Anthony came home in June, just before the general election. On the evening of 26 July William and I made our way to Transport House to hear the announcement of the results – delayed for three weeks after the election to enable the forces' votes to come in. There was a big gathering of leaders and rank and file. Prominent among the former was, of course, Clement Attlee. All manner of jokes were current about Clem. Later, a favourite one was: 'An empty car drove up to Number 10 Downing Street and Mr Attlee got out.' In fact this was a grave misjudgement of his character. William, who later served in his Cabinet, said Clem was the complete master of it, as his colleagues soon realised. He had good experience as Deputy Prime Minister during the wartime Coalition under Winston Churchill, and I was told by various members of this Cabinet that everyone was thankful when Winston Churchill's absence put Clem in charge. Business was all put through quickly and quietly without any of Winston's inevitable ebullient monologues.

I was looking at Clem when it became obvious that a Labour landslide – unexpected by us all – was inevitable. It was fascinating to see the change of expression that came over his face as he realised that this would make him the first Labour Prime Minister to preside over a majority government. It was a mixture of many emotions – astonishment, delight, acceptance, resolution. We went home to prepare for what would be in every sense a new day.

On it, Clem duly kissed hands at the Palace, and that evening the telephone rang at our flat: it was a summons to Number 10. William was given the job of Secretary of State for Air, and the next day Clem invited us to spend his first weekend in office with him and his wife, Violet.

We drove with them down to Chequers, the Prime Minister's country house, set in lovely grounds. I was particularly delighted with the accommodation. It was none other than the suite that had been used by Winston Churchill, and had only been vacated by him a few days before. It was a good-sized room with a pleasant view, and richly furnished. On the mantelpiece stood a large clock in decorated gilt wood. The armchair and curtains were of tapestry. A switch on the wall labelled 'Prime Minister's Bath Water' promised a luxury unknown at home since pre-war days.

The main feature in the room was a king-sized double bed with an immense dip in the middle. I cannot imagine why, having, presumably, created the obstacle to a good night's rest, he went on enduring it. Churchill is said to have done a good deal of his work there in the daytime, so perhaps he did not notice any discomfort. Certainly for a chance occupant it was otherwise. All night long I kept rolling into the dip, hearing in my dreams the great voice that had inspired us during the darkest days: ' . . . we shall fight on the beaches, we shall fight . . . in the streets . . . ; we shall never surrender.'

In the daytime we moved between the dignified hall with its crackling logs, a smaller parlour, the dining room, and the so-called Long Gallery with its many interesting objects. Chief among these was a ring which had belonged to Queen Elizabeth I and which she is reputed always to have worn. When a spring is released it opens to reveal a microscopic portrait of her cherished mother, Anne Boleyn. There was an oil painting of the Lord Protector, Oliver Cromwell, wearing a yellow satin coat. 'They did themselves well,' remarked Clem tersely, ending with his usual sniff.

The weekend enabled me to make my first acquaintance with Violet Attlee. We were about the same age, and alike also in possessing husbands older than ourselves of whom we were exceedingly fond. 'I cannot imagine', she would say, 'what life would have been or could ever be without Clem.' We had both had four children. She told me a great deal about her early married life when Clem had been a social worker at Toynbee Hall in the East End of London. Often short of money, they were given a great deal of help by Clem's elder brother. Even so, she had to do everything herself, which was most unusual for a middle-class couple of that time. 'Was Clem domesticated?' I asked. 'Not at all,' she replied with a laugh, but he made up for it by the support he gave her. He was good in his relations with the children and kept them in line with her routine. Equally important, in the long evenings he stayed at home and read aloud by the hour while she endlessly mended and ironed all their clothes.

But now what about the present? In the beauty and peace of Chequers I talked with Vi about how we could help the Government. She spoke of the 'inadequacy' she felt having to follow Clementine Churchill. There would be entertaining of supporters, of course. That would be easy. But what about distinguished foreign politicians and their wives? They might speak English or they might not. We decided the best thing we could do was to improve our French, the accepted international language.

I easily found a tutor with an excellent reputation and we arranged that she should come to Number 10 once a week to coach us and help us to acquire the sort of vocabulary we should need. Vi knew very little beyond school French and I was not much better off. It is true that I had spent two years in France between the ages of three and five and so had an excellent accent and a colloquial turn of phrase. But on the whole this did not help me much; indeed, it was slightly ridiculous to utter grammatical gaffes in an impeccable French accent!

Our French lessons continued for many months and proved to be very helpful and also good fun. From time to time I lunched with Clem and Vi in their small private flat looking out on Horseguards Parade. Vi had daily domestic help but did a large amount of the cooking herself. Once, I had just been invited by Bert Alexander, the First Lord of the Admiralty, to launch the light cruiser *Tiger* on Clydebank, and wondered what I should say on such an occasion. I told Vi about this and, turning to her husband, she said: 'Help her, Clem.' With great deliberation, first taking a cigar, cutting off the end and lighting up, Clem began: 'My Lord Provost, Members of the Town Council, my Lords, Ladies and Gentlemen . . .' and went on for ten minutes without a break while I scribbled feverishly, trying to take down every word. When I transcribed it into readable English I soon saw that from Clem it would have been first-rate whereas from me it would sound impossibly pompous. But nevertheless it amused me to think that, once, a Prime Minister had been my speech writer!

I enjoyed the launch immensely and was thrilled to be given an old Spanish silver inkpot – which I still have on my desk. It was an appropriate gift because the first *Tiger* had fought against the Spanish Armada. The one I launched became famous twenty years later when Harold Wilson used it for talks with Ian Smith after he had unilaterally declared the independence of Rhodesia.

One other memorable occasion of these immediate post-war years was a large fireworks display given to mark the final victory after the surrender of Japan. William and I were invited to watch this from the rooms in the House of Lords of our old friend Bill Jowitt, who was then Lord Chancellor. Along with Queen Mary, her grandchildren and a host of others, we watched as King George and Queen Elizabeth landed at the terrace of the House of Commons. After they had joined the party we all gathered at the windows to enjoy the magnificent spectacle.

In order to get a better view, Winston Churchill and Bill Jowitt stood on chairs, and Churchill said to him: 'You'd better take care. That chair's not safe – it's a political seat!' Churchill was wobbling about in a most dangerous fashion and at one point he warned Queen Mary: 'You'd better look out!' Her response to this informal remark was to stare straight ahead as if Churchill had not been there. A short while later I noticed with quite a shock that I still had on my bedroom slippers! Fortunately, my dress was long, and I do not suppose anybody bothered to look at my feet.

William's appointment as Secretary of State for Air enabled him to make an important decision concerning women priests. As he set off to 10 Downing Street after Attlee's summons, I ventured to put forward a particular interest of my own. All through the war I had worked with the Chaplains' Department among the women in the Forces and had seen the urgent necessity for women chaplains to be appointed. Anglicans would be barred because the Church of England opposed women priests, but the Free Churches had fully trained and ordained women ministers. I said to William: 'If you are given the Air Ministry would you please appoint the Reverend Elsie Chamberlain a full chaplain to the RAF?' William was in complete agreement. Even though Elsie was a Congregationalist, William went to Lambeth to see the Archbishop of Canterbury to tell him what he was going to do. 'I must go for my wife,' was the response, whereupon William was faced with both Geoffrey and Rosamund Fisher attacking his plans.

William was determined to press ahead, but it took him about nine months to get the appointment settled because the opposition to women chaplains was so intense. It was fought at every stage. This was purely a matter of Anglican prejudice against women priests, for Elsie was an experienced minister. We had studied Theology together at King's College, where she had obtained a Bachelor of Divinity degree. There were women doctors who were members of the RAF, like male doctors, but the chaplains would not have a woman chaplain as a member of the RAF. So although Elsie became a full RAF chaplain, she was commissioned as a Squadron Officer in the WAAF.

Eventually her appointment was announced and *The Times* had a photograph of her in uniform with a caption stating that no woman had ever held her position before. Within a few hours William received, by special messenger, the following letter, which became known in our family as 'the Archbishop's stinker':

My dear Lord Stansgate,

'The Times' to-day announces the appointment as an R.A.F. Chaplain of the Rev. Elsie Chamberlain. I cannot but deeply regret that you have not heeded my warning that this would cause confusion and trouble. It appears that in fact her commission is as a Squadron Officer in the W.A.A.F. To that of course there is no objection, but her description as a Chaplain will certainly bring me enquiries to which I shall have to be able to give a clear answer. May I therefore put the following questions: –

1. Is Squadron Officer Chamberlain in fact also a member of the Chaplains' Department of the R.A.F.?
2. In that case is she as such under the orders of the Chaplain-in-Chief and are her activities as a Chaplain controlled by him? If not, who does control her activities as a Chaplain?
3. In any case may I have an assurance that as a Chaplain she will not be permitted to exercise her ministry or take Services for Church of England personnel? In particular, under what conditions, if any, will she be allowed to administer the Sacraments of the Congregational Church and what steps will be taken to secure that all Church of England personnel are strictly warned that under no conditions must they either intentionally or by inadvertence attend Services at which she administers the Sacraments?

   I am sorry that the position has arisen in which I am compelled to put these questions. They need never have arisen if the admirable example of the Army had been followed and she had been appointed as a Chaplain's Assistant.
4. May I also be assured that in no circumstances will any Church of England Chaplain be put into the position of accepting orders about Services or their conduct from her or of being associated with her in their conduct?

William replied with the utmost courtesy and things went on just as planned.

A further problem arose when the Air Force annual described her as a welfare worker. William, realising that this had been done out of pure prejudice, called up the editor to complain. 'Very sorry, Minister, but it's done.' William was not accepting that reply. 'It's no good telling me that. You can just pulp the whole thing and put her down as a Chaplain. Print it again,' he said.

We next discovered that Elsie Chamberlain had been engaged for eight years to an Anglican curate, John Garrington. They had delayed their marriage because Bishop Wand of London had warned the curate that if he married Elsie he would never be given a parish. 'He can go and be a butcher's boy if he wants to marry this welfare officer,' was the Bishop's comment.

When I told this to William he was very angry and went straight to the Lord Chancellor, who had livings in his gift. Bill Jowitt was as furious as William. 'How very, very wrong,' he said. As a result, John Garrington was given a parish and he and Elsie were married. They exercised something of a joint ministry as Elsie's own church was nearby and they often preached at each other's services.

Elsie Chamberlain proved a very great success as an RAF chaplain, but the opposition in principle to any woman with the rank of full chaplain, even a Free Church one, remains implacable in the Chaplains' Department. No woman has ever held her post since.

Another example of Anglican prejudice concerned a Chinese deaconess. During the war Hong Kong was under the control of the Japanese, who deported all the clergy. In 1944, to enable Christian congregations to receive the sacraments, Bishop Hall of Hong Kong, on his own authority, ordained Deaconess Li Tim Oi, who thereby became the first Anglican woman priest. After the war the Society for the Propagation of the Gospel threatened to cut off aid if she remained a priest, and the Synod of Chinese Bishops put pressure on the Bishop of Hong Kong to ask for her resignation. Not wishing to see the dismissal of Bishop Hall, Lei Tim Oi agreed to resign, and in 1946 resumed her duties as a deaconess. I held a meeting in my house at which a very indignant Bishop Hall told us about the enormous pressure that had been placed upon him. A few years later on a visit to China I was told that all the Chinese Christians had supported Li Tim Oi. If it had not been for her there would have been no sacrament celebrated.

In April 1946, while I was with my parents in Scotland on a brief visit I heard on the radio that William was very shortly to be dispatched by Ernest Bevin, the Foreign Secretary, to Cairo to lead a British delegation to renegotiate the 1936 Anglo-Egyptian treaty under which British troops occupied bases in the Suez Canal zone.

Everything was to be arranged with the utmost speed, and I only just arrived home in time to hear what was proposed and see him off. His absence was likely to be a prolonged one, during the intense heat of the summer. This was the worst possible climate for a malaria victim and my first thought and question was: 'Would I be allowed to accompany him?' William unwillingly agreed to sound out Ernest Bevin. The answer was an uncompromising 'No.' When the treaty was finally concluded Bevin proposed to come to Cairo with his wife, Florence, for the celebrations. I would be allowed to go then, but not before.

It was a long, dreary summer. William made no mention of the heat, but the tale needed no telling. As the months passed, the letters I received were often blotted by perspiration. Finally the situation became intolerable and the traditional move to Alexandria took place. Although very concerned about William's health, I had to be satisfied with a situation which there was no means of changing. At least William was comfortably housed with every convenience at hand.

The mission itself did not go well. William put the Government's case that Britain would agree to evacuate troops from the military bases only if they had the automatic right to send them back in an emergency. When the Egyptians would not accept this, William, who for many decades had supported Egypt's right to self-determination and believed that British troops should withdraw from Egypt unconditionally, persuaded Attlee and Bevin that more concessions were needed, but in the event the talks broke down because Britain would not accept Egypt's claims over the Sudan.

One man who was pleased with this outcome was the Leader of the Opposition, Winston Churchill. On learning of the Egyptian mission, he had said to William: 'While remaining personally friendly, I shall make your life as difficult as possible.'

In the early autumn of 1946 Attlee reorganised the Defence Services under a single Minister of Defence and looked for younger men to take over as service ministers outside the Cabinet. William received a brief cable to this effect and was asked to come back at once and then resign. The British authorities in Cairo insisted that he must wait for a plane that measured up to the safety standards required for Cabinet Ministers. On hearing this, Clem, in his businesslike way, ordered William to resign at once and to take any plane that was going.

Political life is full of such ups and downs. They are only to be expected and have to be taken in good part. A party leader, especially if he is Prime Minister, must be free to make what changes suit the needs of the moment without having to consider the personal feelings of those affected. In general the Tories have shown themselves to be better at this activity than the Labour Party, but Clem was an unusually good butcher.

After his return from Egypt William devoted himself to his duties in the House of Lords. At first he found the restrictions placed on him by Labour headquarters somewhat tiresome. Although he was in genuine sympathy with Labour aims in the widest sense, from time to time the old Liberal 'independent' broke through and he felt compelled to act on his own. I believe that this clearly illustrated the difficulties that anyone born and brought up as a Liberal always experiences when he has joined any other party.

Without the restraining influence of a constituency, William simply used, more and more, the freedom his seat in the House of Lords provided. He remained popular and on the most friendly terms with his colleagues, but they came to think of him as someone outside the party discipline – no cautionary advice was ever whispered – and in the course of time summons to the regular party meetings of peers simply ceased to arrive.

William always said he did not really like being in the House of Lords, describing it, with affectionate disrespect, as 'old gentlemen's political croquet', but I felt that this great House of Commons man began to enjoy himself in the Lords, of which he ideologically disapproved, more than he had done in the House of Commons since 1927 – even as a Cabinet minister. He relished his increasing independence.

Officially he was described as retired but this expression had no meaning. He continued to read *The Times* daily for a couple of hours, filing all the important pieces of world news. By the time he took his seat in the House of Lords in the afternoon he was up to date – no one more so – with what was going on everywhere. When challenged he could, as always, give chapter and verse in support of his statements and attitude. This professional performance gave him immense satisfaction and won a wide respect. Nevertheless, at the age of seventy, he did not imagine that he would ever again be called upon to play a central role in international affairs. He could not have been more wrong.

CHAPTER 12
1947–1957

In the midst of this active and enjoyable 'retirement', William was invited, in 1947, to become World President of the Inter-Parliamentary Union. The IPU, as it was familiarly called, had been founded in 1889 by an English MP, William Randal Cremer, and a Frenchman, Frédéric Passy, with the intention of promoting international peace and understanding. In each member country it functioned at the level of the Speakers and private members, many of whom, like William, had held Cabinet rank in the past. The headquarters were in Geneva.

The IPU had no actual political power and some people expressed doubts as to whether it had any influence at all. But after thinking it over, William concluded that the existence of the IPU, and the holding of its conference in a different country each year, under the aegis of that country's government, were valuable ways of keeping and extending international contacts. There was a great deal of tension in these early post-war years between the Western countries and our wartime allies the Soviet Union and her satellite states. Anything that might produce holes in the Iron Curtain would be worth trying. Having decided this, William threw himself into the service of the IPU with characteristic vigour, and for the next ten years he, and I, as his personal aide, visited a large number of different countries, learnt much, and made many lasting friendships. I believe we were able to 'get understanding' of each other.

The duties of President kept William in close touch all the year with the Secretary General of the IPU, an office filled first by Léopold Boissier, then by his successor, André de Blonay, who invited us to stay with his wife and himself at the Château de Blonay on Lake Geneva, which he had just inherited. This visit proved to be a most charming interlude in the business life of the IPU. From sunrise till the moonlit night hours the lake and the mountains provided a changing panorama of marvellous beauty, and we could hear the bleating of hidden sheep high up in their pasturage on the slope above us. Sometimes André de Blonay, a superb pianist who had missed his vocation, would play something by Beethoven. In these days of rest and refreshment there seemed nothing more to wish for.

Each spring a particular pleasure was the visit to Monte Carlo, in the Principality of Monaco, for the annual Council meeting. It is difficult to convey an adequate impression of how delightful it was, after long months of wintry bad weather in England, to go by plane or, even better, by train, for anticipation was prolonged, into the sunshine of the Riviera. We would touch down – or wake up – to find brightly coloured flowers and a blue sky. At the Hotel Metropole we were always given a large room facing the sea. Everything on the morning breakfast tray, although familiar, tasted better than ever before in such welcome circumstances.

On one occasion we enjoyed a memorable lunch with Prince Rainier. The whole atmosphere of the palace was of the eighteenth century: the armed guards in their old uniforms, footmen with their braided coats, the band playing for lunch, and the family portraits hanging round the room, with its massive Italian fireplace.

The proceedings were of a most formal kind. As we gathered in the ante-room the soldiers drew their swords to salute the Prince as he entered with members of his family. We sat on either side of the Prince and William reminded him that an earlier Rainier had fought at the Battle of Hastings. The Prince spoke perfect English and was most charming, but there were times when he looked a little gloomy, and I was very glad for him when he married the actress Grace Kelly a few years later. A beautiful and vivacious wife was exactly what he needed.

After Prince Rainier had left the drawing room, passing between the drawn swords of the guards standing at attention, the Chamberlain returned and asked William to see the Prince for a moment to be presented with the Order of St Charles. We were then shown round the palace and I was intrigued to see a bedroom furnished in eighteenth-century style known as the York Room. This turned out to be named after Edward Augustus, Duke of York, a brother of George III, who had been taken ill during a visit to Monaco and died there.

As well as the Council meetings in Monte Carlo a conference was held each autumn. The 1948 gathering was held in Rome, but I did not accompany William as I was involved with the first Assembly of the World Council of Churches in Amsterdam. Just as William and I saw the IPU as a universal organisation which might counter the increasing division of the world into two camps, East and West, so we hoped that the World Council of Churches might play a similar part. It was therefore a great pity that many of the Eastern churches were not represented and that the Pope would not allow any Roman Catholics to attend. Nevertheless, there were representatives from over forty countries.

I was asked by the General Secretary, Dr Willem Visser't Hooft, a Dutch priest, to join the Study Commission, and to be a member of the committee that was considering the Nature of the Church in God's Design. As I was also a consultant on the Place of Women in the Church, I was there for the whole month the Assembly took place. When the news of my appointments reached Dr Fisher, the Archbishop of Canterbury, he wrote to Dr Visser't Hoof warning him that my views on the ministry of women in the church were not those of the Church of England. This was the final straw for me. Now that I knew I was not a welcome member of the Church of England and that there would be no progress in the near future on the issue of the ordination of women, I decided that when I returned home at the end of the Assembly I would become a Congregationalist.

I enjoyed my work at the Assembly and met many interesting people, including Pastor Martin Niemöller, who had spent eight years in Nazi prisons, and Professor Karl Barth, the controversial theologian who was creating quite a stir with his extremely otherworldly approach to religion which ran counter to the views of many liberal theologians, including those of another leading participant at the Assembly, my friend Reinhold Niebuhr. I was amused some years later at a meeting held to commemorate Karl Barth's seventieth birthday when the Archbishop of Canterbury introduced William to him with the words, 'here is another rebel'.

At the Assembly Karl Barth had the room opposite mine. No one dared to put him in any of the dormitories shared by eminent theologians. 'The spoilt boy of Europe,' complained the wife of an English bishop, separated from her husband. I ventured during the debates to ask the eminent professor a polite question. I got a very short answer. Dr Barth, I could see, did not suffer amateurs gladly, nor, for that matter, experts either.

At that time he was in a perennial state of argument with Dr Emil Brunner. This he pursued in an atmosphere of lofty disdain which unfortunately the very sensitive Dr Brunner could not share. Reinhold said of Dr Barth's treatment of the Bible: 'He takes what he likes and allegorises the rest,' a remark with which Dr Brunner joyfully agreed.

The following year in London I found a note, from my helper, on the telephone pad saying: 'A foreigner rang up about religion.' This mysterious message was happily followed by a letter from Dr Brunner saying he would shortly be in London and asking: 'Would you care to hear me lecture on the Christian Idea of Time?' Unfortunately, I had the greatest difficulty in doing so as he gave no place and the wrong date. By dint of much effort I traced him to King's College and we had a happy reunion afterwards.

The first annual conference of the Inter-Parliamentary Union that William and I attended together took us to Stockholm in the summer of 1949. I had special cause to feel happy at that time because, a couple of months before, I had taken my first and only university examination: the special entrance allowed to 'mature' students in place of London Matriculation. This consisted of papers in English, French, New Testament Greek and Logic. It was an altogether new experience and one I thoroughly enjoyed in spite of being questioned by the board of examiners, some of whom were professors of University College, London, of which William was an Honorary Fellow. One of the great moments of my life was when I rang up my father to announce my success.

The voyage to Sweden was a delight. William always chose to go by some means of transport owned by the country we were visiting. Only if pressed for time did we fly. We both preferred a journey that showed us as much as possible of the local land and people. On this occasion, as soon as we boarded the liner, we were taken into a world far removed from the shortages of post-war Britain. Our first lunch brought before us the long-forgotten luxury of an unrationed meal. This, being Swedish, began with an immense variety of smorgasbord – hors d'œuvres – which in themselves would have constituted an entire repast for me. Much else followed, then, and at every meal.

The only note of anxiety on the brief journey was sounded by the Captain, who had to be on constant look-out for 'magnetic mines', laid during the war and still wandering about the sea ready to attach themselves to any ship they came across and blow it up. Fortunately, nothing disturbed the calm of the voyage and we arrived much refreshed at the Swedish capital. Sweden, a neutral country during the war, seemed at that time, to a Briton, a singularly normal and untroubled country. But we soon found that its inhabitants regarded themselves as having been very much in the middle of the war because of the number of refugees of all kinds who had sought asylum there.

It so happened that my mother showed more interest in this visit to Sweden than she had done in any other that I had ever made. I knew that my mother had received several proposals of marriage, but I had been told few details. Little by little it came out that, as a young woman, she had visited a Swedish friend at her home and there met and fell in love with a compatriot. The affection was warmly returned and he wooed her with great determination over several years. Only one thing stood in the way of their marriage: her mother's opposition. The suitor made one last effort, some years later, by letter. He wrote to my mother's old address at her father's home, not knowing she was married. It so happened that my nurse took me along that day to see my grandfather and I was given the letter to 'hand to Mummy'. At the time I had not realised the significance of that incident.

What I particularly enjoyed about the conference was meeting MPs from so many different countries. For me the most interesting of all came from the newly established State of Israel. In 1947 the United Nations had decided that Palestine should be divided between the Jews and the Arabs; but the Arabs, refusing to accept the partition, launched attacks on the Jewish areas. Eventually, in May 1948, David Ben-Gurion proclaimed the State of Israel and, after further fighting, an armistice was declared in the spring of 1949. At the end of the war the land was divided between Israel and Jordan, with the Egyptians administering the Gaza Strip. Jerusalem itself was partitioned, the Jordanians controlling the old city of East Jerusalem, including the Temple area and the Wailing Wall, while the Israelis had the 'new', western part. This situation lasted until 1967, when the Israelis gained control of the whole of the city after the Six Day War.

The Israeli Government under Ben-Gurion, the first Prime Minister, was anxious to take every opportunity of becoming part of the comity of nations and lost no time in joining the Inter-Parliamentary Union. They sent as representatives Rabbi Mordecai Narock, the Minister of Posts, and Moshe Rosetti, English born, who was the Clerk of the Knesset – the Israeli parliament. William knew Rossetti from his London days when he had worked in the Mayor's office in Stepney in the East End of London. When William had been an MP in the same area before the First World War many of his constituents had been Jews who had fled persecution in Russia. This had given William his lifelong interest in the Jewish cause.

Rabbi Narock spoke to the IPU in Hebrew, and for the first time ever a modern international conference was addressed in the language of the Prophets and one in which Jesus himself had been proficient. We had many conversations with the Israeli delegates and they expressed the hope that we might visit the new state before long.

The conference ended with a performance at the beautiful Royal theatre near the palace, followed by a meeting with the King and Queen of Sweden, with whom we took tea. Both spoke perfect English, for Queen Louise was the sister of Earl Mountbatten of Burma, and King Gustav's first wife had been Princess Margaret of Connaught, granddaughter of Queen Victoria.

Next year we were invited to hold the conference in Ireland. Among the British delegation there was some trepidation as to how things might develop, because the Republic of Ireland, established the year before, had left the Commonwealth and disapproved of Northern Ireland's being a part of the United Kingdom. William, who had always supported the cause of Irish nationalism, was interested to observe the new situation.

For my part a visit to Ireland presented an entirely new experience. It might have been a completely foreign country as far as I was concerned. A rough sea passage from Holyhead took us there and we arrived tossed and weary. Immediately, we were made welcome by delightful hospitality and at once felt at home. I was much struck by the European atmosphere of Dublin, which gave me no sense of being the capital of an island.

The only discordant note came when, during a session held, as usual, at the Dail, it was found, for the first and only time, that a demonstration hostile to Britain had gathered outside. In consequence the authorities would not allow any members of the British delegation to leave by the front door. We were spirited out by a side entrance into waiting cars. When we reached our hotel we were disturbed to find that the genial and popular Conservative MP for Ealing, Sir Frank Sanderson, was missing. Someone had heard him refuse to come with the rest of us and, indeed, had seen him disappear into the thick of the demonstration.

We awaited the outcome of this recklessness with some anxiety. Fortunately, half an hour later Frank arrived in fine trim. 'Did you have a rough time?' he was asked. 'Rough time?' he replied. 'Certainly not. I just went through the crowd shaking hands right and left. They were soon all slapping me on the back.' This reaction was in keeping with Frank's own friendly nature, which would not allow of anyone exhibiting hostile feelings.

Our journey to the conference in Turkey in 1951 remains memorable because it was while we were on our way there that we learnt that we had become grandparents for the first time. I had not been happy about leaving London, as Anthony's wife, Caroline, was due to give birth to their first child at any moment. Her parents were in America and we, would naturally have liked to have stood in. During our first night on board ship we worried about what was happening, but were delighted when we were greeted the next morning with a telegram announcing the joyful news 'wonderful green-eyed grandson arrived safely this evening'. The news got round among our fellow members of the IPU, and at dinner that night we were presented with so many pink carnations that every table on the ship was able to have a bunch of them to celebrate the birth of Stephen Michael Benn.

We enjoyed the few days on the Mediterranean between Marseilles and Istanbul, relaxing in congenial circumstances and society. As we passed Mount Etna it obliged us with an eruption. Red-hot lava rolled down its sides into the sea, to be extinguished with a hiss that was felt rather than heard. Very late on the last evening we passed by the island of Castelorizo, which, once again, brought back so many memories to William of his wartime experiences.

This was my first visit to Istanbul since 1926, and I was looking forward immensely to returning to this city of enchantment. We were housed by our hosts in the best hotel the city afforded, but, alas, we soon realised that paralytic plumbing and a resident colony of grey rats were going to make life very uneasy once the day's work was over. I could not but admire the skill of the rats at getting what they wanted. They somehow managed to enter the drawers where I kept gifts of chocolates and, having carefully slipped off the silver paper that covered them, devoured each one.

They also took a great interest in my clothes, and if I left the wardrobe door open I would waken at dawn to see them running backwards and forwards on the rail, inspecting my various outfits. This made me shiver as I thought of the parasites they might be leaving behind. Not surprisingly in all these circumstances, many of us fell ill, and the one British doctor in our party found himself very busy indeed even when he was stricken himself.

Happily, William and I recoverd sufficiently to set out for convalescence in the beautiful holiday village of B'am Doune high up on the hills above Beirut in the Lebanon. There we stayed for a week or two, occasionally going down to the city for diplomatic parties. We were very anxious to be fit and well so that we could proceed to West Jerusalem, where we had been invited to stay as guests of the Israeli Government. From the Arab city of Beirut we had no direct access to Israel, so we flew to Jordanian-controlled Old Jerusalem, from where we knew we should be allowed entry to the Israeli part of the city.

Although Jerusalem was supposed to be composed of two entities completely closed to each other, it was run in many ways as one. This applied, for example, to the whole drainage system, which was impeccably managed. On our arrival we spent a few days at the American hospice, where everything was perfection. We were able to visit old friends and spent many hours walking in the old city and visiting again the Church of the Holy Sepulchre.

It was obvious that the two authorities were in touch by telephone, because after we had been there for about a week we were told: ' "They" have been ringing through to know when you're going over to the other side.' We fixed a date a few days ahead and duly presented ourselves at the Mandelbaum Gate – actually a road barrier with huts – with our luggage and our two necessarily different sets of passports. In the first we were shown as leaving Arab countries; no mention was made of where we were going. The Jordanian frontier officials, adhering strictly to regulations, pretended to have no knowledge whatsoever of the existence of Israel. As far as they were concerned we simply vanished like Elijah, transported straight to Heaven.

The other passports, on the contrary, were innocent of any mention of Arab countries. We were coming out of the blue into the sovereign state of Israel. Our old friends shook hands in farewell. We took a few steps and our new friends greeted us with the traditional 'shalom' – 'peace'. Among this small group we were delighted to see our old friend Moshe Rosetti, and a youngish rabbi, Shlomo Nathan – known to his friends as 'F. G.' Nathan – who had been the chief Jewish RAF chaplain in the Middle East during the Second World War. He and his charming wife, Eva, were to become great friends of ours. Sadly, he died very prematurely some years ago.

William and I were given a suite in the King David Hotel. Our rooms opened on to a terrace facing the old walls of Jerusalem, and we found much to think about as we sat there and watched giant bats hovering over the tombs of the Herods. Our hosts were more than generous, and as well as dinner parties we were taken to see everything we could wish.

This city that has seen so much and suffered so much and given so much over the centuries always speaks in a wordless intimacy to those who have ears to hear. Time stands still in its streets as nowhere else on earth. It seems as though one might at any turning see all those who have ever walked there in the past.

At that time Operation 'Eagles' Wings' was proceeding almost daily. This was the programme under which whole Jewish communities were lifted back to Israel from countries where their ancestors had settled for centuries. We saw this in action one morning at sunrise. Together with Moshe Rosetti, we stood on the tarmac at Lydda airport and watched a large plane land. Out of it came about forty immigrants from Persia and Afghanistan, their humble possessions wrapped in sheets. But they were not rustics. In their midst stood the rabbi carrying a Torah – the scroll of the Law – wrapped in rich scarlet. These were dedicated Jews brought up on the Law, the prophets, and the writings of their religion. 'These are the same people as myself,' declared Moshe Rossetti, almost overcome by his emotions, 'and we haven't met for three thousand years.'

We asked if we might convey our heartfelt good wishes to them in their new life. Surprisingly, it was a little old lady who came forward, not the rabbi. Through two interpreters we talked. She told us something about the community and its feelings. 'We have not come for privileges,' she said, 'but to work in our own land.'

We were told that the newcomers neither expressed nor felt surprise at the hitherto unknown experience of flying. Had it not been promised that 'They who wait upon the Lord shall renew their strength; they shall mount up with wings as eagles'? The only thing, we were told, that they later found astonishing was that the bus from the airport did not in its turn rise from the ground.

Every day there was something new for us to do and experience. Among the highlights was a Kiddush – the sabbath meal – at the home of the Chief Rabbi of Israel and his wife. Dr Herzog had been Chief Rabbi of Dublin before taking up his new position and we were interested to observe that his son, Chaim Herzog, the future President of Israel, spoke English with an Irish accent. Mrs Herzog met us in the hall a minute or two before her husband appeared. During this brief time she whispered a warning in my ear: 'The Chief Rabbi does not shake hands with ladies.' Thus warned I advanced carefully towards Dr Herzog with my right arm firmly held behind my back. After a very cordial greeting we entered the dining room, where a solemn sabbath meal was to be held.

For a Christian the Kiddush is of great interest. The word itself is derived from the root meaning 'holy'. It is of course the origin and on the pattern of the Last Supper held by Christ on the night of his arrest and on the day before the crucifixion. In Christian churches of a hierarchical nature women may not participate in the consecration and distribution of the bread and wine. This function is for the priests only, and the service takes place in church always on the first day of the week and often on other days as well. Jewish people celebrate their service at home on the Friday evening. It is a meal for family and friends at which women take the leading part.

I can think of few more joyful occasions than the service of the Kiddush celebrated in Jerusalem. The Chief Rabbi and Mrs Herzog proved to be delightful hosts. They were able to tell us much we wanted to know about the exciting days of the new State of Israel. At one point in our conversation Dr Herzog startled me by asking: 'Do you ever preach any sermons?' 'It has happened,' I replied, wondering what I was calling down on my head by this admission. 'In that case,' he said, 'I'll give you a text for your next one.' He recited verses about the rebuilding of the Temple. When the stones were put in place there was no noise, for they had been moulded to the right shape before they were brought there. This, said Dr Herzog, expressed the function of the Jewish home. There children were moulded from earliest days by the influence of the family so that when they attended synagogue they fitted to perfection.

Perhaps the most memorable event of our visit was an audience with the Prime Minister. Once met, David Ben-Gurion was a man never to be forgotten. Short of stature with distinctive tufts of white hair, he was to the last degree a down-to-earth, tough character of great determination. Like all the Zionist leaders we met, Ben-Gurion was totally dedicated to the practical vision of a homeland for his people. During his early days in Palestine he had endured great privation and knew the meaning of bitter and prolonged hunger. This spurred him on to greater effort and now, as he told us, 'Israel has been redeemed.'

The first thing I noticed about the room was the presence on his desk of a large copy of the Hebrew Bible – the Book of Books. Just beside it lay a small glass case containing a line or so of writing in Hebrew. This, I was to learn, was changed every day. It was the Prime Minister's habit on coming into his office in the morning to read very studiously a portion of the Hebrew Bible, then to take from it a short passage which expressed and emphasised for him the central message of the whole. This provided him with both his course of action for the day, and a travel guide on how to get there and so fully achieve the objective. This was the man some people told me was not an observant Jew.

We began talking about the political situation, but the whole conversation took a different course when, to my great surprise, Moshe Rosetti told Ben-Gurion of my interest in Hebrew. At this politics instantly vanished into the background. Pushing the Hebrew Bible across the desk to me, the Prime Minister demanded: 'Read to me out of it.' What a daunting prospect! Fortunately, I had been studying Genesis in depth and, opening it at the first chapter, I read bravely in a confident voice that masked inner trembling. After a few verses, he stopped me, seized the book, shut it with a bang and, with every appearance of displeasure, remarked: 'You'd never make a Zionist – you know too much Hebrew!' So it all turned into great fun, and his wry joke remains one I have always cherished.

During that same visit he invited me to attend a session of the weekly Bible class held at his official residence. I was placed next to him at the large table around which were gathered a whole variety of people: politicians, scholars, craftsmen. My attention was drawn to the most knowledgeable Bible student – a working man – and the special honour given to him. It was a lively evening. The enemies of Israel were active, despite the armistice, and above us we heard the constant movement of planes coming over and being chased away. No one took any notice, and I wondered in how many capital cities one could find the Prime Minister and his colleagues quietly studying the Bible while enemy planes flew overhead. Here, I knew, I had come across the living heart and soul of Israel, the very reason for its unconquerable existence down the long millennia of time.

I went back to our beautiful suite at the King David Hotel and walked for a little while on the terrace, overcome by the timelessness of Jerusalem. I came back to the present with a jolt. The next day William and I were to be the guests of the Knesset at lunch: supposing – knowing, as the MPs did, of my deep interest in Israel past, present and future – just supposing I was asked to say a word as well as he? I was alone and sat down in complete silence with my eyes shut. Suddenly a speech came into my mind fully formed. If asked I would speak about Israel under four aspects: the people, the land, the language and the Book of Books. These four were not separate things but one entity. I felt no more fear. It would all be easy and natural: what comes from the heart reaches the hearts of others. I went to bed at peace, without a word written.

The lunch was most enjoyable, and afterwards I was indeed asked to speak. I said the words that had come into my mind the evening before, and although I spoke without notes the ideas came fluently. By great good fortune I recalled the words of a leader of the English Reformation, 'There is yet more light and truth to break forth from the Holy Word,' to which I added, 'and here in Jerusalem we have seen it happen!' I am pleased to say that my speech was very well received and some of the audience were overwhelmed with tears of emotion. Later I was told: 'Your speech was the talk of Jerusalem.' It was written down and printed in the daily newspaper.

We left for home in happy possession of a bottle of Jordan water for the christening of our first grandchild. It had been collected for me by a Jew with the words of goodwill, 'May he be a good man and a great friend of the people!' I took a photograph of this event which my eldest grandchild, Stephen, possesses, and he is certainly living up to the words uttered.

The conference held in Washington in 1953 was an outstanding occasion for the IPU and for us. William presided at the opening meeting, which was held in the House of Representatives. To the strains of 'Hail to the Chief', President Eisenhower arrived with his supporters. To see William in the seat of authority with the President of the United States seated below him seemed like a topsy-turvy dream. As Commander in Chief of the Armed Forces in Europe during the Second World War, General Eisenhower had been based in England, and had long been a familiar figure to us all. It was reassuring to see the degree of trust he inspired in his own people.

Afterwards we were all entertained in the Oval Office of the White House. I was particularly charmed by Mrs Eisenhower, who greeted me with a friendly wink. Soon after arriving we were taken in charge by a young-looking man with rows of decorations. 'This young officer has got a lot of medals,' said William with great respect, picking out those he knew and explaining them to me. When the anonymous hero left us we heard him say to the next guests: 'I'm General Gruenther.' The 'young' officer turned out to be the Supreme Commander of NATO Forces in Europe!

In the early 1950s the tension between the West and the Soviet Union had deepened and the East European states had refused to continue participating in the Inter-Parliamentary Union. The death of Stalin in 1953 improved the diplomatic climate, and by the time of the 1955 conference, held in Helsinki in Finland, parliamentarians from the Soviet Union and the East European states were in attendance.

The conference was notable for the great effort William made to get China admitted to membership of the IPU. American opposition remained the one powerful element that stood in the way. This was expressed forcibly by members of the delegation. 'You don't think, do you,' exclaimed one Congressman, 'that we're ever going to sit round a table with the Chinese?' More politely, our Secretary General, André de Blonay, reminded William of the financial considerations: much of the money necessary to the IPU came from the United States. This, of course, was the side of things that least appealed to my husband.

The Chinese themselves were so optimistic that they sent a carefully chosen group of 'observers' to the conference, men and women ready to become members immediately if permitted. They were charming people: highly educated and well versed in foreign affairs. Unfortunately, the 'Noes' prevailed, and to the grief of many they returned empty-handed to Peking.

Leaving Helsinki at the end of the conference, we set off to pay our third visit to the Soviet Union. We were very pleased that our son David, fluent in Russian, was able to accompany us. The political situation was

somewhat different from the days of Stalin. The Soviet Government had
recently recognised the existence of West Germany and we were fascinated to see Dr Adenauer, the German Chancellor, standing with the new
leaders, Khrushchev and Bulganin, at a performance by the Bolshoi
Ballet, while a special choir sang the German anthem, 'Deutschland über
alles'.

I was particularly interested in the religious situation and noticed that,
while things seemed a little easier since Stalin's death, there were obvious
shortages of such things as prayer books. Both William and I were asked
to give addresses in public at Baptist chapels. Our Communist guide
seemed concerned as to what we might say, but David told us that she
translated correctly with emphasis in all the right places. The service
finished with a hymn sung to the well-known tune 'God be with us till
we meet again', after which everyone took a large white handkerchief
out of their pockets and waved them and gave us a long and most moving
farewell. We asked David to thank them all for the wonderful experience
and he received the warm reply: 'It is we who thank them for coming.'

Our Soviet hosts generously asked us what we would like to do and
encouraged us to see as much of the country as we could. Travelling in
low-flying planes, we had a good view of the land of Soviet Central Asia.
Samarkand was very beautiful, but, alas, there was no hope of seeing, let
alone buying, any of the beautiful rugs for which the region was famous,
as this kind of skilled handwork was apparently looked down upon. We
were offered any amount of machine-made carpets as the latest thing.

After visiting the oilfields of Baku on the Caspian Sea, we flew to the
headquarters of the Armenian Church at Erevan, from where there was
a wonderful view of Mount Ararat. A new head of the church – the
Catholicos – was in the process of being elected. William and I were
invited to attend the service and were accommodated with seats in front
of the high altar, where a large number of bishops from all over the
world were conducting the ceremony. It was a brilliant gathering and
the singing of the young priests was very beautiful.

From there we went to Sochi on the Black Sea coast, where unfortunately I was struck down with bronchitis. I was assured by the doctors
that they would be able to 'interrupt' the condition by a strange treatment known as 'cupping'. The only result was that my back bore about
twenty bright brown raised marks! Antibiotics were tried next, but they
were administered in such quantity and strength that I developed problems with breathing and swallowing, and nearly died. I was sent to
Moscow and recovered under the care of the British Embassy doctor.
While I was there I received the sad news of my sister Hermione's death
from lung cancer after a long illness. She had lived in South Africa for
many years, but had been able to make an extended visit to England not
very long before.

Later that year it was with great anticipation and delight that we accepted an invitation to visit India. At last we should see the country that had been constantly in our thoughts during William's period of office as Secretary of State. Arriving at the airport, we were met by officials who duly greeted and garlanded us with much warmth. Our first visitor, Mr Speaker Mavalankar of the Indian Parliament, promised us an extremely interesting series of experiences.

For the first time William met many people whom he had imprisoned, most unwillingly, during his period of office as Secretary of State. It was quite usual for a fellow guest at a dinner party to say to him, good-naturedly: 'I wrote to you, sir, from prison but, alas, you did not release me.' One of these former prisoners was now the Prime Minister: Pandit Jawaharlal Nehru. He entertained us at his official residence and afterwards took us to see something of which he was exceedingly proud – a pair of giant pandas, the gift of China, which had settled down exceedingly well and shortly afterwards produced a number of young. He said: 'I'm very pleased they've given birth, I'm so delighted.' That day, as every other day, he donned gloves after lunch and went and fed them himself.

The beauty of New Delhi, as planned by Sir Edwin Lutyens, remains vividly in mind, but no less interesting was the old part of the city with its ancient buildings and the 'sacred cows' wandering through its streets. We visited the ashram where Mahatma Gandhi, tragically assassinated in 1948, had lived with his religious followers. It was full of memories but sadly rat-infested.

We had planned to travel from Kashmir down to the south, but, alas, William fell ill with his old enemy, malaria, and we were only able to spend a few days at Agra to visit the Taj Mahal. This unforgettable sight – viewed at all hours of the day and by moonlight – did something to compensate for losing a view of the Himalayas and Kashmir as well as Southern India.

We spent a short while in Bombay. The problems confronting the Indian Government were vividly in evidence in the early mornings, when pavements were covered with sleeping people covered by old coats who stirred into uneasy life a little later on. Our headquarters were vastly different and illustrated only too painfully the great gulf between the privileged and the rest. We were housed in Nehru's holiday bungalow on the edge of a cliff high up above the Indian Ocean. The superb view and the peace and quiet made it an interval of dreamlike recuperation.

In January 1956 we visited Egypt as guests of President Gamal Abdel Nasser. The withdrawal of British troops from the Suez Canal bases which was then in progress had eased relations between Britain and Egypt, but now the main internal problem for Egypt was arranging finance to build the Aswan Dam. The day after our arrival we drove by appointment to visit the President in his modest home in Cairo. On arrival, William, leaving me in the car, went up to the house and rang the bell. We were both surprised by the lack of security guards. The door was opened by a youngish man in his thirties. William explained that he had an audience with President Nasser and the young man replied: 'I am President Nasser. Is that your wife in the car? Bring her in and I will get my wife.'

After ushering us into a living room he vanished into the kitchen and presently returned with Mrs Nasser. A very pleasant hour followed. Mrs Nasser did not speak fluent English but dispensed coffee and orange juice in the most friendly fashion. She gazed on her husband with obviously deep admiration and devotion. The President himself struck us as an impressive patriot totally committed to his country and its needs. He greeted William as 'a good and true friend of Egypt'. Referring to William's attempt at renegotiating the Anglo-Egyptian treaty, Nasser said it would never be forgotten how well he had understood the situation *vis-à-vis* Egypt and the Sudan and the need for Egypt to have control of the waters of the Nile. 'You understand our situation, which your governments have never done.'

Nasser was very concerned that the American and British offer to finance the dam had many conditions attached, whereas the Russians had offered to pay for it without restrictions. 'I must feed my people,' said this modern Pharaoh. 'To do so I must have money to build the dam. Where will I get it? If I call in the Russians will they ever leave? I have no experience of their ways. I would rather have help from the British than from anyone else. You are gentlemen and you know when to get out. But all the pressure is from the West; the smiles from the East.' William and I recalled this conversation when, later in the year, the West withdraw the offer of finance for the Aswan Dam, thus starting the train of events that culminated in the Suez crisis.

At the time of our visit, and for many years afterwards, there were no diplomatic relations between Egypt and Israel and, like everyone else with whom we talked in Egypt, Nasser was greatly concerned about Israeli intentions, fearing that they wanted to take over his country. Speaking with great anger and bitterness, he declared: 'The all-important thing is how long are the Israelis going to let us live?' Out of my long and deep interest in Israel I attempted to reassure him. All the Jewish people wanted, I told him, was to return again to the plane of political existence as a nation based on Jerusalem; they had no aim whatsoever to conquer other nations and set up an empire. But he was sure he knew better.

Before leaving Egypt, we went by train to Luxor and visited the tomb of Tutankhamen in the Valley of the Kings. After walking down long, cunningly concealed passages, lit originally by light transferred from mirror to mirror, we arrived in a hall of stupendous majesty and grandeur. There in the midst was the young Pharaoh in the place where he had been laid to rest in the year 1352 BC, surrounded by the possessions he had treasured in his earthly life.

His mummy had only recently been returned to Luxor as a result of a government decree which stated that the bodies of the Pharaohs were to be taken out of the Cairo Museum and sent back to the Valley of the Kings. This operation had been organised in a highly inventive fashion. A date had been fixed and at midnight, when all was quiet and the population asleep, a fleet of ambulances had been called out to transport the mummies of the departed rulers to a special train that took them to their original burial places.

After our visit to Luxor, we embarked with great expectations of enjoyment and restful stimulation for a journey up the Nile to Khartoum in the Sudan. There were only two other English travellers, and to our surprise they turned out to be Somerset Maugham, the writer, and his companion-secretary, Alan Searle. We found Maugham exceedingly charming, very modest and unassuming and, indeed, quite unlike the somewhat cynical image of him that his photographs suggested.

He had just come from paying a visit to the Aga Khan in Cairo and had some amusing tales to add to our own about the Prince's sense of humour. 'How is it', Maugham had asked him, 'that you, the head of a large body of Muslims to whom alcohol is strictly forbidden, do in fact consume it daily?' The Aga Khan looked at him pityingly. 'Did you not know', he asked, 'that as soon as alcohol touches my lips it becomes orange juice?'

The days passed delightfully. Whenever the boat stopped, William and I went out to explore the local country, together, as often as not, with Somerset Maugham, always his congenial self. Then one afternoon I had a strangely different experience. This time, unusually, William had remained below and I was lazing on the deck on my own. I came to attention as Somerset Maugham seated himself beside me. His whole expression had changed from one of light-hearted relaxation to one of great concentration. Leaning forward with his arms crossed, he asked me several questions of a personal nature, and I began to feel like an inexperienced fly that had somehow strayed into the web of a sophisticated and very determined old spider, pursuing a well-worn course of action. This was the other side of the man – the literary artist at work getting the raw material from life that he would later turn to use in his incomparable stories. He obviously enjoyed prodding. I equally enjoyed parrying the prods! It was all an interesting experience that enabled me to obtain an increased understanding of the great story-teller.

The last lap of our journey to Khartoum was a long train ride across the desert. Although we shut all the windows the sand got into William's malaria-disturbed lungs, and soon after we got to Khartoum he took to his bed. He had just had time to contact the Mahdi, the leader of the Sudanese, and accept an invitation to dinner for both of us. This, I hastened, with many apologies, to cancel. I was told, however, that it could not be done and I must go alone, as the Mahdi had prepared an address of welcome to William.

William immediately wrote a reply to this which he said I must deliver on his behalf. After making myself word perfect, but not too obviously, I put on a party frock and set out. The dinner was a very grand affair. I was put next to the Mahdi, who appeared little interested in me. After dinner he duly made his speech, which was translated by an interpreter. I made ready to reply, but nothing more happened. It was plain that to him – a good Muslim – women should be seen but not heard!

During our visit, however, something happened which showed that Sudanese women felt very differently. I was asked to attend a large gathering of about eight hundred women in a high-walled garden. I was the only European present. The others were all Sudanese, wearing traditional white robes. They belonged to the Sudanese Women's Council and had met to discuss women's rights, about which they all felt very strongly. It was one of the most interesting gatherings I have attended. Two demands were urgently voiced: 'For every woman full political rights, and for every man *one* wife only!' It reminded me of the suffragette meetings I had attended with my mother before the First World War.

Our next port of call was Israel, where we had a long talk with the Prime Minister in his office. To meet Ben-Gurion so soon after being with Nasser was almost like seeing them together. On all sides in Egypt, and especially in our interview with the President, we had been struck by the intense fear and apprehension about Israel's aims. We conveyed this to Ben-Gurion. He picked up a stick and, pointing to a map, burst out: 'How much more sand does Abdel Nasser think I want?' He went on to detail the Israelis' one great hope and desire, which threatened no one: to have a land of their own and be able to live in it at peace according to the hope and promise of centuries. He concluded with the words: 'The world didn't believe we would return; *we* believed.'

During this stay in Jerusalem, accompanied by my friend from the Ministry of Religious Affairs, Rabbi Nathan, I climbed what is said to be the Hill of Zion, containing the Tomb of David. There had been considerable doubts among the authorities as to where exactly this was to be found, but eventually a suitable hill was picked out. Traditionally every step should be accompanied by a prayer. I did this in spirit. At the summit stood a building commemorating both Jewish and Christian events of great moment.

On the ground floor was a museum in memory of the six million Jews who had been murdered by the Nazis during the Holocaust. It contained objects of a harrowing nature that were almost impossible to look at. Lampshades made from human skin, and sticks of shaving soap made from human fat, were among the appalling relics that bore witness to the horrific events of just over a decade before. A reference to the 'righteous Gentiles' who had helped to save Jews, and a quotation from the philosopher Maimonides expressing hope and belief in resurrection and life beyond the grave, gave me consolation.

After visiting the Tomb of David, containing objects rescued from a desecrated European synagogue and in the care of a rabbi who was a survivor of Buchenwald concentration camp, I passed up to the Christian place of commemoration – that of the 'upper room' where the earliest followers of Jesus are said to have met, first with him, and then, after the crucifixion, with each other. I was greatly touched to hear from Rabbi Nathan how much personal trouble and care he had taken over this for the sake of Christian visitors. Many came to worship here individually and in groups. For me it was a most important contribution to one of my greatest interests in life: the cause of Jewish–Christian understanding.

The two faiths are necessarily different and can never become one. While it is not for me to say whether a knowledge of Christianity is of value to Jews, I am quite sure that Christians need to understand Judaism. Of crucial importance is the Jewishness of Jesus. According to the theologian Dr Martin Buber, Jesus is 'a great son of Israel who cannot be put into any hitherto known category'. Jesus never moved outside his own religion; he never thought of himself as founding a new one; and neither did any of his contemporaries. We who follow him have today to look at things from there. We cannot read the New Testament except in the light of the Old Testament. I can honestly say that there is no place in the world where my religion is more real to me than Jewish Jerusalem.

I was able to discuss these issues with Dr Buber when I spent an unforgettable hour with him in his study. I had very much wanted William to meet the great scholar who, like him, was working for Arab–Jewish friendship, and I was delighted when the Ministry of Religious Affairs readily arranged an interview. Alas! On the morning of the appointed day, William had one of his severe attacks of emphysema. His temperature was high and the doctor ordered him to stay in bed. Consequently I went to the interview myself, accompanied by a rabbi.

I set out to learn as much as I could about Dr Buber's theology. He proved to be most kind and welcoming. 'Dr Buber,' I asked him, 'how would you advise a Christian like myself to read what we call the Old Testament?' Immediately his face lit up. 'Don't read it,' he said, 'listen to the voices in it: the voices of these and those.' As he said this his hands moved in opposite directions. 'The ones who understood what is being said to them; and those who do not. They represent a great argument that has gone on through time and is going on still.'

Then we went on to speak of the Soviet Union and of the deep religious life which I had witnessed there. It seemed to me that the Anti-Religious movement had never understood Christianity well enough to attack it intelligently. It saw only a Tsarist-sponsored

superstition observed through the spectacles of Karl Marx. I saw the
Soviet Union as being well inside the biblical picture of life. It was as if
the Jewish heart of Christianity, demanding a good, moral caring life,
had risen up as from outside the churches when it was, in fact, a distorted,
secularised but still recognisable form of Old Testament prophetic ethics.

At that time there was a complete separation, which I greatly regretted,
between biblical scholarship and the worship of the synagogues. The
rabbi was very pleased when Dr Buber told me to go straight to the
Bible for inspiration. 'Ah then, Dr Buber,' he said triumphantly, 'we
may take it for granted that you have no use for biblical scholarship.' Dr
Buber silenced him with the reply: 'You may take nothing for granted!'
As we left, Dr Buber cheered me greatly with his parting remark: 'You
permit me to say it? I like you English Christian lady and I like your
ideas.' On my way back to the hotel the rabbi said wistfully: 'Don't you
wish we had had a tape-recorder under the table?' He had been greatly
enlightened by the whole interview.

From Israel we went to Nicosia, the capital of Cyprus, then a British
colony. The majority of the population were of Greek origin and wanted
Cyprus – against the wishes of both the Turkish minority and the British
Government – to be united with Greece. Supporters of union with
Greece had formed a guerrilla organisation called EOKA, and in 1955,
the year before our visit, had launched a terror campaign against the
British authorities in which many servicemen were killed. In response
the British Government had appointed Field Marshal Sir John Harding
to be the new Governor, and at the time of our visit he and the British
Government were involved in a series of discussions with the leader of
the Greek Cypriots, Archbishop Makarios.

Sir John Harding told us that he could not understand Makarios. In
that case, I pointed out, he would find a good deal in common with the
Soviet authorities in their dealings with the Greek Orthodox Church in
the Soviet Union. We went on to have an interview with the Archbishop
at his headquarters, which were sporting a Greek national flag. Makarios,
a most striking figure with his heavy black beard, told us his demands:
there must be a Greek elected majority; security must be handed over
to Greek rule in, say, a year; and an amnesty should be allowed except
for personal violence. In addition Cyprus must be free to choose to unite
with Greece. The British Government had obviously decided to end the
discussions for, just two days after our meeting with him, Archbishop
Makarios was arrested and deported to the Seychelles, where he was
detained for a year.

One of the most interesting IPU assemblies took place in Siam, now
Thailand, in the autumn of 1956. We went to Burma en route, where
we met the Chinese Prime Minister, Chou En-lai, who was paying a
visit to Rangoon. He told me he had learnt English from the YMCA
and was very grateful to them. On arriving in Bangkok we were most

hospitably accommodated in the government guesthouse for foreign visitors. At that time the romantic film about old Siam, *The King and I*, was for the first time being shown all over the Western world, and we were fascinated to find ourselves having an audience with the contemporary monarch, the young King Bhumibol, in his magnificent palace. For me the occasion brought difficulties as well as interest. Slippery floors added much peril to the necessity of walking backwards out of his presence, but somehow it was accomplished.

Bangkok, with its palaces and temples, is a place of rare beauty, and I particularly enjoyed seeing the early morning market in operation on the river. In the evenings there were diplomatic parties in waterside gardens. At one of them I was startled by the attack of a large black crab that reached my knee before it was caught and removed by the French Ambassador, acting with all the diplomatic aplomb and presence of mind associated with his profession. After dinner we lit candles on little flower boats and launched them on the river. The Thai custom was to place a coin in each boat in order to remove sin. The Soviet delegates were already unpopular for resolutely defending their government's recent invasion of Hungary, and so it was particularly unfortunate that it was their boats that set fire to the others. After the launch we danced to Western music on a stage in the river.

From Bangkok we continued under our own steam to make unofficial contacts within the Communist or near-Communist world. We flew to Cambodia, which had recently gained its independence from France, and, after spending a short while exploring the vast and impressive temple at Angkor Wat, made our way to the capital, Phnom Penh. Finding that no bookings had been registered for us at the hotel used by foreigners, we went to one favoured by local people, the Cambodia Hotel. At first sight we could see that this was startlingly different from any we had ever stayed in before. The wall that separated one bedroom from another reached neither the floor nor the ceiling. Thus the conversation and movements of neighbours were audible and sometimes partially visible.

Any sense of privacy was completely banished. As usual William enjoyed 'going native' in a new country, but I must confess to a feeling of dismay as I tried to settle down for a visit of as yet unknown length. I need not have worried. Within half an hour we were told that a visitor had called to see us. This turned out to be Peter, now Sir Peter, Blaker, the future Conservative minister, then a diplomat at the British Embassy, whom we had met in England. He came with a supremely welcome invitation from his wife, Jennifer, and himself to stay with them at their home. This generous hospitality made a wonderful background to our visit to Cambodia. I recognised it as a woeful weakness in myself that this British connection made it so much more enjoyable, whereas William would have been happy anywhere. There were many people to see, and we attended frequent lunches and dinner parties given by the diplomats.

William went to the royal palace, built by the French in 1863, to meet
the ruler of Cambodia, Prince Norodom Sihanouk. There was a rather
uninspiring museum where the chief exhibits seemed to be a bust of
Emperor Napoleon III which had originally been that of his uncle, the
first Emperor Napoleon, and now had a new, and poorly executed, head;
and a bowler hat, a gift from Mussolini, which had been decorated by
the attachment of a diamond brooch to a spike on the top.

As a guard of honour presented arms, a large door at the head of the
grand entrance staircase opened to reveal Prince Sihanouk. His facial
expression changed between smiles and a sort of grimace and he had the
national habit of putting hands together and crouching. The meeting
went well and William felt that the Prince was in favour of Cambodia
joining the IPU.

Living conditions in Phnom Penh were very primitive, with open
drains running through the streets. The subjugation of women was
painfully obvious. I recall the sight of a young husband, carrying nothing,
walking in carefree fashion a few yards ahead of his heavily pregnant
young wife. She was laden with many bundles and was carrying a baby
on her back.

From Cambodia we went on to Laos, whose parliament had just joined
the IPU, and then to Saigon in South Vietnam. We stayed with the
British Ambassador, Sir Hugh Stevenson, and his wife, friends of William's nephew Glanvill Benn. They made us very welcome, but were
not pleased to learn that we intended to go on to Peking and then, if
possible, to Hanoi in North Vietnam. They so loathed Communism that
they asked us not to talk about the next stage of our journey.

We visited China in a private capacity as guests of the People's Bureau
for Foreign Affairs, which contained a number of the delegates who had
come to Helsinki. William and I were concerned, as in all the Communist countries we visited, to meet Christians and see how they were
getting on under the new system of government. Christmas was approaching and as we drove around Peking we were pleased to see all the
churches – some sixty of them, we were told – open for worship. Parties
of carol singers were quite a familiar sight, going from church to church;
the newspapers mentioned the festival; and even the government-owned
Peking Hotel set up an immense, glittering Christmas tree in the hall.
But I also noticed that the Roman Catholics had made a gesture towards
the new regime by having a red star over the nativity tableau in their
cathedral.

There were many denominations at work, including the Salvation
Army where we spent an enjoyable hour or two. As we said goodbye I
brought out, as I usually did on such occasions, my small camera. To
my dismay everyone recoiled in horror. It took just a minute to understand why. Strange as it may seem, the only time I was ever refused

permission to take a photograph in Communist China was when the Salvation Army considered it to be an improper activity for a Sunday.

Christmas week was a very busy one with so many churches and meeting halls to visit and Christian gatherings to attend. On Christmas Eve the YMCA gave a great party for some hundreds of its workers and their children. I was unexpectedly invited to address them, and the Communist intellectual who interpreted found himself saying things about Christmas he can never have thought to utter. But he took this and everything else in immensely good part. Very soon the gathering relaxed into a great party with talk and games and much laughter and Father Christmas bringing presents for all the children.

Among my warmest memories was that of a service at the principal Congregational church in Peking. It was the first Sunday of the new year, 1957, and the church was full of worshippers. There were familiar hymns set to the same tunes as ours. They sang in Chinese, we in English. They followed the lesson in a Chinese Bible, we in a British and Foreign Bible Society edition. When it came to the sermon there was a whispered translation. We felt completely at home.

One young minister in a New Year sermon summed up the situation in Communist China as he saw it: 'Much has come to us in recent years and a great improvement in our standard of life, but material things are not enough. We Christians are called to be Light and Salt in the New China.'

During our stay in Peking we visited the university, and while we were being shown round the women's residential block I was astonished to see a Bible on every desk in the students' bed-sitting rooms. 'Are the students here all Christians?' I asked the professor. 'Oh no,' she replied, 'they are studying for a degree in the English faculty, and you cannot understand the history and literature of the English people if you do not know the Bible.' This attitude pleased us very much.

After leaving China we went on to Hanoi. William had been unwell, and when we met the ruler, Ho Chi Minh, he arranged for us to have lunch with him in a chalet in the grounds of his house so that William would not have the exertion of climbing a large number of stairs. I sat next to Ho Chi Minh, and he told me about all his travels and how he had spent some time as a cook in London.

Leaving Hanoi we went on to Ceylon, now Sri Lanka, where we stayed in the capital, Colombo. The Prime Minister, Mr Bandaranaike, and his wife – later, after her husband's death, to be Prime Minister herself – entertained us at their home. We ourselves were hospitably lodged in the official guesthouse, where we mingled most enjoyably in leisure hours with other state guests, including Prince Sihanouk of Cambodia.

We enjoyed sightseeing in the capital. On the main street there were a number of shops with English and Scottish names over the door.

Obviously these belonged to old-established settlers. The scenery was beautiful but flying foxes presented a new type of menace. We could not keep our windows open at night because they flew right up to them. By day dozens of the sinister black creatures slept hanging from the branches of selected trees. These looked like Christmas trees, presents and all, that had been blighted by the curse of a wicked fairy. Our only disappointment in Ceylon, and it was a big one, was that on the invitation of the authorities we handed in all the many photographs we had taken for development, only to learn on leaving that they had been stolen.

These overseas visits were a most rewarding aspect of William's duties as President of the Inter-Parliamentary Union, but there were also interesting activities at home. We very much enjoyed being guests at various embassies in London, where we were able to meet and get to know many different people.

Apart from a handful of left-wing Labour MPs and Communists, few people from Western countries attended receptions at East European embassies during these years of the Cold War. Sometimes members or representatives of the British Government would make an appearance; a more lively note would be struck if someone from the world of the arts made an appearance – the sculptor Jacob Epstein, for example, accompanied by one or two of his models. William and I were trying to 'get understanding' of people from different political systems, whether we approved of them or not. But our presence at these functions was occasionally misinterpreted as giving support to Stalinism. Meeting William in Parliament one day, Nancy Astor teased him, in her characteristically straightforward manner, by asking: 'Why don't you join Stalin right away?' She was, however, as warm and friendly as ever!

True to his passionate attachment to the principles of freedom of belief and expression, William was totally opposed to discrimination against Communists; and I gave him my full support. In 1949 the John Lewis Partnership made a decision to dismiss partners who were members of the Communist Party. William asked a question about the matter in the Lords, and as a protest I closed my small account at the store.

When, the following year, Lord Vansittart, the former Permanent Under-Secretary at the Foreign Office, alleged that the Church of England and the Civil Service had been infiltrated by Communists, William proposed a motion of censure against him. No other member of the House of Lords supported William, who was accused by Vansittart of having 'taken his ticket and labelled himself as a fellow-passenger of fellow-travellers'. William, who never worried about comments like that, replied: 'My Lords, we Nonconformists have a hymn: "Dare to be a Daniel, dare to stand alone." That is what I propose to do.'

In November 1950, William was joined in Parliament by Anthony, after he won the by-election in Bristol South East, caused by the resignation of Sir Stafford Cripps, who was seriously ill. We were delighted by Anthony's success, especially as, at twenty-five, he became the youngest MP – a distinction William had enjoyed almost half a century before. For the next ten years they were able to support each other's causes from their respective Houses. In 1954, for example, William and Anthony took up the case of Paul Garland, who had been expelled from the Boy Scout movement in Bristol for being a Communist. On this issue William had almost no support from the other peers.

William was also incensed when Paul Robeson, the great singer and actor who had campaigned so hard against Fascism in the Thirties, became a victim of the McCarthy witch-hunts and had his passport confiscated for so-called 'Un-American activities'. After an eight-year struggle a Supreme Court ruling led to the return of the passport, enabling Paul Robeson to visit London in 1958. It was a most joyful occasion, and William was one of a large crowd of supporters and well-wishers who met him at the airport. Later he came to a tea party we were giving in the House of Lords for the eightieth birthday of our friend Margaret Buchanan. When I told Paul Robeson that we were celebrating Margaret's birthday he looked at her and began to sing the song with which he will always be associated, 'Ol' Man River'. She was enchanted, and everybody in the dining room – peers, guests, waitresses – stopped whatever they were doing and listened to the beautiful deep voice. There could be no doubt as to the identity of our guest!

At the time of Paul Robeson's visit, William was no longer President of the Inter-Parliamentary Union, having retired in 1957 at the London conference. During his decade in office, William had put new spirit into the IPU and the membership had doubled. At the conference the American delegation nominated William, and the Russian delegation seconded him, for the position of President of Honour, which he held until his death. At the height of the Cold War, honouring William was, I am afraid, about the only thing on which those two countries agreed. Sceptics would point to the tension between East and West as evidence of their belief that institutions like the IPU had achieved little. But William believed that any opportunity for people of differing views to meet each other must be taken. He used to say: 'What do you see first? That it's raining. Then you see the sun shining. Then one day you see the harvest.'

CHAPTER 13
1958–1991

After his retirement from the presidency of the Inter-Parliamentary Union, William was as determined as ever to commit most of his time and energy to his parliamentary work, and regularly contributed to debates in the House of Lords. I continued to pursue my theological studies and was very pleased when my friend Elsie Chamberlain, then working in the Religious Affairs Department of the BBC, asked me to take part in 'Lift Up Your Hearts', a daily programme she produced. Calling my week of talks 'Divine Challenge', I chose to consider the meaning of six questions put in the name of God to people in the Old Testament.

I spoke, for example, about the prophet Elijah, who tried to defend the religion of Israel against the heathen Queen Jezebel. When the effort proved too much he ran away to the desert, believing himself to be a complete failure. But this was not the case and God said to him: 'What doest thou here, Elijah? Go, return!' He was not to be discouraged, but must go back and work even harder. I very much enjoyed working out the implications of these questions for us in the present day. William enjoyed the talks and was very pleased that I was giving them. Sadly, these talks were to be one of the last happy events we shared together, for only a month later William died.

On 16 November 1960 William was in the chamber of the House of Lords waiting to speak against the Central African Federation, which he believed had been devised to perpetuate white rule in Rhodesia and Nyasaland. This would have been his second speech in two days. Indian affairs had been debated the day before and, as it turned out, the last words he spoke in Parliament were: 'We must never lose that most precious thing: the friendship of the Indian people.'

As William sat on the back benches he suffered a heart attack and was taken to Westminster Hospital. I stayed the night there and the next morning was relieved that he seemed better. First he insisted that I should go straight home and fetch his job list, adding firmly: 'Don't think you can keep me here!' With a full heart I thought, 'How blessed we shall be if we can.' But it was not to be. Anthony, David and I had been with him for some time when he became worse. We were asked to leave for a while but were not called back, and at twenty minutes to eight that evening the doctor told us that William had died.

It was 17 November 1960, the fortieth anniversary of our marriage – our Ruby Wedding Day. We had planned to spend it seeing *My Fair Lady* in a family party. Now our sons and I spent it sharing a grief which for each of us had, besides its mutual aspect, its own agonisingly personal edge. My son David, at the age of only thirty-two, lost a father to whom he had been particularly close and whose political views he shared. For Anthony there was not only the loss of the father he adored but, with the death, the loss of his whole career in life – the work to which he had been dedicated from his teens. He was now, against his will, the second Viscount Stansgate and was deemed to have ceased to be a Member of Parliament. On a different level, but still the cause of grave anxiety to a married man and the father of four young children, he lost his parliamentary income.

It was a day of unassuageable sorrow for all of us. For me, above all, it was a day of testing. The thing I had always thought of with most dread was upon me. For the first time that gulf of the twenty years between us had triumphed. What judgement would it pass on me? How could I ever come through the certainty of 'not seeing, not hearing'? How could I endure the knowledge that from now on the rest would be 'silence'? As I faced the certainty of no longer possessing William's blessed companionship, a line of verse by W. E. Henley that William had often quoted came to mind: 'Shall we not take the ebb who had the flow?' This, I knew, was my answer. I must set myself in the most positive manner to turn away from any morbid concerns and look outwards. There was first of all the family, my great blessing. More than ever I saw my role in relation to them to be that of a 'ministry of reinforcement'. This must not consist of any proffering of advice unless it was asked for – which was unlikely.

One must never be what C. S. Lewis, in a shattering *aperçu*, calls 'the sort of woman who lives for others'. As he goes on to explain, 'you can always tell the others by their hunted expression!' Reinforcement consists above all in the possession of an understanding spirit which identifies itself with the hopes and desires of another. Beyond the family lay the many causes which I cared deeply for and had already sought to serve as well as might be.

The kindness of friends was all around me: letters poured in. I cherish to this day one from Dr Sidney Berry, the head of the Congregationalists, who bade me, as he was sure I would, to go through the duties of the next few days with 'uplifted heart'. Giving the address at William's memorial service in St Margaret's, Westminster, Dr Berry spoke in the truly characteristic fashion of the shrewd, lovable and humorous saint that he was: 'Our beloved Independent has gone, and let us be thankful that he has been spared any time of debility and handicap because he would have been an intolerant and intolerable invalid!' That was perfectly true. Dr Berry had always enjoyed teasing William about politics, and I remember one occasion when he said to him: 'I'll believe anything you tell me except that you are a socialist. You are a Gladstonian Liberal!'

There were many obituaries and tributes. Clem Attlee, speaking in the House of Lords, said this of William, using the name by which he had been known to his parliamentary colleagues:

What always struck me about 'Wedgie' was that, although he was now well on in years, he still had the heart of a boy. He had an extraordinary zest for life and he was always a knight errant, ready at all times to take up a cause for anything or any person in the world whom he thought to be suffering injustice. He was a great character.

One of my most immediate concerns was to give Anthony all the help and encouragement I could in his fight to renounce the viscountcy. In 1955, with William's support, he had made an unsuccessful attempt to get a bill passed to enable peers to renounce. Would he succeed now? He returned his Letters Patent to the Lord Great Chamberlain, but was told that that would make no difference. According to the law a peerage was 'an incorporeal hereditament affixed in the blood and annexed to the posterity' and could not be given up. The next setback was when his Bristol seat was declared vacant and a writ was issued for a by-election to be held in May 1961. But neither Anthony nor his constituency party were deterred by this and he was re-adopted as the Labour candidate.

The result was a resounding triumph. The Conservative candidate, Malcolm St Clair, was decisively beaten and Anthony's majority had doubled. But when he arrived at Westminster to take his seat the door of the House of Commons was shut in his face. Indeed, the doorkeeper had been instructed by the Speaker to use force, if necessary, to keep Anthony out. St Clair took him before the Election Court and a serious problem arose when the court not only declared the defeated candidate to be the member for Bristol South East but ordered Anthony to pay £8,000 costs – a considerable amount of money in those days.

Fortunately, Anthony's supporters organised a public appeal and the generosity displayed was overwhelming. The whole costs were paid by the British public – from the £500 given by a Tory Cabinet minister to 2s 6d postal orders from old age pensioners. Churchill supported Anthony's cause, and a member of the Royal Family gave money, saying he did not want anyone to know: 'Keep this dark!' The press was truly marvellous in its support. 'He only wants to be plain Mr Benn,' said the leading article in the *Evening Standard*.

Unable to hold out any longer, the Government set up a Joint Select Committee of members of both Houses to consider possible changes in peerage law, and at the beginning of 1963 the committee reported in favour of renunciation. Events now moved rapidly. A Peerage Bill introduced by the Government quickly passed through all its stages and the date for the Royal Assent was fixed for 31 July 1963. On the morning of that day *The Times* carried a front-page column headed: 'Lord Stansgate will be Mr Benn today.' In the afternoon I went with Anthony and his wife, Caroline, to Parliament. Dozens of photographers and cameramen were crowding round outside the St Stephen's entrance as we arrived.

We had tea and then took our seats in the gallery of the House of Lords. As soon as the Royal Assent was given to the Peerage Bill we left the chamber and went straight to the office of Sir George Coldstream, the Clerk of the Crown. After Sir George had seen that the Instrument of Renunciation was in order, Anthony put his thumb on the seal and, giving the Instrument to Sir George, said: 'This is my deed and my act.'

Sir George said that he was glad Anthony had been the first to arrive, as he had feared that some other peer might have robbed Anthony of 'his rightful place' at the head of the list. He showed us the register in which the names of those who renounced would be entered. As we left, there occurred an incident that epitomised for me the whole story of the transient peerage. One of the messengers of the House of Lords, with a casual nod, remarked coolly to Anthony: 'Goodbye, sir.' Just thirty minutes before, another messenger had approached him and with a deferential bow had asked: 'May I take your brief-case, my lord?'

As he had promised, Malcolm St Clair resigned his seat, leaving Anthony free to return and fight the resulting by-election, which was to be held on 20 August 1963. As Caroline and the children were on a brief holiday in France, I went down to help and enjoyed my last experience of electioneering: speaking at indoor meetings, street corners, and from the backs of lorries. The result was not in doubt, as the only other candidates were two Independents; there was no Conservative or Liberal standing. Nevertheless, it was extremely exciting when we learned that Anthony had won with a majority of over 15,000.

For the family it was an outstanding victory that would have delighted William's heart as it did ours. But for Anthony the three-year struggle had been too painful to bring him any joy even in victory. He put it out of his mind as quickly as possible and has often said he hoped he 'wouldn't be remembered for that'. During those anxious years in the wilderness, when everything seemed lost and he could see no future, he felt the full strength and weight of the Establishment and its power over individuals. This lesson was never to be forgotten. More and more he has come to feel that from Magna Carta onwards progress in democracy has only been achieved, and can only be achieved, by making active protest against laws that stand against present and future liberty.

After William's death I continued with my religious interests. I lived and worked happily within the Congregational Union, serving for many years as the Free Church President of the Society for the Ministry of Women in the Church. But I was not only attracted to Congregationalism because it enabled women to fulfil their vocation to the priesthood. Congregationalism is a very democratic movement, built on the concept of the 'priesthood of all believers'. This very much appealed to me, as I do not think the Almighty wants us to accept dictatorship and have our minds made up for us by bishops. People should arrive at their own beliefs in the light of biblical religion.

Believing in the importance of independence, I was unhappy when it was suggested that the Congregational Union should merge with the Presbyterians to form the United Reformed Church. I am ecumenically minded and can work happily with other denominations, but I felt the fundamental principles of Congregationalism would be submerged if we joined the more authoritarian Presbyterians. Consequently, a group of us, including Elsie Chamberlain, opposed the move and we founded the independent Congregational Federation. At the age of seventy-five I became the first President and, after my year in office, was made Emeritus President. I spoke at many meetings, explaining our case, and found it a most enjoyable experience.

The other cause dear to my heart is the promotion of understanding between Christians and Jews. I feel that our paths lie together and that for too long there has been misunderstanding and even hostility between the two faiths. I am very proud to be a Vice-President of the Council of Christians and Jews, an organisation established in 1942 to combat discrimination and promote understanding against the backdrop of the Nazi atrocities. During the war the Council urged the British Government to allow more refugees into Palestine.

At the end of the war there was a big meeting to relaunch the Council. Anthony and David came with me – William was in Egypt – and we were delighted that Reinhold Niebuhr was able to attend. It was a most moving occasion. At that time there was a great desire on the part of Jews to have a national home in Palestine, and frustration with the attitude of the British Government. The Council took up the cause of the Jewish refugees on board the ship *Exodus*, who were prevented by the British Government from landing in Palestine. Today the Council of Christians and Jews puts much emphasis on educational activities, and talks are given to schools and societies.

Since its opening in 1925 I have always taken a great interest in the Hebrew University in Jerusalem, which fosters the great Jewish love of learning. Most countries exist for many centuries before they produce a university, but not so Israel. The Hebrew University was there a generation before the state itself and, indeed, was one of its creators. When the foundation stone of the University was laid on Mount Scopus in 1918, the foundation stone of the state was laid as well. Albert Einstein truly called it 'the greatest institution in Israel since the destruction of the Temple'. It not only serves Israel and Jewish people everywhere but has the universal aim of serving humanity at large.

After the war William and I attended many fund-raising dinners and balls in aid of the University, and I worked with the women's group of the British Friends of the Hebrew University. To my great delight, when the British Friends had collected a substantial sum of money they founded, in 1975, the Margaret Stansgate Library. I was particularly happy that it was part of the Martin Buber Institute of Adult Education, which takes a special interest in educating the disadvantaged. It is appropriate that I am associated with an institution to help people catch up with their education, for that is what I have been trying to do ever since I started school!

The authorities of the Hebrew University invited me to go out to Jerusalem for the opening of the library and most generously paid all my expenses. I lunched with the President of the Hebrew University and his wife, and then attended the opening ceremony. There were many people there, including the British Ambassador. I felt very much honoured, and it was such a delight to see my name written in Hebrew.

One further honour awaited me. When I was eighty-five I was made a Fellow of the Hebrew University. To be in fellowship with the Hebrew University of Jerusalem is to be in visible partnership with one of the greatest creative enterprises in the world today and it makes me feel extremely proud. The University gave me a beautiful framed plaque which I have on the wall of my flat.

I was given the opportunity of talking on television about my interest in the Old Testament when I was asked by Dr Barry Lynch to take part in a series for BBC Wales called 'A Lasting Impression', in which I was required to choose a book that had greatly influenced my life. I chose *The Book of the Twelve Prophets* by George Adam Smith and spoke especially about Amos, one of the greatest of the Old Testament prophets. I explained that what comes burning through the words of the prophet Amos is his great passion for righteousness and justice. From him I learnt that there can never be social and political harmony in a country unless there is social and political justice. Society will not endure if it is founded on wrong thinking and wrong doing, and religion is of no value if it is indifferent to these things. The Old Testament is full of the idea of the necessity of a just society and it is not sufficiently remembered that this idea comes originally from the prophets of Israel.

All through the years of my widowhood I have loved nothing better than to be with my family. I not only have six grandchildren but six great-grandchildren as well. Anthony and Caroline have four children: Stephen, the Parliamentary Affairs Officer of the Royal Society of Chemistry; Hilary, who works for a trade union; Melissa, a journalist; and Joshua, a computer expert. David and his wife, June, have a son, Piers, who is an academic, and a daughter, Frances, who works in publishing. They have been a great help and comfort to me in the years since William's death.

Many of us as we grow old begin to wonder why we are left so long. Is there any purpose we can hope to fulfil, anything we can give and hand on to our descendants, especially the youngest generation of all – the 'great-grands'.

One of the youngest members of the family, my eldest great-grandson, then four years old, gave me a clue about this a few years ago. I used to rest in the afternoon and he would come in to preside over the operation. The attraction, it must be admitted, was an electrically controlled bed. This, which brings great independence of movement to the occupant, offers entrancing opportunities to the experimenter.

He loved to possess himself of what is appropriately called a 'wand'. Press one switch and up comes great-grandmother's head and shoulders to an upright position. 'No, that's a little too far . . .' Another touch and down she goes. Then a further switch is pressed and up come her feet. This is adjusted until she is jacked up to a position in which perfect rest is assured. Every aching joint is supported, arthritic pains have disappeared and it is like lying on a cloud. Then there would be a final touch: massage, gentle and vigorous, may be applied as desired to both legs and shoulders. When this is over the operator would vanish, his work done.

But on one occasion he did not move. Suddenly there was something on his mind. With concern on his little face which moved me greatly he asked in a quiet, distinct voice: 'When are you going to die?' I was aware of my brain working in two different directions simultaneously. This was certainly the most important question he had ever thought of or asked. Pray God I would not let him down. There might never be another such opportunity. At the same time I heard my voice saying: 'What a good question. The answer is I don't know. Nobody knows. We all have to wait until we are sent for. But when I do die it will be lovely because I shall see my mummy and daddy again. I haven't seen them for a very long time. They were born more than a hundred years ago. And I shall see your great-grandfather – my husband – and my son Michael, and my baby Jeremy.' He did not say anything in reply, but just looked happy and ran out to play.

How astonishing that so young a creature should be able, in Reinhold Niebuhr's phrase, to 'abstract himself from the sea of life' and ask an ultimate question. Pray God that he will be able to lay a secure foundation on which to build, never looking just at life but also through life for its meaning.

As my own life reaches on towards its inevitable close, I feel more and more as if I am living in a tent. The sunshine of other days is bound, to a certain extent, to be muted, but more and more the canvas becomes transparent as light begins to filter through from the other side. I seem more and more to be living at the junction of matter and spirit. In these latter days I can draw near to the writer of an old Scottish evangelical hymn – a woman who lived in my father's native Irvine, and who sang her life's song of thankfulness and praise, using the homely imagery of cloth-making:

> With mercy and with judgement my web of time he wove
> And aye the dews of sorrow were lustred by his love.
> I'll praise the hand that guided, I'll praise the heart that planned
> Where glory, glory dwelleth in Immanuel's land.

Margaret Stansgate

An Appreciation by Tony Benn

This book brings back with great force, clarity and authenticity the mother and grandmother whom we knew, and with whom we used to talk, over all those years from our childhood right up until her death.

My brothers and I were greatly influenced by what we learned and heard discussed at home, which helped to shape our view of society and the world which left a deep and lasting impression on us all.

First a sense of the central importance of social justice, and the need to seek out truth, and distinguish right from wrong in political, as well as personal, choices, a command that is not always easy to follow, but which at least identifies what it is that everyone should attempt.

This was combined with a genuine and deeply felt internationalism, which was underpinned, in my Mother's case, by a spiritual conviction that we were all the children of God.

Her own approach to the Christian faith derived from a belief which she had arrived at quite independently, and when very young, as a child in Scotland, that there was a kindly spirit at work in the universe, and her approach to the role of Jesus himself was that he embodied that spirit, rather than that he was the incarnation of God on earth – a very unusual and interesting analysis of the Bible story and the Christian Gospels.

We were all brought up on the Old Testament stories and learned from her of the relevance and importance of the Prophets of Israel who preached righteousness against the Kings who exercised power – and regularly abused it.

These were the roots of the radical dissenting tradition to which both she and my Father belonged, he having been brought up as a Congregationalist, and Mother having become a Congregationalist quite late in life.

Congregationalists believe in the 'priesthood of all believers', offering to everyone a direct line to the Almighty, which liberates them from the uncertain mediation of bishops or priests, a view that encourages freedom of thought and inculcates a spirit of questioning all those in authority in both religion and politics.

Her move from the Church of England to the Congregationalists came after the World Council of Churches meeting in Amsterdam in 1948,

which she had attended as a delegate, and where she was offended by
the negative attitude adopted by the Anglicans to Christians from other
denominations.

It was this same independence of thought that led her, and others, to
establish the Congregational Federation, after the formation of the
United Reformed Church, which she feared would swamp and over-
whelm the traditional Congregational values and spirit.

It was this very controversy which encouraged her to develop her own
idea that Christian unity should be a Mosaic rather than a Monolith,
requiring us to cherish the rich and diverse traditions of the faith rather
than submerging them into one vast Christian multinational organization.

Mother's committment to freedom and her desire for justice also lay
behind her life-long support for the cause of women, and specifically
their right to be ordained as ministers in the church.

Inevitably this led her into conflict with successive Archbishops of
Canterbury and what was the main body of opinion inside the Anglican
communion in those early days, and although she lived to see the
American Episcopalians ordain women and even consecrate a woman as
Bishop, the final acheivement in England was – sadly for her – not
reached by the time of her death.

Mother's love of the Bible and her determination to learn to read it
in Hebrew and Greek, as she did, stimulated her interest in Jewish-
Christian relations, and explained her work with the Council of Christians and Jews, her support for the Hebrew University which she always
believed was a shared resource for humanity, and her enthusiasm for the
rebuilding of Jerusalem.

She was always a great believer in the Ecumenical movement, and she
supported the Congress of Faiths which allows all the world's great
religions to share their spiritual experiences, and ease the suspicions and
tensions that, in the past, have led so often to conflict and war.

When my father was alive mother saw it as her first duty to support
him and his political work. She travelled with him all over the world
and, when he was ill she took over his responsibilities in election
campaigns.

During the war, when he rejoined the RAF, she took over his volu-
minous constituency correspondence, and handled it all herself.

As the daughter, wife and mother of members of parliament, this was
how she saw her role, and, although she never liked us to say it, the
thirty years, after father's death gave her much greater freedom to
develop her own interests to the full.

She became more active in all the campaigns in which she was involved, travelled, broadcast and lectured until, towards the very end she
was incapacitated by her age and infirmities.

But at all times she took the very keenest interest in her children, her
grandchildren and her great-grandchildren, welcoming their visits, and

looking forward to our family holidays at Stansgate where she had her own self-contained flat, and was always engaged in the most interesting and enjoyable conversations with a veritable queue of descendants who came to see her.

We all appreciated her great sense of humour and the time she gave to talking to us, asking about our own plans and putting her own immense personal experience, stretching back in politics and religion to the beginning of the century, at our disposal.

Although she had, as a child, been denied a proper education herself, she was a natural academic, always anxious to learn, loving to delve into biblical history and fascinated by higher theological scholarship, so that she was familiar with all the complex issues raised, and ready to answer any questions which we put.

My brother and I especially appreciated listening to her talking on politics because she had a phenomenal memory, clearly recalling people and events from eighty years ago, and possessing a very shrewd judgement about contemporary affairs.

Her influence extended far beyond the family, as we were reminded by all the letters we received after her death, and the fact that hundreds of people attended her memorial service who had equally enjoyed her friendship.

Perhaps the greatest test of her religious faith, and her personal courage, came as she suffered the disabilities which old age brings, all of which she bore uncomplainingly.

'I would not wish this on my worst enemies,' she would say as her sight began to fail her, and when she suffered a succession of strokes.

She viewed the prospect of her own death with total equanimity and this inspired the title for an autobiography on which she had been working, all made possible by Gillian Shepherd, who has drawn on Mother's own notes and diaries and in many sensitive interviews has brilliantly re-created her exact tone of voice in her writing.

I hope that readers of this book will have enjoyed it and gain some inspiration in the story that she has told, for it was a very full as well as a very long life, with much happiness and her share of grief as well when she lost one still-born baby, an eldest killed in war, and her own husband, leaving her a widow for over thirty years.

Certainly for those of us, who knew her best, this book will be a constant reminder of the friend we had, and of one of the main influences of our early and later years.

Tony Benn

INDEX